Cows home from Aspen November 15, 2002
Tim, Bruce, Mike, Leigh and Steve
18km Drive to Fraser River Benches

BRANDING CREW

Branding Crew - 2002

T-BONE

A RANCHER'S STORY

Tim Brewin

◆ FriesenPress

Suite 300 - 990 Fort St
Victoria, BC, V8V 3K2
Canada

www.friesenpress.com

Copyright © 2018 by Tim Brewin
First Edition — 2018

Photographs by LeRae Haynes

All rights reserved.

No part of this publication may be reproduced in any form, or by any means, electronic or mechanical, including photocopying, recording, or any information browsing, storage, or retrieval system, without permission in writing from FriesenPress.

ISBN
978-1-5255-3985-5 (Hardcover)
978-1-5255-3986-2 (Paperback)
978-1-5255-3987-9 (eBook)

1. BIOGRAPHY & AUTOBIOGRAPHY, PERSONAL MEMOIRS

Distributed to the trade by The Ingram Book Company

Tim Brewin grew up with six brothers and three sisters on the family farm at Purple Springs, Alberta. He helped his brothers Gerald, Frank, Rod and his sister Eleanor develop the family farm under the guidance of their mother and father. He built up his own farm and raised four daughters and one son with his first wife, Marj.

At age 50 he relocated to B.C. where he was manager and president of three different ranches, and where he built up a herd of 1,800 beef cows. He also expanded and developed the range and irrigation on these ranches with his partner and wife, Pat.

He was often called 'T-Bone' by his brothers and good friends because of a T-Bone steak.

The Way it Was

I saw the pivots near Purple Springs as I was passing by
They stood stark and solitaire against the summer sky.
I recalled the endless grasslands there and the sagebrush, gray and dry.
The days of youth are too soon gone, only memories stay.
Those selfsame fields now lush and green were my haunts of yesterday.
But the carefree rides through that pristine range progress swept away.

I can see it now and hear it too, the silence that solitude brings.
The only sounds, the rustling grass and the odd whir of the prairie chicks wings
And over the hills a few miles to the west, the little store at Purple Springs.
The old timers would father at that little store, what stories they would tell;
Of the early times, the hardship times and the happy times as well.
But what would they say of this place where they used to dwell.
Do they wonder with awe wherever they are of fields of lush green hay,
Of rows of corn and potatoes too, and they make it rain near every day.
And glory be there is a huge factory too just a mile or so away.

But would they, like me, miss the endless range and the silence that solitude brings.
But gone forever the rustling grass and the whir of the prairie chicks wings.
But folks gather still and spin their yarns and friendship reigns
at the little store at Purple Springs.

Gerald Brewin
Copyright, 2000

Much of the native grassland and open unfenced range land that was part of, and surrounded the Brewin home ranch a short fifty years ago, today is cultivated and rows lush green irrigated crops.

A RANCHERS NIGHTMARE

The Scribe pulled up a chair and ordered a beer
And one for the old rancher as well.
For the Scribe had a story he was longing to write
And the rancher had a story to tell.
He told how he trailed a small herd of stock
Beyond the mountains of the Canadian Northwest.
How he built up a ranch on the range that was there
That any man would be proud to possess.
He reminisced of friendships and prosperous times
And seemed to have nary a care.
But the Scribe pressed on, this sounded so good
There had to be times of despair,
When disease hit the herd or prices were low
Or wild animals took the odd cow.
The old-timer smiled and thought for awhile
Then a frown appeared on his brow.
No, diseases have cures and prices turn round
And wild animals gave us some sport.
But if you persist there is one thing I dread
And that is a weather report
That predicts a late spring, cold temperatures too,
And a foot or tow of new snow.
For I many have worried and watched as winter pressed on
And know that my feed stocks are low.
So I ration my feed and I hope and I pray
That somehow I'll still make it through.
So you ask my friend if I've had times of despair
And I must reply if I'm true.
That is sure if hell when you have fed your last bale
And the cows are still abawlin',
And the warm west wind has switched to the north
And a March storms ahowlin'

Gerald Brewin
Copyright, 2002

The idea to write the above poem came to me after I heard a media interview with "Panhandle" Philips, a rancher from northwestern B.C. Philips and his partner Rich Hobson opened up a new area to ranching there in the 1930's. Hobson wrote his book, "Grass Beyond the Mountains" based on that venture.

In the interview Philips told of his wonderful life as a rancher. But after being pressed admitted that it was pure hell if on rare occasion he ran short of teed in the winter.

Dedication

I dedicate these memories and my story to my wife Pat, who worked by my side for over 30 years. She was a great companion and dedicated wife and was truly talented and capable.

She also loved to garden, was a great cook and worked extremely hard on the ranch. She helped with calving with feeding and the health of the cattle herd. She also helped with the irrigation and field work. Truly she was a dedicated rancher's wife, and was also very active in the community, and with cattle associations.

Pat made sure all ranch employees were treated fairly and with respect. She helped me plan many of the irrigation improvements and design the calving barn and the ranch yard. She was always active.

Pat was a very proud person but was also very fair and was truly respected. She did the cattle records. She could not tolerate vindictive people, or gossip. She could not accept employees who did not do their part, or who took advantage of the other employees.

She did her part to make sure the ranch moved forward. She truly loved all the grandkids, and was well-accepted by my family, including my brothers and sisters.

I also want to pay special attention to my mother, who worked so very hard on the farm. She brought up 10 kids and was truly loved by all of us. My brothers Alfred, Norman and sister Monica left the farm in the early 1940s. This left the development and expansion of the farm to Gerald, Frank, Eleanor, Rod and myself. My father was a fur buyer and used the income from that to supplement the farm. He was also a councillor on the Municipal District of Taber, and was on the Taber hospital board, where he was instrumental in building the first hospital in Taber.

He held both of these positions for over 30 years – these were the years following World War II.

I am truly proud of all of my family: my brothers, sister, and my children and grandchildren. My grandkids often asked me about my life, and encouraged me to write my memoirs, as did Linda, my partner since 2013. They helped me put all this together. I also want to acknowledge LeRae Haynes for helping me to put these memoirs together and doing the typing.

I have written my story mostly from memory, therefore some of the dates may not be accurate. I did research several sources to attempt to be as accurate as possible, and to avoid controversy.

I researched the old school records, the Taber municipal records to help confirm the date of my leg injury and some operations. I researched the American Air Force flights and bomber fly-overs in southern Alberta in the early 1960s. I researched the St. Mary's irrigation district records, the sugar beet and cattle feeding induction in southern Alberta, the Taber rodeo records, as well as my own records of expenses from my farm at Purple Springs, including house repairs.

I researched the trainees and their placements on my farm, the ranching records in B.C., my involvement in the Cattlemen's Associations, predator control and Animal Health.

My intent was not so much to have dates, etc, accurate, as it was to record these events. For sure, some of my memories will be controversial. This is perhaps a good thing, as it helps spur the memories of others.

Note from LeRae Haynes

I sat at Tim's kitchen table and typed his story as he remembered it. I made no attempt to edit it, change it or alter his 'voice.' I just listened and typed with the laughter and tears from his memories. It's his story, and no one should try to change it. You will find errors, some repetition but also a story from his heart. You will find the appreciation of his crew and his neighbours. What comes out most is a tremendous love and admiration he has for his family and how very proud he is of every one of his grandchildren.

Carroll

Please enjoy reading this

Best Wishes

HAPPENINGS

A – Arrests, murders and killings
1. Bus arresting convicted murderer.. 35
2. Murder at the Bobtail... 149
3. Murder of Alfie and Helen's grandson.. 140
4. Knifing and murder of Jim Heaton at FRR..................................... 180
5. Drowning in the lake.. 42

B – Accidents
1. Tim's hand getting caught in combine.. 69
2. Tim's three accidents.. 79
3. Pat's eColi.. 211
4. Bale falling on Pat.. 211
5. Dan falling into lagoon... 77
6. Horse crushing Tim's leg.. 210, 121, 232

C – Ranch maps
1. FRR.. 186
2. Three ranch layouts... 229

D – Close Friends
1. Alden and David... 246
2. Frank Sitter... 246

E – Bear Encounters
1. Bear at Magnussen property... 179
2. Bear problems... 204, 205
3. Bear while feeding cows..

F – Trainees
1. Erik... 70
2. The Ruddenklaus... 81

G – Mother playing tricks
1. Tim overhauling the tractor.. 44
2. Dad in the car on the trip to Edmonton... 67

H – SPF pigs..59

I – Collins Creek at FRR.. 190

J – Forest fires
    1. Fire in 2003 202
    2. Forest fire in 2010 203

K – List of friends 293

L – Cattle drives
    1. From Aspen 208
    2. From Skiff 80
    3. From Emerald Lake and Pre-Emption 210

M – Tim driving combine at age 13 47

N – Rod scaring Tim on combine 71

O – B52 bombers 97

P – Veterinary friends
    1. Don Hamilton 86
    2. Darwin Lund 87
    3. Importing cattle from Italy 90
    4. Chianinas 82

JOHN PALLISER

In 1856 the British Government commissioned John Palliser to chart out all of western Canada. He determined that the area from west of Moosejaw following the Cypress Hills west to the Milk River, north of Ft. MacCloud, northwest to Brooks, further northeast to Oyen following the South Saskatchewan River to Piapot, back to Moosejaw, to be wasteland and of little use for agriculture production and said that no development would ever take place.

120 years later Lethbridge, in the heart of the Palliser triangle, was slaughtering 69% of the meat in Canada and 60% of Canada's domestic sugar requirements. Today 260 different crops are grown to enhance food production, including 80% of Canada's hemp, 40% of its seed potatoes and 30% of its onions.

John Palliser was very wrong. I grew up in the centre of that triangle. In the early 1800s ranchers established large herds of cattle on the north slopes of the Sweet Grass hills. There was warm weather, good grass and open winters encouraged ranching. Ranchers moved their herds from Colorado, Wyoming and Montana to what now is known as the Milk River Plateau.

Milk River Ridge gets high rainfall amounts and mild winters. Growing up we often seen the clouds and Chinook conditions develop in the southwest. The hills west of Purple Springs seemed to turn back the clouds and rainfall amounts; Taber may receive a half inch of rain in a rain storm, but 11 miles east and on our farm, we might get nothing.

The weather man in Lethbridge would often give his weather reports, issued by Environment Canada, and then he would tell us what might really happen based on an Indian chief in the Cardston Mountainview area. This chief would forecast the weather by looking at Chief Mountain east of Waterton Park.

When I was growing up most of the area was prairie and rolling hills, but you could see open spaces – you could see for miles in many directions. To the west were the hills southeast of Purple Springs. To the north were the sand hills. These were areas that settlers broke up the sod for farming at the turn of the century.

During the drought years and the Depression of the 1930s there was not enough rain to support grain or grass. The wind started the soil to blow and drift; the top sod all blew away and nothing was left but sand.

Some of the sand hills were 15 to 20 feet high. To the east you could see for miles – it was as flat as a table. It was excellent farm land farmed by many Mennonite families who were conscientious objectors during the war.

They were able to take advantage of the fact that many of the young men in the area had gone to fight in the war. The Mennonites bought up a lot of the best farmland; to the south were the beautiful Sweet Grass hills that adorned the skyline like mountains.

There were miles and miles of native prairie grass that was called Sweet Grass. It did not grow very high - 6 to 8 inches and was very rich and high in protein. Cows would get fat on this grass that looked barren to many people.

The rolling coulees provided shelter and protection from the wind in summer and winter - it was truly a paradise to ride. Wildlife was limited but in the spring it came alive with crocuses and the very beautiful wild roses.

They were very aromatic: I can still smell them.

There were also areas of patches of sand grass and other areas of sagebrush. It was the original home of the buffalo path leading to their water holes and valleys of the Old Man River which criss-crossed the prairies.

Huge rocks were rubbed shiny and the area around them were wore deep from buffalo rubs. When irrigation was introduced the whole structure of the land changed in just a few years, and for cowboys like myself and my brothers this was very sad to see.

But we also broke up many acres of this pristine prairie to make a profitable and rewarding lives for our families.

But make no mistake - we still longed for the great yet demanding life of the natural prairie.

Growing up it was not uncommon to see prairie chickens. I watched their mating dance and circles on several occasions. We would also see Medium Grouse and Barred Brown Grouse, but my favourite bird of all was the Meadow Lark. Its song truly is music to your ears. We seen Lucy Warblers, Chickadees and Grey Beaked Thrush and the Caroline Wrens.

Water and shore birds such as Long Tailed Jasper, the Red Knot Sandpiper and Spoon Billed Sandpipers, and Killdeer were often seen. They did their imitations of being hurt to lead you away from their young.

Hungarian Partridges were very plentiful: they were good hunting and good to eat. There were many kinds of gulls, like Franklin, Eskimo and Little Gulls. We sometimes seen the Common Crane and Blue Crane, as well as the Pintails and Mallards that we also hunted.

Birds of prey included the Prairie Falcon, the Peregrine Falcon, the Ferruginous Hawk, the Red Hawk and the Coopers Hawk. Pigeons were common, as were the swallows, plus the Small Burrowing Owl.

In the winter we often seen the Great Snowy Owl and the Great Horned Owl and large flocks of snowbirds. You could easily determine if a bird was native as the feathers grew all the way down their legs to their feet. If the bird was introduced from Europe or the southern U.S. the feathers stopped at the top of the leg.

Foxes were common, as well as weasels and wild mink; the Jackrabbit and Snowshoe rabbits were also common.

We had many sparrows and a few Robins

We often seen rattlesnakes, Garters and occasionally a Bull snake

I truly enjoyed walking or riding on the prairies watching out for birds or wildlife.

Crows and Magpies were also a real nuisance.

MOM AND DAD

My dad was born in 1888 in Wales; his dad, my grandfather, was a games keeper, which was a prestigious thing to be. He provided pheasants, etc, for the wealthy.

Dad grew up being kind of a loner; he was very involved with hunting and following dignitaries around.

Grandad's house was preserved as a heritage house and was not allowed to be torn down. Today the people who own the property have this old heritage house in the middle of their home – they built their house around it.

My brother Gerald visited England and Wales several times and researched about dad in church records.

Dad was sent to school in Wales, and he said he was a terrible scholar. He was enrolled in a school to learn carpentry. His dad told him he was too dumb to go to school and needed to learn a trade. He was a bit of a little renegade back then, and joined what he called the army for two years.

On a side note, when Dad, Mom and my brother Jack went to England in 1973 they visited the area where Dad grew up. He kept saying, "I've been here before," and Jack kept saying, "No you haven't." One morning Jack came downstairs in the hotel where they were staying and Dad was sitting there by himself looking at the fireplace.

He told Jack, "I've been here before. I'll prove it to you." He went to the front desk and asked for a measuring tape, walked over and measured the fireplace, which was about 20 feet long. One side was about one inch longer than the other side. The innkeeper said, "How did you know that?" and he answered, "When I was 16 years old I was fired for building it wrong."

On that trip Dad got quite sick and ended up in the hospital in England for about three months. He was sure he was going to die. It was in his stomach and bowel. All the health care was free there, and that helped him big-time.

When they brought him back to Canada, Frank picked him up and took him to the hospital in Lethbridge. He was there for a couple more weeks before moving to the hospital in Taber.

When Dad was 16 years old his parents were going to immigrate to Africa. Grandad knew Cecil Rhodes, who asked him to come when starting Rhodesia. Cecil Rhodes died, however, before Grandad and Grandma left England.

When Dad was 17 he had made up his mind he wanted to travel and decided to come to Canada instead of Africa.

Granny Brewin with Dad as a baby in 1888

My dad, Roland Frank Brewin at Wokingham, Berkshire 1907

Mom – Marjorie Brewin 1925 – age 26 years

Uncle Jack, Mom on the right, and their sisters

Mom and Dad

Roland Frank Brewin and Monty

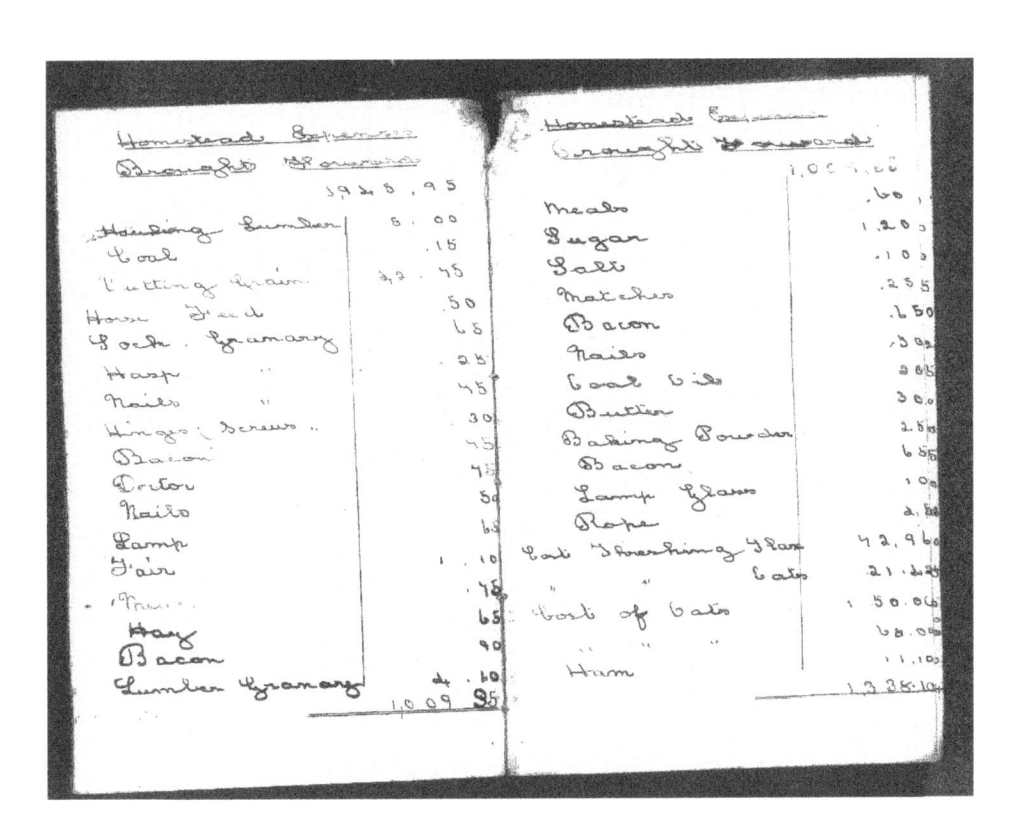

Dad's ledger page one 1908

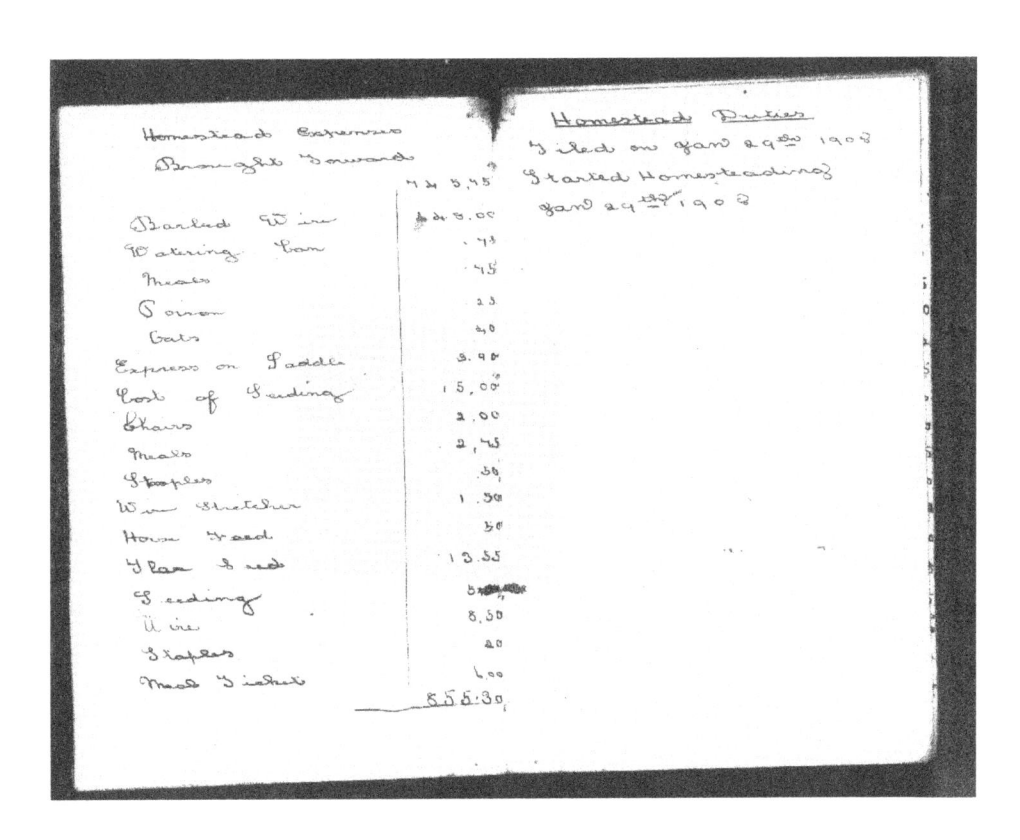

Dad's ledger page two 1908

On a side note, my wife Pat and I went to Pier 21 in Halifax. That is where most people land in Canada from Europe, and all soldiers left from there. We looked up the records on Dad's travels and found that he didn't come through Halifax - he sailed from England to Montreal and then headed west to Calgary.

In Calgary Dad met up with Eager Westlake, who he had been in the army with in Wales. Dad took on several jobs around Calgary; it was extremely hot and he wandered around looking for work for a couple of weeks. He went to the English consulate and they said, "Get rid of your English clothes and get western clothes," and the next day he got a job at the Palister Hotel in Calgary as a carpenter.

He worked there for a while, as well as odd jobs around the area. In 1905 he was told to go to Taber because you could get 160 acres for $10 and homestead on it, so he did. He met up with Eagar Westlake again; a group of 10 of them all decided to homestead on land northeast of Taber, bordering on one another. It was SW-14-9-14 W-4.

When Dad went in to fill out the papers for the homestead, he accidently put down the wrong township. The land that the rest of them homesteaded on was sand hills and very dry. Dad's land had been previously filed by another homesteader who had built a shack and a well. This homesteader couldn't make his payments and do the work for a homestead so he had to let it go.

When he went out to look at the homestead, he went out on a nice warm fall day; but by evening a blizzard settled in. He had no gloves or warm jacket. He stumbled into a sheep camp of Albert Greene's. Greene looked after him for a few days, then put him on a train from Purple Springs to Taber, said "You dumb Englishman, you'll never survive here." They ended up becoming lifelong friends.

This land was in the middle of land that a bunch of Americans had homesteaded on, so as an Englishman Dad was not real welcome. They did a lot of things to discourage him like blocking his chimney and chasing his horses around. They really tried to drive Dad away.

Then Dad married a lady named Hilda Yates, whose parents were school teachers at a small country school along the railroad tracks called Antoinia. There was a school every six miles, according to an agreement between the government and the rail road.

Dad and Hilda had three children: Alfred, Monica and Norman. We always called Norman 'Bus' because as Dad got older he had seven sons and couldn't remember our names. He called us all 'Bus' short for 'Buster' but it stuck with Norman.

They lived on a farm until 1921, when Hilda died in a flu epidemic, leaving Dad with three small children. After a couple of years, he met my mother, Marjorie Shenfield, a school teacher in Purple Springs who taught school to 65 kids from Grades 1-9. As Mom grew older, kids she had taught told her how much they appreciated her and how much they learned from her. They all had tremendous respect for her.

Dad went in for their first date with her and bought a tennis suit with white shoes: he was really going to impress her. They married after a couple of years, in 1924.

He said he was so lonely.

He must have pulled a really good con on her. Mom and Dad had five boys and two girls: Jack, Gerald, Frank, Rod, Tim, Eleanor and Marjorie.

MY EARLY LIFE

I was born in Lethbridge. Marjorie and I were the only ones born in a hospital. The rest were born at home. I was named after Timothy Eaton and Winston Churchill, who were two prominent people in the war effort against Germany.

Winston Churchill was really big in my family: he was a hero and we had pictures of him all over the place. We read everything we could about him, and one of the things I always enjoyed was reading about his wit and humour. When he was in the government, there was a lot of opposition to a lot of his thoughts and ideas. At one big banquet, he was sitting by a lady who had no use for him. She leaned over and said, "Mr. Churchill, if you were my husband I'd put poison in your drink." He replied, "Madam, if you were my wife I'd drink it."

We suffered some shortages, I truly do not remember feeling we suffered or were in need.

Growing up, we got along very well and were well-behaved. Mother seldom had to discipline us, and I never remember getting a spanking. A few times, stern words were used, but for the most part, my older brothers disciplined me. I always wanted to look good in their eyes and tried hard not to misbehave.

This write up is about many traumatic experiences I had: crimes, thefts and even murder.

The first is our house burning down when I was three years old. I remember neighbours and men on the roof fighting the house fire. My brother Rod and I were sent to play in a dirt pile some distance from the fire. The house was completely demolished. For the next year and a half, we lived in three work cars and storage units from the M.D. Each one was 10' by 16'.

Monica had left home and moved to Lumby, B.C. and Alfred went to work in Lethbridge for two years until he was old enough to sign up in the Air Force. Norman, or 'Bus' as we called him, followed in 1943. They both signed up with the R.C.M.P. at the end of the war. Bus also trained as a prison guard for one year. He told us many stories and experiences. Both Bus and Alfred took boxing lessons as teenagers and were very good. Bus won the Alberta Golden Gloves in the 165lb weight class.

We were all raised on the farm at Purple Springs. Besides raising mink and badgers for pelts, Dad started buying furs from other farmers and shipping them to Winnipeg. He went to Winnipeg a few times with the furs to make sure everything was done fairly.

This was the 1930's and very few people had any income. Many times, older people would come to me and say if it weren't for dad they would have starved to death.

There was an abundance of coyotes, rabbits and weasels so the farmers and their sons would spend most of the winter trapping.

My first real memory was when our house burned down when I was three years old. I remember men on the roof trying to put out the fire. My brother Rod and I were told to get way back, and we played on a dirt pile while the house burned down.

The only things saved from the house was Mom's canary, which she grabbed on her way out, and a big silver spoon, found later, that had been taken out when the dogs were fed that morning. We lost everything.

At the time Dad was on the council for the municipal district and he arranged for three of the cook cars to be brought to the farm. They were all 10'x16', and Mother set one up as a cook house and the other two for sleeping. J.R. Fletcher also gave us a cook car from his harvest crew.

The first night after the fire my brothers have told me we were all sent to different neighbours for the night. Next morning at 6am Mom sent my two oldest brothers to pick us all up; she wanted us all together.

We lived about two years in the cars. Dad owned some land about four miles away with a house on it and he pulled the house over to the farm and we lived in it.

Because of the war, it was probably tough times. I don't remember wanting anything or needing anything. Mother always had chickens and pigs and sheep; we were provided for. The Government gave us coupons for things like sugar, salt and some clothing, but years later when we opened Mother's safety deposit box at the bank, we found a pile of those coupons. She didn't have to use them; she was saving them for 'tough times.'

As a family we were really close. Frank, Eleanor, Rod and I were especially close: always playing together and always supporting each other. Gerald was three years older than Frank and he was a big brother that looked after us and kept us on the right track.

I guess I have three real heroes in my life--one is Winston Churchill, the second is my mother and the third was my brother Gerald, who always supported me in what I did.

I remember at the end of the war Mother and Dad had a large bonfire that they lit to symbolize Hitler being burned. To this day, the only time I ever heard my mother swear was when she threw a log on that fire and said, "Burn, you son of a bitch, burn!"

She was so glad the war was over.

For many years my dad had large numbers of sheep. He would hire sheep herders to look after them.

In the summer months when my brother Gerald was 11 and 12, he often looked after the sheep, and stayed in these wagons. This was a lonely, boring job. When I was only four or five years old, he would occasionally take me with him for company. These wagons were very hot, as you also cooked in them, making it very difficult to sleep at night.

I remember one night asking Gerald if we could sleep outside, and he gave me a very definite 'No!'

The next morning, about 200 feet from the camp, he showed me a rattlesnake all curled up. I never asked to sleep outside again.

My sister Eleanor remembers going to the camp with Dad to check on the sheep herders one spring. The sheep herder he had hired abandoned the sheep, leaving them still locked in the corral without any water. A few sheep were dead. Eleanor and dad pumped water for hours to save as many as they could.

Photos taken at Remington Carriage in Cardston Alberta in 2010

As a family we stayed very close, especially the five of us, for the rest of our lives. We always said we weren't brothers and sisters, we were friends.

One of my earliest tasks was bringing in the firewood and coal for the cook stove. When I was about six or seven I was put in charge of the chickens: clean the pens, feed them and get the eggs. The chickens served me very well. Within a couple of years we had about 100 hens, and I was allowed to sell the eggs. So, I had some spending money. I shipped eggs twice a week by rail to the Co-op in Lethbridge and would get a cheque for between $6 to $10 a week.

My two oldest brothers, Bus and Alfred, had left home when I was a baby, and my oldest sister Monica left before I was born. She married Jim Berryhill and they moved to B.C. and logged and had a small dairy. It was always great to have these older brothers and sister come home; they spoiled us, and when Alfred got married his wife Lillian was a real big sister to us. She would come home and really look after us.

I remember the Berryhill kids coming to visit - there were five of them, plus the four of us, and we would get on the two saddle horses we had. I have pictures of nine of us on our horse Tony; it was so much fun.

Mom looked after the hired men after the war, and Eleanor was always busy helping Mom with the housework and looking after these guys. I will always remember Eleanor with a great deal of respect for how hard she worked. She left home to go to Olds Agricultural School when she was 17 years old.

She met a boyfriend there. He come to the farm to take her to the show one night. Of course, her four brothers weren't going to accept that. We went to the theatre (Gerald could drive) and sat behind them in the theatre, and when they went to the restaurant after the movie, we sat behind them there, too. I don't think she ever quite forgave us. That was her last date with Henry.

When she got out of Olds, she went to secretarial school in Calgary. Dad didn't really want her to go and he give her some money but it wasn't enough. She knew that. I lent her about $250 from my egg money, and she paid that back with her first paycheque from work. That speaks to how close we all were.

There was so much happening between 1945 and 1948--such progress. There was a huge irrigation canal built that went right by our house. During that time, we must have had some excellent crops: Dad bought a lot of new equipment. Dad continued to buy furs and also was very involved in the stock market.

He helped with the farm and provided direction, but the work was mostly done by us boys with Gerald and Frank leading the work.

We had excellent crops; I remember piles and piles of grain on the ground. Mother had the hired men, usually two or three. They were bums, but she kept them working.

Dad only went back to England twice. Once was in 1929; he was there when the stock market crashed. When he came home Mother had taken good care of the farm, but times were tough again.

When Dad was about 60 years old, Gerald had the idea at Christmas time to arrange a phone call to his sisters in England. Gerald talked to them first (he'd been to England and had met them) and put Dad on the phone. Dad talked to his three sisters for a few minutes. He got off the phone and said, "I just can't understand them. They're just too damned English."

As a young child, I had a German Shepherd named Sport. We did everything together - we were best buddies. My brothers and sisters were in school, so we hung out. I used to walk down the quarter mile to meet the school bus when my brothers and sisters would get off the bus. One day I decided to go meet the bus and I didn't tell my mother.

I walked down to where I met the school bus, but it never came. It was about two in the afternoon and it started to storm. Sport took me by the sleeve and led me home and by the time we got there it was a real blizzard.

When I got home I opened the door and walked in covered with snow. Mother asked me where I'd been, and I got a real talking-to. That was one time Sport saved my life.

When I was about seven years old, Dad would take the hired men to the field and I really wanted to go with them. One day they came in for lunch and I went out and crawled under the truck so I'd be there when they came out, and I'd get to go with them. I fell asleep. Dad put the truck in reverse and looked in the rear view mirror, and saw Sport dragging me out from behind the back wheels.

There was another time I got hell for being in the wrong place at the wrong time. We had chickens that ran around in the yard. Dad fancied himself a pretty good shot, and when Mom wanted a chicken, he'd sit on the back step and shoot one for dinner. The yard had a lot of tall grass that I would play in, and one day I was out there and suddenly I heard Dad shouting and hollering at me and giving me hell. My head popped up right between him and the chicken, and I ruined a good shot.

My brothers and sisters all went to a school about a mile and half from home, at the Sherbune School. I started school in a one-room school south of there named Hudson school. There were about 30 students in Grades 1-9. We were bussed six miles east of there to Deer Park School after that. Deer Park had two schools in the yard; the other was Wild Park.

In those days, the school district provided very little in sports equipment so you played your own games. The big thing we did in those four or five years was dig tunnels and caves at school. We were tough little boys. I always thought, 'Poor guy who farmed that after us.' We'd smoke weeds for cigarettes and really thought we were somebody, I guess.

In Grade 9 they closed those two schools and we attended Chamberlain School in Grassy Lake.

By the time I was in Grade 9 and Rod was in Grade 11, Dad needed us at home to help on the farm so we got to miss a lot of school. If we had taken the bus to school we had to leave at 7:30 so he bought us a car and Rod drove us 10 miles to school.

Rod got married after he finished Grade 12. From then on, I drove myself. At the school in Grassy Lake we had a gym and sports equipment; I also took a big interest in drama and was in all the school plays.

Gerald Brewin in front of the house that burned in 1938

Monica Brewin, house on Brewin farm in 1920

Bus at Granny's in 1957

Alfred Brewin driving horses 1938

Alfred, Monica, Tim, Eleanor, Gerald, Frank and Rod

Brewin farm 1945

Combines and oil rig on Brewin farm 1952

Grassy Lake Grades 9-12

Air Cadets 1955

Oil rig on sec-13-9-14 in 1955

Dad and Bus 1948

Rod and Eleanor 1940

Three generations: Alfred and Bob (front row) Bob Jr. and Jim (back row)

T-Bone

Carson Jones, July 16, 1991, seated in Grimshaw heritage chair made in early 1700s. Grimshaws were Mother's family

Alfred, Eleanor, Frank, Tim, Rod and Gerald in 1980

Frank and Gerald (back row) Rod, Eleanor and Tim (front row)

Frank, Eleanor and Tim in 2017: the three remaining family members

FIRST YEAR AT OLDS COLLEGE

I then went to Olds Agricultural College for two years. I loved Olds because I got to be on the wrestling team, boxing team, gymnastic team, played a lot of badminton and excelled at basketball.

The Dean of Men at Olds was an excellent mentor. He called all 200 boys his boys and was like a dad to us all. Unfortunately, they had a policy at the school that there was no alcohol allowed in the dorms. When we went back for the second year, we found out that he had been dismissed - caught drinking in his room one night.

He called me and five other boys into his office and told us what had happened and asked us to gather all the other male students together and tell them what happened. He couldn't face the rest of the boys.

Years later we had a gathering with more than 600 kids to honour him; he was so well regarded.

One day in class we were examining the laying hens, and as I walked by a classmate named Andy, and he said, "Tim, I can't get this chicken to sit still, what do I do?" I said, "Just wring its neck." And he did. I got kicked out of class for a week.

Another time I got kicked out of class - Journey class. One of the boys would throw a penny or nickel at the blackboard to aggravate the teacher. One day I was really interested in the lecture, and this boy Leroy tossed a penny. The teacher looked around and everybody but me was laughing: I was busy writing notes. He thought I did it and kicked me out of class.

I was told I couldn't return to class until I apologized to the instructor. I refused to because I hadn't done anything. I was out of class over a month and was told I wouldn't be able to graduate.

But I guess I was a stubborn as the principal. He came to me and said, "I know you didn't do it, but just apologize." I wouldn't. He got a group of professors and instructors to put together an exam for me, and if I passed by 80% I could graduate.

The exam was on field husbandry, which was what I had done all my life. When I wrote the exam it was supposed to be two and a half hour exam. I finished it in under an hour. And got 98%.

MY SECOND YEAR AT OLDS

I met my first wife Marj at Olds during my second year. She starred on the girls' basketball team and I was one of the better players on the men's team.

When I graduated in 1957, I wasn't sure if I wanted to go back to the farm. I had been offered a job with the irrigation specialist in Lethbridge, and I accepted it. That's what I was going to do, but when I went home, Dad and my brothers convinced me there was an opportunity for me at the farm; they rented me some land and I farmed.

EARLY YEARS FARMING AND STARTING A FAMILY

We worked well together and moved the farm ahead. Dad had wanted to buy another ranch but my older brother Jack was dead set against it so we all stayed.

Marj was from Blackie, Alberta where her parents had a farm. The next summer she got a job in Taber at the bank and moved there. We started dating full time and were married in 1960.

Bev was born in 1963 in Taber, Dan was born in 1964, Sandra was born in 1969, Dixie in 1971 and Naomi in 1980.

Dan, Marj, Dixie, Bev, Sandra and Tim in 1971

I am so proud of my kids. They all got a good education and have their own lives.

The Manyberries pasture was a huge natural grass area and ran 2,500 cows. When I was about 35 years old I was asked to assist with the A.I.

I drove down every other day for the nine days and another A.I. technician from Medicine Hat, Don. did the same. It was great to ride this area. No buildings on site, only coyotes, badgers, foxes, deer and antelope for wild animals. There were many hawks, meadowlarks and small birds.

I truly enjoyed the days I worked there. I sometimes rode with Gerald on our ranch. He loved to ride into the Prairie Chicken dances. Nothing is more peaceful than riding on the wide-open prairie.

I want to share with you an incident I had when herding cows when I was 11. I was walking back to the Jeep on an old buffalo trail when I seen a badger following me. The faster I walked, the more it increased its speed. It was, in fact, chasing me. Badgers have sharp teeth, long claws and you do not want to tangle with one. I was very glad to reach the Jeep but it tried to get at me until I got the Jeep started and out of there. It chased the Jeep for several hundred yards.

My dad raised badgers for their hides, along with wild mink. His dens were accessible from the house before it burnt down. They were kept underground. When I was a boy the badgers' den dugout was very evident for years after the house burned.

I will touch on two irrigation ditch rider incidents. One ditch rider was always up early, checking his water and would be very upset if anyone tinkered with his head gates. There was a lot of Indians that came to southern Alberta to hoe sugar beets. The ditch rider did not like them or get along with them and vice versa. They were often drunk and teased him.

One morning I went out at 4am to move my irrigation water in my field ditch. As I drove through the trail on the pasture, I seen the ditch rider truck surrounded by a lot of drunk Indian ladies.

They were having a grand time teasing the ditch rider, who was about 65. Many of these Indian ladies had taken their clothes off, pissing on his trunk. They were trying to get money from him. Two of these Indians were part of a crew that had hauled bales for us. When I suggested they move on, they left with no problem.

Another incident was when we had a young ditch rider. His first name was Dave. Again, I was out changing my irrigation water early on Sunday morning. He came driving like a maniac, honking his horn and very scared. He had been cleaning out weeds in one of his head gates when he pulled up a hand and body. He threw his weed fork. Never did find it. I went home, phoned the R.C.M.P. in Taber. They said it was not in their area. I phoned Bow Island R.C.M.P.; they did not want to deal with it, so said it was not in their area.

I phoned Lethbridge and they made Taber R.C.M.P. attend. The police wanted my help to retrieve the body but I refused as it was not something I wanted to do.

As Dan grew up he worked with me on the farm. We experimented with a lot of things like canola, lentils, different grains and sunflowers. We put up and sold hay and straw. Farming was a real challenge. We borrowed a lot of money and went into debt.

In 1989 Dan decided that farming did not seem to hold a lot of future for him and he wanted to go back to university. We both decided that it was time for us both to move on, so we sold out. I knew several people with the Bank of Montreal and they made two suggestions to me. One was an offer to manage a small Purebred Herford ranch at Princeton, B.C.

The other was to manage a large beef ranch owned by the Natives at Merritt B.C. There was a lot of problems, theft cattle shortages, etc at that operation and the bank wanted someone to protect their interests. I wanted and accepted the position at Princeton.

The house there had been built by the notorious Billy Minor. But the bank phoned and asked me if I would instead take on the position as manager at the Bobtail Ranch in Penticton.

During my time farming at Purple Springs I was the victim of some crime: stolen batteries, gas, tools, etc. Dan had a motor bike stolen out of the shop. It was his pride and joy. They recovered it but it was spray painted a terrible purple colour.

My brother Rod had an older house he rented out to some Indians. His wife Louise was driving the grain truck and they ran her off the road. Rod came down and got really pissed off. There was four Indian men and three women living in the house but Rod marched in and told them to get out.

He called me and Gerald and told us to look out for them, and sure enough, they came to our yards trying to get gas. Had in fact stole some blankets, etc from Rod. We followed them to Frank's yard and I pulled up tight behind them so they could not back up. We seen a lot of tools in their car and that the front license was Alberta and the rear Sask. They were from Saskatchewan.

We called the police and kept them there until the police came. They walked around; the women pretending to cry a lot between the vehicles. When the police came, they would not charge them, as they could only charge the drivers. Instead, they escorted them out of Alberta.

The next morning my hired man went to fill up my truck with gas and noticed sugar on the top of the gas tank. The squaws had opened up a bag of sugar in their car and were walking by my truck with hands full of sugar, putting it in my tank. I had only driven two miles. We took the heads off my truck and the carb and filters.

Luckily, we caught it soon enough and no damage was done.

The Hutterites had a reputation of being dishonest. This was not my dealings with them. They came to buy a boar, picked one and asked what I wanted for it. I said $125. The three men looked at one another, thanked me and said they wanted three boars and 10 gilts.

They said they checked around and knew what I sold my pigs for. They said everyone else tried to take advantage of them, but because I was honest then would take more. They became good customers, usually buying four boars a year.

I always tagged my cows with a large dangle - a plastic tag with a number on it, and a small metal tag with the same number and my name on it. One fall I was missing six cows I could not find.

The auction market in Taber burned down, complete with all the records. About four years later the brand inspector in Lethbridge phoned to say that a farmer from Warner had tried to sell one of my missing cows in Baylog auction in Lethbridge. I had very good descriptions of the cows I was missing and was able to clearly identify the cow as mine.

The farmer claimed he had bought the cow and one other in Taber before the market burned down. The next spring, he tried to sell four more of my cows in Fort Mcleod. This time the stories did not match up and he was charged. I got my four cows back but was out possibly 30 calves over the years.

Questionable practices on Bobtail

When we took over management of the Bobtail Ranch in Penticton B.C. we experienced a lot of questionable practices. The ranch was owned by Bob Gibson from Calgary, and the cow boss was Kenny Mclean.

We would buy our salt and minerals in bulk, 10 tons at a time in spring.

I caught one of the crew selling salt blocks one at a time to a neighbouring ranch.

Dixie came to stay with Pat and I and that is where she met Steve. I did get along good with Dave Rolston, a previous manager. Over the next three years he helped me out a lot, particularly with the Natives.

Going back to when I was 16

I had raised market hogs ever since I was 16. We had three small farrowing barns and sold about 200 weaner piglets each year. Marj and I were married in 1960. In 1963 I borrowed $160,000, bought some land and designed and built a heated confinement barn with slotted floors, and a lagoon to facilitate manure disposal.

I bought my own portable grinder. The barn held 1,100 pigs from weaners to market. They were all hand fed. I had four farrowing crates and 80 sows that farrowed three times a year.

As disease was a problem with hogs, I purchased 16 S.P.F. bred gilts. S.P.F. stands for Specific Pathogen Free, or disease free. This was done by taking the piglets from their mothers by caesarean section in a sterile environment. The little pigs did not even breathe the same air as their mothers. They would go to market at 210lbs in five months as compared to other hogs that took seven to seven-and-a-half months. This saved a lot on feed, drugs and health costs.

This procedure was started by Dr. Greenway and the Lacombe research station. I bought my breeding stock from certified S.P.F. producers in central Alberta, of which there were only 10. I was number 11. I was named to the Alberta Agriculture Herd Health where we developed strategies for swine health as well as beef and cheep health.

This proved to be a big benefit to me; it was headed up by Dr. Jim O'Donahue, who was highly regarded all over the world.

Years later I was asked by his staff to be a field auditor for various Alberta sponsored subsidy programs. More about these programs, its problems and dishonest cattle producers later. I worked for three years part time as a field auditor. My headquarters were in Medicine Hat, but I audited beef herds, swine operations, poultry and sheep operations for eight months a year, all over southern Alberta. It paid very well and provided me with the funds to start my own cattle herd in three years, and to buy more land, irrigation equipment and machinery.

My association and partnership with my brothers Gerald, Frank and Rod played a big part in this. We worked well together, shared equipment, and supported each other.

We formed a company called Purple Spring Cattle Co. We imported Chianina and Romagnolo cattle from Italy to flush and breed the embryos. Our company bought 1,100 acres of pasture land and 60 head of cattle to breed to new breeds from Europe. I was elected to care for, breed and house this herd. Under an arrangement with American Breeder Service, I fall-calved this herd (in November) for four years. The calves were placed on feed trials and tests at Bassano, Alberta and tested against Chianina and Romagnola, and many other European breeds, and Welsh Black cattle.

Two of the four years our calves placed 1st in rate of gain and carcass tests.

We tried many new ventures and were:
1. First to breed and calve Chianina calves in Canada
2. First to import Romagnola bulls and heifers from Italy
3. Firsts to breed and calve out Romagnola cattle
4. First to sell Chianina embryos to United States
5. First to import Romagnola and Chianina cattle from Italy to Britain
6. I was the first person to export S.P.F. hogs to the U.S.
7. Gerald, Frank, Rod and I were the first Canadian farmers to form a farm syndicate that enabled us to borrow money form Farm Credit Corp. to purchase farm equipment
8. We were the first to put Romangonola bulls in an A.I. stud and sell semen
9. Rod was the first person in Canada to successfully artificially inseminate a horse with frozen semen. When I moved to Williams Lake I was the first producer to utilize liquid fertilizer in pivot irrigation systems.
10. I was the first person to utilize triticale grain as a silage grain in B.C.

I want to note here that we put our Romangonola bulls in Universal Breeders A.I. stud at Cardston. Various A.I. technicians would pick up the semen directly from Universal Breeders and pay us directly for it. We sold it for $2 per ampule or straw.

I mentioned Dr. Greenway was involved in the S.P.F. technology. He had moved to Williams Lake, actually bought grassland there and it was named after him.

Another coincidence was when I was 10 or 11 years old. Dad hired a hired man named Harold. He often told us of the large sheep ranch in B.C. that he had worked on. It consisted of 5,000 sheep and four flocks that they would turn out with herders in the spring. They would do a circuit of about 80 miles up the mountains every summer, returning to the ranch headquarters in late October.

On the Bobtail Ranch that I managed there was evidence of many sheep camps. When Gerald visited me at the Bobtail we figured it out that the Bobtail originally was the Gardener Sheep Ranch 30 years before.

As a boy of 10 and 11 years old one of my duties was to look after and herd our 300 cows and corral them every night. Dad bought a 1949 army style jeep for me to do this. I did this for three years at 10, 11 and 12 years of age, until adequate fencing was put up to keep the cattle out of the grain fields.

1952 and 1953 were very good years for growing grain on our farm. Dad bought three no. 55 John Deere self-propelled combines and a large three-ton grain truck. At age 13 I was given the job of driving one of these combines, Rod another and Gerald the other one. A lot of the grain was piled on the ground and delivered to the elevator in the winter. We grew mostly Durum wheat, pearling barley and flax. These were very good years and our farm really expanded.

I also played a lot of ball in June and July on our local men's team; I was pitcher. Thanks to Dad and George Wesley who coached the Lethbridge White Socks and their contacts, I was invited to attend the White Socks baseball school in Pennsylvania when I was 15.

This school was run by Ken and Cletus Boyer. Dad did offer to pay the $2,000 school costs. But we were also very short of help on the farm and ranch. I did not go. At age 16 I got a letter from the St. Louis Cardinals baseball camp, again inviting me to their school. Again, I found excuses not to go. I think I was either afraid to leave home or did not think I was good enough.

When I was nine years old my brother Jack was infected with polio. He spent over a year in intensive care in the University Hospital in Edmonton and lost the use of his right arm and had a long and difficult recovery.

12 years later he contracted Brucellosis from the cattle, which he also took several years to recover from. I continued to work very hard on my farm, experienced several crop failures, could not afford any help until 1965 when I hired my first agricultural trainee, Erik Hothe from Norway.

I continued to grow grain and run a small herd of cattle. I had over 400 acres of flood irrigation. I was often up at 4:00am to change irrigation setup. I also did the health and A.I. work on my brother Jack and Dad's 350 cattle.

We did all our own machinery repairs. Bev, Danny, Sandra and Dixie came into our lives and were a big help.

I also became good friends with a local vet, Dr. Darwin Lund. We were on the agricultural board and rodeo committee together. Darwin travelled to Australia as well as Zambia in Africa to rodeo. He won the Australian All Around; his dad had won it 20 years earlier.

He got me to look after his cows and horses while he was gone. For this, he gave me two very good horses: Swede and Cherry.

Before that my main horses were Jingles and Billy.

When we imported the heifers and bulls from Italy, they had to go through three months' quarantine in Italy - three months on an island (Irish property). All the feed was shipped in from

Ireland. Everything had to be from a country that never had had Foot and Mouth Disease. This was followed by six months' quarantine on an appraisal sit in Calgary. They were under close supervision by Health of Animals and regularly blood tested by veterinarians.

We were not allowed to visit any of these sites or see our cattle until they were released to us after learning quarantine time and no semen was to be kept or used.

But the vet service in Calgary hired to do some of the inspections did drain semen and breed cows. Darwin somehow found out they had done this, and in fact had bred 60 cows to our Romangonola bulls. We lodged a complaint with Health of Animals and those bred cows were all destroyed. This was an enterprising attempt by these vets to try to cheat the system. But it did put us in good standing with Dr. Woodward at American Breeders Service (A.B.S.).

In 1972 Frank and I took an artificial insemination course with A.B.S. at Pincher Creek. It included instruction on cattle anatomy and how to preg test. We both did very well at the school and became friends with the instructors.

Several times in the next year I was asked to help A.B.S. at the schools as what they called a checker. I would check to see the students were doing the procedure correctly. The pay for that was usually travel expenses, hotel and good steak suppers and meeting good farmers and ranchers.

I was asked to help out at schools in Medicine Hat, Brooks and Claresholm. I was also asked by a local vet and a few farmers to preg test their cows. I would only charge travel expense and $3.00 per cow.

The farms I helped out were all local: Taber, Warner, Vauxhall and Hays. I got a letter from Health of Animals that informed me not to do this as what I was doing was considered diagnostic medicine and as I was not a vet. It was illegal for me to do it.

The complaint came from a 4H parent from Vauxhall whose cattle I had checked three years in a row. The S.O.B. never did pay me.

Flashback to Dad

My dad, Roland Frank Brewin Sr., was elected to the municipal council of Eureka, Alberta in 1936, which later became the Municipal District of Taber. He served on that council for over 30 years, many as Reeve.

During the Depression many had lost their homes and businesses, so Dad helped implement a tax relief and debt relief so they could get back in control of their land and property. During the war years, many Japanese people from the west coast resettled in southern Alberta, as did many Doukhobors. Many settled on farms, and over the years became successful and respected citizens.

A lot of them settled on land with very limited access, and Dad worked hard to encourage the municipality to help these settlers.

Growing up and farming in southern Alberta, many descendants of these settlers were my neighbours. They had been uprooted from their homes, placed in internment camps and resettled in southern Alberta.

As Reeve of the municipality, Dad and the mayor of Taber, Doug Miller, took steps to build a hospital in Taber to serve Taber and the surrounding areas. They lobbied the provincial government and secured funding for this effort. Work started on this hospital in 1942.

The hospital was opened in 1943 and the nurses' residence was built in 1949. Dad served for 31 years on the hospital board, most of this time as chairman

My mom, Marjorie Shenfield, was born in Bowden, Alberta; she had four sisters and one brother. Her dad was the postmaster and also a notary public in Bowden.

Later her parents moved to a farm in Innisfail, Alberta. When I was young I remember taking the train from Purple Springs to Bowden. I remember my grandmother and my aunts always making a big fuss of Rod, Eleanor and me. My uncle Jack loved to joke around and tease us. He was very adamant that mother never be allowed to make a cake without putting icing on it.

He lectured me time and time again: "Don't you let her make a cake without icing."

My mother worked very hard raising 10 kids and was sometimes in charge of two or three hired men. She met Dad while teaching at Purple Springs. She boarded with a local family who also owned the store.

I had some traumatic experiences in my life.

When I was a baby Monica went to Lumby, and Alfred went to Lethbridge to work at Fefferman and Davis, which traded in furs and hides. Norman, or Bus, enlisted in the Air Force in 1943. They both later signed up with the R.C.M.P. at the end of the war.

That's where Bus also trained as a prison guard;

During the depression years water was very scarce; Alfred raised and trained a lot of horses; he would have to drive them to the Old Man River about 15 miles north every other day for water and he was usually alone when he did this. We have photos of his teams of 24 head pulling combines, wagon trains, etc.

Both Alfred and Bus were shy and very good looking. All my life I would run into ladies who had real crushes on them. Bus won the Alberta Golden Gloves in the 165lb class, and this served him very well as a prison guard when a couple of the prisoners tried to overtake him with knives.

He took the knives away and prevented a prison break and a riot.

During his training as a pilot in the Air Force, Bus was taught that if there was ever a fire in your plane, to make sure you close the cockpit and the fire would soon go out. This happened to him-- and he remembered his training and was able to close the canopy tight and stay in the aircraft.

When I was about 10 years old Bus arrested a hired man wanted for murder

Buster brought a friend to dinner. Mom was to take us all out of the kitchen when she seen him pull in. The other man with Bus was an R.C.M.P. in plain clothes. They came in and grabbed this Larry, put handcuffs on him and arrested him. Bus had recognized him from a mug shot he had seen.

Larry, the hired man, had escaped from a prison down east where he was serving time for murder. The other hired man that lived in the bunk house with Larry said Larry had several loaded guns in case the police came for him. I believe the action of Bus got him a promotion.

What happened was, Bus came down one evening when we were swimming and noticed Larry's hair colour on his head was different than the rest of his body. The next day he went into Taber and searched the wanted posters at the R.C.M.P. He phoned Mom to tell her to get us all in the other room. He and a plain-clothes R.C.M.P. officer came to the house and arrested this hired man.

When Bus was in the R.C.M.P. he did some investigative work and some undercover work, simply because he was a bit of a renegade. On one occasion three men in a car were following him closely.

Bus made the mistake of turning into a blind alley. He knew these men were very bad, and out to get him. He turned his car around fast and headed straight at them. There was barely room for both cars to pass, but the other guys chickened out first and drove into the wall.

Alfred also had many experiences, and a long proud career in the R.C.M.P.

He spent most of his career in different detachments in Saskatchewan. He retired as a staff sergeant after 28 years and became a sheriff and a bond officer.

Bus served most of his career in R.C.M.P. headquarters in Ottawa, both in the firearms registration and the fingerprint department. During the FLQ uprising in Quebec and the murder of Cross, the training Bus had provided to his successor played a huge part in the conviction of the perpetrators.

Greg Brewin, Bus's son, spent time in the Army with Canada's Black Watch unit, and later with the Ontario Provincial Police. He also did a lot of underground work, and trained a highly recognized dog for sniffing out drugs, etc.

He trained his dog not to eat unless Greg fed him. One day he found some raw meat in his yard that had been thrown over the fence. The dog had not eaten any of it; it was full of strychnine.

When we visited Greg and his wife in Ottawa, they also had a pet cemetery that was quite profitable.

Bus was always quite adventurous. He became part owner of a scuba diving operation in Hawaii, where his lady partner cooked the books in her favour. He was asked on one occasion to sail a small sailboat from Florida to Ottawa. He was caught in the middle of a very rough storm. The Coast Guard found him and said they couldn't believe he sailed through that weather.

Another nephew, Jim Brewin, Alfred's son, was with a dog unit with the R.C.M.P., mainly in B.C. Yukon and N.W. Territories.

His adventures are a book of their own. He was responsible for many rescues and investigations and enjoyed telling us about his adventures. He'd come visit the ranch and always had to wear a cowboy hat because that's what his uncles did.

On one occasion he and his partner were responding to a serious accident with their lights and sirens, when a young fellow passed them. Jim know that the accident was a life and death situation and didn't want to waste time with a stupid traffic violation.

But they did pull the young fellow over. Jim got out of his car mad as hell. He asked the young guy what he thought he should do with him and explained how stupid he was. The kid said, "Well, officer, I guess you could just hit me."

So Jim did, knocking him down the ditch bank. Jim was always glad this was never reported.

Monica and Jim Berryhill started a logging operation and dairy farm in Lumby, B.C.; they raised a large family of four girls and one boy. Their daughter Joan was shot and killed when she was 13 years old when a neighbour was loading a hunting rifle in the next room. The bullet went through the wall and hit her in the head.

My two older brothers both visited the farm often. One of them would visit at least once a year. The family remained close and still is. Alfred made a concentrated effort to attend any Brewin function. His daughter Janet and her family have remained great family supporters and she, like her dad, attends every gathering possible.

Janet's son Jim Preston, also joined the R.C.M.P. and he is with the dive unit on the west coast. Her son-in-law Matt Haas is also a member of the R.C.M.P. and is stationed in Terrace.

When I was going to school at Hudson in Grade 1, two of my classmates were Alden Fletcher and David Mulner; we became lifelong friends. David's dad worked as an equipment operator for the municipal district and would often visit Dad or attend meetings where Dad would take me. David and I spent quite a bit of time together.

David became a well-known hockey player in his teenage years. Alden was very involved in community work, and he and his wife Millie are still two of my best friends.

I remember on one occasion when I was seven or eight years old a few of our friends came to the farm for a visit. We had quite a few sheep and we spent a lot of time riding them. Eventually the sheep got very tired and just laid down. Rod and I were very scared that we had killed a few. We couldn't get them to get up.

We went in for supper too afraid to say anything. We were very relieved when we got up in the morning, expecting to see a bunch of dead sheep, but when we looked out the window we saw them all grazing and very much alive.

Growing up, several different religions influenced our lives. We were Anglicans, but Mennonites, Catholics, and Mormon families were very much part of our community. Friction was very evident between the different religions. This was a particular problem when we attended the school in Grassy Lake. I had been used to only three or four kids in my class, but in Grassy Lake there were 15 and the majority were girls.

I had always been very good at Arithmetic and Math. Myself and a student named Kathleen Jones were very competitive and were always first and second place in all the exams.

We were taken by school bus to Taber, 20 miles away, to attend shop and woodwork one day a week. I still have a wooden filing chest I made at the shop.

In Grade 9 one of the boys who joined our class was Frank Sitter; I have a lot of respect and admiration for the Sitter family. They purchased 160 acres of land without a lot of extra cash or resources. They worked very hard and developed a very nice farmstead and family operation.

Frank loved baseball and always had his ball glove on his belt ready to play catch. Frank also became a very close friend and remains so to this day.

When we were in Grades 10 and 11 our class often traveled to other schools to play basketball. Several times we took my car; once such time was to Conqerville.

There would be a dance after the ball game. We could buy beer at the Hotel Burdet, and after the dance I was not in very good shape, so I asked David to drive; He wasn't sure how to get back to Grassy Lake; I told him go straight north on the gravel road for 13 miles. Then he would get on the highway, turn left and go the nine miles to Grassy Lake.

I fell asleep, and all of a sudden we went over a huge bump and it woke me and Frank Sitter up. I asked what it was; he said he thought we just crossed the highway and the railway tracks. David hadn't been paying attention. Finally, I got him to stop. We turned back for three miles. And sure enough, he had crossed both the highway and tracks, but was still content to drive on. His next stop would have been the river bank.

We often talk about that and wonder whose fault it really was.

At 11 years of age, I joined the Boy Scouts in Taber for two years. Gerald and Frank usually took me to the meetings. I learned to tie all the knots.

At 14 David and I joined the Air Cadets in Taber. We both won trips to the west coast Air Force base in Sea Island. I will never forget an Indian squadron from central Alberta.

They were so well trained, they won every inspection and march we had. It was a real treat just to watch them. There was a game we played called Borden Ball, and because six or seven of us on the Taber team were in good shape and bigger than the other cadets, we won most of the games.

On the last day we came up against the Indian squadron; many were small but in very good shape.

There were about 2,000 cadets at the camp, and almost all of the cheered against us. We lost the cup.

Jack and Dad set up a feed lot where we fed about 300 steers to market; much of the grain was fed by buckets. Frank went to school in Taber, so the feeding fell on Rod and I. Rod and I and one hired man would do the feeding night and morning. By the end, it took 200 buckets each time

Our weekends were spent grinding barley and filling the chop bins.

Dad had traded a lot of land that was needed for the irrigation reservoirs for grassland. When I was 10 and Rod was 12, our summer job was to herd our 250 cows and keep them out of the crop land. The following year Rod was needed more to do farm work, so the job of herding cows was left to me.

Dad bought me an old army jeep and for about six weeks every summer I herded cows in the daytime and corralled them at night. I got to corral them early when I played baseball.

Our small community hall was very active and busy in the winter time. David and I played badminton two times a week. When I was 15 the Alberta government implemented a program to upgrade all rural telephone service in the province.

We had many new farms not supplied with telephones. A new line that was 42 miles long was designed from Taber to our area. The farmers themselves did all the work; they took down the old lines, put up new poles every 250 feet, and installed new wires.

David and I somehow were given the job of climbing the new poles and fastening the two wires to the insulators at the top. Most of them were 20 feet off the ground and 25 feet at the roadway. We both got quite good at this and would race to see who could do this the fastest. Believe it or not, we got so we could do this in less than two minutes.

We had spikes on our legs and a belt around our waist for safety.

There was a crew that checked the old poles to see if it was safe for us to climb on them and take the wires off. The crew I had loved to visit. They checked a pole and said it was safe. Up I went. When I undid the wire at the top, the pole started to come down. I undid my belt, took about four large steps with spikes digging into the pole as it fell.

I ended up about 10 feet from the ground for my last jump. I was only 15 years old, and those men were much older, but they learned how much cussing out a kid could give.

Dad had us break up some land and farm, with 1,000 acres for Jack. This extra farm work, looking after 250 cows, etc, made us grow up very fast. Dad was a very capable manager and Mother also kept us all organized.

This all helped Gerald, Frank, Eleanor, Rod and I learn to work closely together and rely on each other. I look back now and am in awe of how the farm expanded, and all that was accomplished from the time I was about 10 years old in 1950 until I was 15.

I always wonder if Frank and Gerald ever slept. I know I picked a hell of a lot of rocks and helped build miles of fence.

Dad hired a German family – a father and three sons. They were great carpenters and built a very large barn or shed, 200 feet by 40 feet.

We took many trips to the mountains every fall in our farm trucks. We usually went to Elko, B.C. and brought home lumber and slabs for the corrals. These were fun trips: usually I rode with Frank and Rod rode with Gerald.

When I was young the municipal district introduced a program to try to reduce the number of crows and gophers. They would pay two cents for a gopher tail and five cents for the left leg of a crow.

I remember at home we rode bicycles a lot and played a lot of tag and kick the can.

One of the teachers at Deer Park School was Mr. McGowan. He was not well-liked. We would hide in the caves we dug during recess and he would get crazy when we were late coming in from recess. From Deer Park School we went to Bow Island, where he lost control and badly beat one of the male students.

Growing up, we had two horses we would ride: Buck and Tony. Often three or four of us would ride together on their back. When I was 10 or 12 Daisy was our main horse. I also remember using her to harrow the garden and to herd cows.

One time, Donnie Kraft wanted to ride. He got on Daisy by himself and she walked right out in the middle of the slough, about two or three feet deep and covered with green algae.

Daisy promptly laid down. Donnie was very scared – he started yelling and jumped off. I had to walk out and help him out of the slough and they go back to get Daisy. I was not happy, as the saddle was soaked.

When I was 13, Dad and Gerald and I went to a horse sale in Calgary. Dad bought two horses and Gerald bought one. One Dad bought was a Shetland named Tiny for my sister Marjorie, plus a couple saddle horses. One was part Tennessee Walker that was a good saddle horse: we often rode her bareback. Gerald bought a very good saddle horse named Dot.

Dad purchased a carload of yearling steers from Douglas Lake Ranch; they were unloaded in the CPR stockyards at Purple Springs. We had to drive them the nine miles to our feedlot. They had never crossed a highway or railway track before and were not used to wide open spaces. When we turned them out they took off in every direction. It was a real chore getting them rounded up and home to our corral, and in the process two of our horses fell and got scraped up on the pavement.

The second winter Dot and Tiny got into a pail of chop and both died. Tiny was not a huge loss as we could never ride her without a saddle - only bareback. That year we also bought a mare from Lee Haynes, and two years later Gerald bought a registered five-year-old stallion we called Davey, with a full sister named Cindy.

They were out of the Dexter bloodline, which was known for having a very quiet disposition. He used him as his main saddle horse, and also as a stud in the area. He produced many good saddle horses.

I dated a few girls as a teenager but my first girlfriend was Alice Reti when I was 16. She lived on a farm approximately eight miles north of Taber. She was an attractive girl with a good personality and we had a lot of respect for each other. Her family was also well respected, and they treated me very well.

Her brother won the Alberta Golden Gloves award about nine times and won the bronze medal at the Commonwealth Games in Australia. That's one reason I had to treat her good.

Her brother Roy and wife Gerrie were great supporters of the 4-H club I was later the leader of. They had a boy and girl, who both enrolled in the club I was leader of in the 70s and 80s.

When I was 17, Rod had about 80 pigs he was fattening, and one morning he was pounding on my door needing help. His pigs were sick, and when we went up to his pens a lot of his pigs were laying around, many acting very strange. We moved them into an adjoining pen with a lot of difficulty.

We looked around to see what the problem was. The pen they had been in was next to a large shed containing barley. Some of the barley had spilled out and got wet from the rain; some had sprouted and was growing green.

Several puddles had formed around this grain - it had fermented and smelled a bit like alcohol, which it actually was. His pigs were drunk. It took a couple of days for his pigs to recover, but I don't think he ever lost any.

When I was 13 Dad hired two hired men, and both were very lazy. I was sent with them to do some fencing one morning, and they would not work. As we went home for dinner, I told them both they were fired. They laughed at me and said they didn't need to listen to me.

When we got home, Dad was just sitting down for dinner. The men marched in for dinner and sat down, and I told Dad what had happened. The hired men listened and said there was no way a kid was going to fire them.

Dad, in a very calm voice, told them both to leave the table, go to the bunkhouse and pack up - he would drive them to the highway so they could hitch a ride.

They were pretty shocked.

In 1954 Dad rented five quarter sections of land, which was 160 acres, two-and-half miles east of Purple Springs and two miles south. This was land that had homesteads on it and was abandoned during the Depression years. That spring and the next spring we broke up about 650 of the 800 acres and seeded it to barley. The Canadian Wheat Board controlled how you sold your grain by issuing you a permit book.

One of these quarters was put into my name. I applied for and got a permit book at age 15 so I could deliver grain to the elevator, but the next summer the wheat board tried to take away my permit book because some of the neighbors complained.

The conditions for issuing a permit book was that you had to be 16 years old, but I had one when I was 15, the youngest in Canada to have one at that time. By the time they investigated and tried to take away my book it was past my 16th birthday which was on June 2, so I got go keep it and had one for 44 years.

The day I turned 16 Dad took me in to get my driver's license. Some of my friends had failed their tests and I was a little worried, but I answered all the questions except one correctly.

Angus Mckay was a notary public in charge of issuing the drivers licenses. I had already been driving around the farm for five years, and Mr. Mckay asked how many miles I had driven. I didn't want to get into trouble so I answered, "About 5,000."

Dad heard this from the other room and shouted, "Hell Angus, he's driven at least 200,000 miles."

Mr. Mckay said, "I can't write that down," and put down 20,000 miles.

I got my license and as we came out of the notary public office Mr. Mckay asked Dad if he would give him a ride home.

Dad threw me the keys and said he had some other things to do in town and I was to drive Mr. Mckay home. When he got out of the truck at his house he thanked me and said, "Hell, you're a better driver than your dad anyway."

Mr. Mckay had a lot of laughs telling that story.

Stu Little was a vet we used in Taber for several years. Around 1964 or 1965 Dr. Don Hamilton and Dr. Darwin Lund bought Dr. Little's practice. They both became very good friends of our family and in fact, we formed a company with them to import cattle in 1971.

At age 17 I was successful in renting 40 acres from the colonization board, and in 1968 the Colonization Department of the Alberta Government took over the 800 acres of land we had cultivated and allotted it out in 160-acre parcels.

Bob Patterson, John Basoski, John Kambites and Steve Sygigli each got one parcel, and my brother Rod got the other. Irrigation was available on this land.

Rod built his own house and buildings on his parcel - he was an excellent carpenter.

He and his wife Louise planted trees for shelter belts and developed their homestead. They built up a very nice farm and raised four sons.

When Eleanor left home for college, Gerald took it upon himself to help Mother a lot in the house. I remember the two of them would work side by side cooking and washing dishes.

The construction camps that were used when they were building the main irrigation canal usually had about 50-80 men in them. I would go ride my bike up and visit them, which made Mother pretty mad because they told me some pretty wild stories.

We had seeded 40 acres to oats right beside the construction camp. My sister Eleanor, who was 15 years old, my cousin Claire and a school teacher boarding with us and I went to pick up the oat stooks. These men seen all those girls out there working, and about 10 of them come over to help out.

There were over 2,000 stooks, and Dad thought it would take us four or five days to gather them and put them all in the barn. With the help of these construction workers it was done in just over a day and a half, and he died wondering how we ever did that so quick.

In the spring of 1953 water was put into the main irrigation canal, running a quarter mile north of our farm. They had completed construction of the canal and dams as far as Burdett, six miles east of our farm.

Eventually the canal went all the way to the Saskatchewan border, just east of Medicine Hat.

During construction a lot of men were involved in the building of the canal, with very few injuries. The main machinery used were bulldozers and a Euclid earth mover.

One accident happened on the bridge a quarter mile from our house.

The Euclid went off the bridge and trapped the operator under the machine. It was about a 15-foot drop to the canal floor. He was extremely fortunate as he fell into the cavity between the seat and the floor and was not killed. They put a large Cat with a cable winch on one bank of the canal and another on the opposite bank.

They literally lifted the Euclid off him and he came out with a big grin on his face.

The first water in the canal was diverted by a series of dams and spillways in order to fill a large reservoir over a two-year period.

A large dam had been built in the east end of the four-and-a-half-mile long ravine, and a large wooden spillway was used for the water to flow out of the lateral canal. This spillway was about 25 feet long.

We used to take tire tubes and ride the water down the spillway. The ended up at the base of the spillway.

One evening there was about eight of us out there swimming. Donnie Kraft could not swim but loved to paddle around on his tire tube. He fell off and started drowning.

Jim Rutherford was only about five feet from the shore; he grabbed Donnie by the hair and pulled him out.

Eventually we were banned from riding down the spillway, but my kids, nieces and nephews also did the same thing as teenagers, but Gerald and I really gave them hell and put a stop to that.

The water in the main canal was sent further along the route to other reservoirs and limited irrigation projects. It was not until 1954 that the irrigation farmland from that system was really put into practice.

The reservoirs were stocked with white fish and trout, but when the native pike fish came down with the water they killed out the trout. It became a very well-known ice fishing spot. This reservoir has claimed at least five lives that I know of: two swimmers in the summer and three ice fishermen.

One winter about 1968 we were working cattle in the corrals north of the reservoir. On the way home for lunch I seen a man standing on the side of the road. It was one of my neighbours, Les Martin.

It was about -10 Fahrenheit and he was wet and covered with ice. I took him to my house to get out of his wet clothes and dry off. He was really delirious and hard to control. Him and his wife did not have a telephone at their home, so I called his family in Lethbridge.

They came right out and took him to the hospital in Lethbridge. He had gone through the ice with a load of fish.

He asked us to get his truck out. Rod, Frank and I went to the lake to see what could be done. The back end of the truck had gone through, but the motor was still on top of the ice.

It was about 30 feet from shore. We could not take the chance of taking a tractor out on the ice, so we had a winch truck come out to retrieve it. Eventually it took two winch trucks because they had trouble locking the wheels. His truck box was full of boxes of fish, with no lids on them, and the fish were swimming out of the boxes on his truck, some even swimming back into the lake.

He was a war veteran and had been given the 160 on that basis. It was very rocky and right on top of the ravine. Les was not a farmer but he and wife struggled on this land for over 15 years. I hired their son to help me on my pig farm many times, and I know this money was almost all they had at times.

Another thing that happened with ice fishermen happened in the winter, but the water was not completely frozen. He was out in a small boat setting his nets; he fell in and drowned.

They dragged the water for his body. Frank and I heard what was going on and went down to see what we could do. Just as they had hooked his net, loaded with fish, and were pulling it out. There were about 50 men there, and we couldn't believe how they were - so intent in grabbing the fish from the net and running over to put them in their own trucks.

Finally, four or five of us made them stop. We asked who knew the guy who had drowned; one fellow said he was with him and he was asked to take the fish and give them to the drowned man's family.

Many were mad at us, but others helped, and eventually about 200 fish were sent home to his family.

During ice fishing season, the R.C.M.P. would often go down to the lake to check the licenses on those fishing. The gate to the lake was right across from my yard in the 1960s. Upwards of 100 fishermen went in out of that gate for three weeks every winter.

One day it started to snow and drift, and I came down the road and was stopped by the R.C.M.P. The officer was really rude and he pissed me off. They were going down to the ice to make their checks, and soon the trail to the lake drifted in. They got stuck and asked the fishermen to come up to my yard and bring down a tractor to pull them back to the road.

It was very cold and I had to start my tractor. I worked all afternoon pulling out stranded fishermen, making it very convenient for the police to sit in their warm car on the side of the road and check the fishermen out.

Just at dark I had everyone pulled out back to the road. The officer came up to my tractor and made a comment about all the business he'd got for me. I was charging $5 for every tow.

He sure got me mad. I gave him a note and a bill for $50 for my time and tractor use. He said, "You can't charge me."

I took the bill into the detachment next time I was in town, and eventually they did pay.

Around 1959 the Grassy Lake irrigation reservoir just two miles from where I grew up definitely changed our way of life and the lives of many in our district.

It also had a big impact on my children and family in future years. The year after I graduated from Olds College also changed a lot of our lives, our workload and our family farm.

Many new farms started up, as well as new farming methods and new crops. The cattle industry was expanding, and many new agricultural societies, meetings and gatherings were put into place to try to adapt to a new way of life.

Our ball team also folded that summer. More people became more interested in golf, fishing and water sports. Hunting for us took on a different outlook: there were more geese and pheasants, and deer, ducks and geese were plentiful. I found myself organizing and planning several goose hunts that fall where we would dig pits and camouflage them for goose blinds.

It became a popular destination for many dignitaries to come and hunt. Bing Cosby and Dan Blocker from Bonanza were often seen in our area.

Growing up we had a 410-gauge shotgun, a single shot with a 22 as an over/under double barrel, and a 12-gauge double barrel shotgun, as well as a 22 Savage with a five-shell magazine bolt action. We also pooled together and bought a repeater 19 chamber Mossberg 22. We wasted a lot of shells with that repeater gun.

Truly there was an abundance of Ring-neck Pheasants on our farm. Dad would not allow hunting on any of his land - he would change vehicles and go chase off the hunters.

Rod and I were each given a heifer calf when I was 12, and two years later my heifer had a heifer calf. Jack kept the cattle records and I didn't get any money for four years for my cattle that sold, although Rod got credit for his calves.

When I was 16 I used my egg money and bought two more cows and made sure I bought my own tags with my name on them. Those four were the base of my cow herd.

Gerald often took a trip in the winter time. We had a small heated shop, and when I was 19 and Rod and Frank were busy building their houses, one winter I decided to overhaul one of our L.A. Case tractors.

It was the year before I got married. I stripped the motor and the clutch down and laid everything out on a long bench. I took the heads and the crank shaft into the Case dealer to have them ground and new valves installed.

I would talk to and get advice from the mechanics at the dealership every time I went to town. They sold me all the correct bearings, etc.

When I reassembled the motor, everything went together very well until I got to the carburetor and the final details. I found I had a short compression spring and a small shaft about 22 inches long that I couldn't figure out where they went. I worked on this problem for a couple of days, and every time I went up to the house to see Mother, she would ask how it was going – always asking if I had all the parts.

I even took that spring and shaft into the dealer; they went through all their parts books and could not find out where it should go. I gave up and had to admit to mom I was stumped.

She got a sly smile on her face and asked, "Why? Do you have a couple of extra parts?"

She said she went downstairs into Dad's workshop and found theses two parts, and once when she came down to the shop to see how I was doing, she simply laid them on the bench.

Her reasoning was that if she had taken something away, I would have found out it was missing, but by adding a few parts it would have been more of a challenge. It certainly was that.

Mother had a great sense of humour; I will always treasure those memories with Mother.

Mother loved telling the story of a hired man they had shortly after her and dad got married. He was sent down to milk the cow. She was quite a large Holstein and she had a habit of swishing her tail and hitting you in the face. This fellow tied a small brick to the end of her tail, and when she swished it, the brick hit him right in the side of the face. Mother had a saying if you did something stupid: did you tie a brick to the cow's tail?

When I was seven or eight we would bring in the milk cow every night. Mother did the milking, but Rod, Eleanor and I were responsible for getting the cow in for her. We had a pasture of about 50 acres. It was very rough and some of it was muddy, so we always walked out to get the cow.

Usually, two of us would go together just before dark. Mother's cow's name was Betsy, and she usually had two or three other cows with her. We could ride Betsy and would ride her back to the barnyard. The cows were anxious to go, as they were fed in the barnyard and we would always pump fresh water for them from the well.

They liked that water over the slough water in the pasture. They were kept in the barnyard overnight and were let out after milking in the morning.

Mother would separate the cream off and we often made butter by letting some of the cream sour just a little and then put it in a jam can and shake it until butter formed.

Mother was very good at putting in just the right amount of salt and the butter was a real treat to put on her fresh baked bread. On occasion, she would have gooseberry jam also.

When I was about 18, Jack took over the milking. He had four cows and would separate and ship the cream. We had a milk barn with four stanchions and a gutter for the manure behind the cows. It was easy to clean but was often also filthy because Jack was not looking after it properly.

About every four or five days Jack would make a fuss and someone else would have to do his milking and clean his barn

When I was 14 we caught an orphan deer and kept it as a pet. It was around the yard for three or four years.

When I was about 13 I ran over a goose nest when I was disking, with about five eggs in it. Two were not broken. I had bought a small electric incubator a couple of years earlier to hatch turkey and chicken eggs. I put the two good wild goose eggs in the incubator, turned them twice a day and kept them a little moist as the mother goose would do.

I also bought 29 tame duck eggs that I kept with the goose eggs; I got 15 baby ducks and one wild baby goose.

I gave them to a chicken hen who was nesting and she raised them. She would get pretty upset when they got old enough to swim and went in the water. I had that wild goose for several years. In the fall, she would fly up to a flock of wild geese migrating south; it seemed she waited for a special flock. In the spring, they would come back, circle the yard three or four times and she would join the ducks and the tame geese we had.

I got a lot of pleasure from her, and she became knows as Tim's goose.

You could always pick her out of the flock because she had a much shorter neck.

In 1955 we got Brucellosis in the cow herd, and the decision was made to breed all the cows by artificial insemination as the bulls could be the carriers of the Brucellosis.

We had to draw blood from every cow in the herd, about 300 at that time. This was a big job. Two government Health of Animal vets came out and we put every cow through the squeeze. We put pliers on their noses and pulled their head around and blood was drawn from their necks. Rod became a real expert at catching their noses.

Every cow that tested positive had to be culled. It took us two years to get a certified clean herd by testing every 60 days.

We continued on with the A.I. program after that. The first two years everything was bred Hereford or Black Angus. When I was 19 the vet, Darwin Lund had become a good friend of our family. He convinced me to breed some of my cows to Charolais.

At that time I had built up to 30 cows. We had to import the Charolais semen from Mexico. Charolais calves were sometimes difficult births, but they went well, and I got a good price for them.

The next year I bred half of my cows to a breed called Hays Converters; this breed was developed by Senator Harry Hays. They were bred up by his cross-breeding program and had Holstein in them. The calves were mostly black with white faces and turned out to be excellent cows.

At this time, we contracted with the A.I. technician to do the breeding. We hired John Lybert and his wife for three years to do the riding and bring in the cows that were in heat.

Jack and Dad had built up a herd of about 12 young horses. Jack made a deal with John to break some of them. One day when I came up to the corral Johnny was working on a young gelding - doing what is called sacking it out. The horse was in a terrible state, scared as hell and sweat just pouring off it. I made it clear to John he was never to treat one of our horses like that again.

In the three years he worked for us he only broke one horse we could ride. We then hired various cowboys to ride for us. A local cowboy, Lynn Ferguson, was one of those. He rode for us from 1970 to 1973 and was using my horse Billy and three horses I had got from Darwin Lund: Cheery, Swede and Blaze.

Jack was adamant that all his and Dad's cows were to be bred Hereford, but in 1968 my brothers and myself started using some of the exotic breeds, such as Limousin, Simmental, Maine Anjou, Tarentaise cattle from France and a breed from Australia called Murray Grey.

When I applied for water rights on the northeast quarter of 22, we had a chance to study some of the old aerial maps that were taken during the war. It showed buffalo paths, used as the buffalo migrated from the harsh prairies to the foothills for winter shelter.

The buffalo had obviously followed the many sloughs and good grass in the lower areas, which also contained the salt in the alkali sloughs. Many old buffalo rub rocks were evident on our land, and I found many old artifacts, such as arrowheads etc. Also, one of my neighbours did find a couple of pouches of pemmican.

One Sunday a neighbour and I followed this route from Chin Coulee to my place. The main irrigation canal was pretty much built, and very close to where the buffalo used for their annual migration.

I have mentioned a few of the hired men who worked on the farm, such as Clarence, who worked for us for approximately eight years. He would ride his bicycle 60 miles to Medicine Hat to visit his daughter. He was convinced that the yellow line down the center of the road was for bicycles.

One Saturday night he got a ride with Rod and me into town. We picked him up around midnight and then were stopped by the police for some reason I don't remember. They were searching the car, and Clarence got out of the back seat, ran around to the other side of the cop car and pissed all over it. We got a bit of a scolding for that one;

There were three young men, Bob, Alan and Keith from Perry Sound, Ontario when I was 12 years old; we had a lot of fun with them. They shared an old car and usually went to town together. They had a common girlfriend and cut cards to see who would date her that particular night.

One time, Bob had a small accident on Main Street with a Hungarian immigrant. Bob had one of those fake driver's licenses that said basically he could do anything he wanted while driving a car. He produced this and the other driver accepted it and agreed not to press charges.

But the Hungarian did go to the police station the next day and demanded one of those driver's licenses that Bob had.

Dad had bought two new Number 55 self-propelled combines that year. He also bought a new three-ton Chevy truck. In harvest, it was decided Bob would drive the new grain truck, Keith would drive a one-ton grain truck we had, and Alan one of the new combines.

Rod operated the other combine. Gerald drove one a year older. Gerald was always the one to do the proper settings for grain separation for all three combines, and also did most of the service and repair on them.

There were many tricks played on one another. One was they'd put grease on the handle that you pulled up to unload the grain tank, so when you reach down to lift the lever you came up with a handful of grease.

We used a kind of lever action grease gun - if you lifted up the lever and hit it down hard, you could shoot a shot of grease out about 25 feet, so many grease gun fights took place.

One day, Alan was driving one of the combines, and Rod another one. Rod got off his combine and ran around the side of Alan's, shooting grease at him. These combines had unloading eight-inch augers that stuck out of the side of the combine about 10 feet. Alan, trying to avoid Rod's attack, crashed his unloading auger into Rod's, smashing them both up pretty bad.

Gerald worked all day and most of the night repairing them. The next day the box and hoist installation was completed on the new grain truck, and Bob brought it out to the field. Everyone had to see how the hoist worked, and Bob pulled up beside Rod's combine right under the unloading auger.

Rod got into the cab of the truck and Bob was showing him how everything worked. He grabbed the lever that lifted the truck hoist and up went the grain box and smashed the auger on Rod's combine again.

Again, Gerald had a huge repair job.

Bob took a lot of stupid chances with his truck, like backing up about ¾ of a mile on top of the narrow road on top of the canal bank, and another time backing up the 10-foot canal bank.

One day, Alan and Bob came to Dad for help. They'd gotten crabs from their common girlfriend, but they did not want to see a doctor because they were afraid their parents in Ontario would find out.

Dad was a good friend of the pharmacist in town; he went in and came home with a small box about 2ft by 2ft full of different creams, ointments and pills. Eventually the boys were cured.

The boys went back east in the late fall after harvest - they had been good men. They were a lot of fun; they liked to play tricks on Mother, such as stealing some of her fresh baked pies.

The next year I was given the combine to operate that Alan had run. I operated a combine every fall for over 45 years; my son Dan did a lot of combining after he was 18.

We did have many good crops for several years after the war and in the 1950s. Dad bought a lot of new equipment and in 1949 he and Jack both bought new cars. Bus and Alfred would come out to visit often. Bus would drive out from Ottawa every second year. He had a Packard car which he took very good care of; he put over 450 thousand miles on it.

Olds College

After Grade 11 I was pretty fed up with high school: it was just boring. I was not sure what path was best for me for the future. my friend Alden decided to enroll in the Olds School of Agriculture.

Olds could accommodate up to 150 boys in the dorm, and the girls had their own dorm on the other side of the gymnasium, which was between the two dorms.

The kitchen and eating areas were underneath the gym, and we could access the eating area and gym without going outside. We all ate at the same time and were assigned seating at a round table that seated eight. We were supposed to stay in our own seats so the staff could easily see who was missing by an empty chair.

The tablecloths were white and were changed once a week, so they got pretty gross. After Christmas several of us traded seats so we could sit with one of our friends. A few were made to move back, but I was one of the lucky ones who got to sit where I wanted.

Several of the students got a job as waiters or waitresses; one of those was a roommate of a good friend of mine. He would sometimes bring us a pie up from the kitchen usually around 11pm.

Don Howard was my friend and roomed directly below me. He would call me to come and enjoy extra pie now and then. There were two boys in each room; we had a desk and a wooden bunk bed.

We also like to wrestle and goof around a lot. I remember one time I was wrestling with Don, and Herman must have thought I was getting the best of him. All of a sudden, he was like a mad man, pulling and throwing me down and yelling, "Don't you dare touch my roommate!"

We had to go to supper around 6:30 and then had a one-and-a-half-hour study time in our rooms. After that we were free to go to the canteen or gym until 10pm. You could play basketball, badminton and take boxing, wrestling or gymnastics. I enrolled in boxing and wrestling and also played a lot of basketball and badminton.

I did not go out for the senior men's basketball team my first year, but played on one of the house league teams. Our team easily won first place that year.

Howard Woodrow and I would often hang around the gym whenever the senior team was practicing, and we got to practice with them. I was asked on two occasions to travel with them to out-of-town games.

In class I sat next to Chuck Blackley; he and I became good friends. Bob Richmond also hung around with us a lot, although he was from a different class.

There were nine of us that hung around together in a group. We often visited in one of our rooms long after lights out. Mr. Rogers was our dean of men that year, and we did learn how important friends are, but also how mean and vindictive some of the boys could be.

Mr. Rogers drove home that every girl was somebody's daughter and somebody's sister. He'd give this lecture for an hour every Monday morning at assembly with all the boys, and when he walked out he was always crying.

There were only 25 girls enrolled, and 150 boys. The girls had to cook a fancy meal and they took turns at this two at a time. They could invite two boys for a meal. We had to dress up fancy and it was all very formal. I was lucky enough to get invited twice: once a great meal, the other time not so much.

We did all our own washing and hung out clothes on some racks in the attic to dry. Some clothing was stolen from other boys while hanging in the attic, and the police were called in. They set a trap to catch any dishonest students. One thing they did was put some cash in an envelope addressed to a boy who had gone home. His name started with a P so they put it in the P mail slot. Inside the envelope, they also put some powder that would only show up under infa-red light.

Herman Penner was one of the waiters at my table. He had gotten a small amount of the powder on his hand, and anyone at his table that night also got a very small amount of their hand.

Herman had not even touched the envelope, but there was enough powder so that everyone whose name began with P got powder on their hand.

I got about a quarter inch spot on my hand; the police checked every boy and everyone who had powder was kept in a separate room and questioned. I was asked a few simple questions then told I could go back to my room.

When I opened up my door, there was about 20 boys in their singing "Hang down your head, Tim Brewin."

They were led by Don Howard on his violin.

One boy was caught with the cash in his wallet; he had given some of the t-shirts and shorts he had stolen off the clothesline to his girlfriend. He was expelled; she was not, as she had no idea they were stolen.

Another boy quit and went home before the police arrested him.

In March our animal husbandry instructor invited four of us to go to the Calgary bull sale with him for the day. One of those was a native boy who was very well liked. Somehow, he got into liquor at the sale, got very drunk and sick the next day and was expelled from the school.

At that time, there was a very strict no-drinking policy at Olds.

There had been a tradition at the school that once a year the boys would have a raid on the girls' dorm. It was just a fun thing. Of course, our dean lectured about it, saying we weren't allowed to do it, but it was planned and done anyway.

We simply had to let the dean of women know so she could monitor it to see that no damage was done.

I went over to the dorm, but only into the waiting room in the girls' dorm. A few beds were messed and garbage tipped over, etc., but the next morning there were panties and bras hanging in trees and one bra up the flagpole. All the boys got a good lecture for going that far.

About a week later I was coming back from the gym and a bunch of girls ran by me screaming and laughing. They never went into my room, but across the hall and three doors down from my room was one of the bathrooms with four shower stalls.

Just after lights out there was a knock on my door. One of the boys was all excited as he had seen two girls hiding in one of the showers.

A few of us went into the bathroom, reached in and turned on the cold water. The girls got soaked and come out like drowned rats. One was darn mad and started throwing punches. We had a lot of laughs trying to figure out why they were hiding in a boys' bathroom.

Our science instructor, Mr. Taite, was a little different. He didn't get along with the students, was often teased and also had quite a temper.

Olds school offered three options: a one-year course, a two-year course and a two-in-one course. I signed up for the two-year course.

I made up my mind at the end of the first year that perhaps the farm didn't have a lot of opportunity for me, and I decided not to return to the farm after my second year.

Norm Thompson, an irrigation specialist from southern Alberta, was a part-time instructor at Olds. He offered me a job with his department, but Dad and my brothers talked me out of it.

When I returned to the farm after the second year, we had excellent crops. With the land I had rented I sold a carload of malting barley, and another 4,000 bushels of feed barley. My income was almost $10,000 and I had been able to use Dad's machinery with no rent.

I made the arrangement to rent another 160 acres of land, plus 40 acres from the Irrigation District.

Rod and I got a contract building fences for three miles on Crown land. Dad had owned a lot of land where the irrigation reservoir was going; he traded the government one acre for three acres of deeded land.

Four years earlier we had put up 15 miles of fence in two years, when I was 13 and 14 years old. It was also split cedar fence post, all dug in with a post auger and tamped in by hand.

Four barbed wires were strung. Our goal was to build a half mile of fence each day. This was all done around the other farm work. I really remember this task well, as a few days were very hot. One day it reached 104 degrees Fahrenheit. We had to wear net masks because of the mosquitos, but we sure put up great fences. Many of those fences are still being used today, 60 years later.

I also got the opportunity to rent 160 acres from Herb Craft. I put a down payment on it and bought it over three years. Because of those positive steps I decided perhaps I had a future on the farm.

Olds college was built as an agricultural college for young people - mostly farm boys to get the education they needed in farming or in the agricultural industry.

Many leaders in agriculture and in the general public in Alberta over the years were graduates of the Olds college.

Six years after I graduated from Olds, the Alberta government put a lot of money into the school and it became a junior college and trade school. Many new programs were offered, and new dorms were built that were coed dorms. The closeness we enjoyed was lost.

Second year at Olds

The second year I was at Olds, Alden and I roomed together. We selected a room on the second floor that year, at the far end of the hall close to the showers and bathrooms. It was one door from the fire escape and had easy access to the outside.

From there we were closer to the metal shop, motors and livestock buildings. It was also convenient for some of our friends that stayed out late after lights out. They would come up the fire escape, leave their coats in our room and if the dean caught them in the hall, they would simply say they were visiting us or another room.

Many weekend mornings we would end up with 10 or 12 coats in our room.

The second week at Olds was initiation. It was just to be a fun get-to-know for the new students. All of us second-year students could select one or two of the first-year students to be their slaves. You could make them carry your books, open doors for you and do your laundry, etc., nothing mean or demeaning.

I had met a ranching boy from Del Bonita at the canteen. He was 6' 1" tall and 190 lbs and seemed like a lot of fun. The new students were all to dress in a certain way during initiation, such as wear a blue a yellow beanie, etc.

The boy I chose was Charlie Barnett; we became very close friends. One of the problems was that he lived at one end of the dorm on the bottom floor and I at the other end of the dorm on the second floor.

It was far closer for him to go to his classes out the front of the dorm and closer for me to go to the metals, motors, etc; out the back way. Being a fun boy, if we ran into another new student he would grab my books or open the door for me and say, "Hey, Tim, I'm your slave!"

At the gym or canteen, he would always stick right with me. One thing a lot of the new students were made to do was push ups. Charlie loved that. If he seen someone made to do push ups, he would say, "Charlie, get down and do push ups," and he would drop down and do 20 push ups and 20 one-arm push ups. He was in great shape.

He soon started to date one of the girls. I had met Marj, so the four of us often hung out together. I convinced Charlie to sign up for wrestling with me. Mr. Warrington was the instructor. I think it was the third night we went to wrestling, when we saw Mr. Warrington standing in the middle of the mats, swaying back and forth.

He stood there telling us. "Always keep your knees loose – don't lock them up and no one can knock you over."

He asked for a volunteer to challenge him and Charlie stepped right up. He walked up to Mr. Warrington, grabbed him by one arm, turned his back and threw him over his shoulder. Everybody laughed: no one liked Mr. Warrington much.

Mr. Warrington was a very large man himself, weighing about 250 lbs. Charlie won a lot of friends for doing that, but wrestling was cancelled for good.

The rest of the year Charlie and Mavis were together as much as possible. They were married two years later, and settled on the family ranch, living in the same yard as his brother.

I ran into him in Lethbridge three years later. He had had a close call with carbon monoxide poisoning. He was working in his shop with the motor of his tractor left running. His brother opened the shop door found Charlie was stumbling around not knowing where he was.

His brother opened all the doors to get Charlie out, but Charlie kept insisting he had to go back and put his tools away. His brother was fighting him, but Charlie kept going back into the shop. Luckily, one of the wives seen them fighting and called a couple of neighbours. They got Charlie to the hospital, where he stayed for several days.

In 1919 Victor Barnett, Charlie's grandad, started monitoring the weather for the government on his ranch. He registered rainfall, hours of sunshine, wind and temperature. Their ranch was only a third of a mile from the international boundary. This duty was passed down in the family.

In 1979 Mavis Barnett, Charlie's wife, took on the duty and still does it today. Some of it is done by sonar, but she also measures high and low water on the Milk River.

This gauge gives amounts for the international boundary and Milk River Ridge between the river and the U.S. border.

Back to Olds. I really enjoyed the metals and welding. Mr. Armstrong was our instructor, and I learned how to make many tools, such as chisels, punches, hooks and chains.

I learned the proper electrodes or rods for welding; we had access to all the metal we wanted so we could learn to weld.

We had to wear leather gloves, aprons and goggles. Our instructor was very strict about safety, but still there was some burns and accidents. One of the boys in another class was welding one day - sitting down and bent over his welding table. He did not have an apron on, and while he was welding with the end of the electrode red hot, the electrode started to slip in its handle.

He pushed it against himself in his crotch area to straighten it out, and it quickly burnt through his pants and shorts and really burnt his penis.

I joined the senior men's basketball that term; we did travel to a lot of other colleges, schools, etc, to play.

We also played the university of Alberta's agriculture basketball team. Olds seldom beat them, as most of them were 23 or 24 years old, where we were boys 18 or 19.

When we beat them, they would get quite mean and aggressive. One day one of their players used both his elbows and came down on top of my face and head, giving me a bloody nose.

The coach wanted to take me out of the game, but I was not hurt that bad, so I stayed in. I got one of my players to pass me the ball real low; the Edmonton boy went towards it, but I grabbed it first. I pretended to pass it away and slammed it right into his crotch. He left the game and I never even got a foul. I guess the ref thought he had it coming.

Marj Newman was enrolled in the home economics course. She also played a lot of sports so was often at the gym. We seen a lot of one another and started to date, going steady by the end of the year. I first met her parents at graduation.

Olds had what they called 'The Little Royal' where every boy had to show an animal. Around six of the boys used one of the farm's dairy cows and there were about 10 sheep. 10 or 12 of the boys brought purebred animals from home and showed them. The farm also had a lot of pigs, and if you wanted you could have one of those weaning pigs to show.

Then you got to keep it and take it home with you as your own. Most of the boys did show pigs.

Don Howard, Alden, Chuck Blackey and myself brought horses from home and showed them. The horse I used was a four-year old palomino of Gerald's named Cindy. She had only been ridden a couple of times and Gerald was going to use her as a brood mare. She was, in fact, my horse Billy's mother.

Billy was the horse Gerald gave me as a wedding present. There were 160 acres of grass a quarter mile from the horse barn at Olds where we could ride, as well as a large arena we could use. We didn't get a lot of time to work with our animals: only three quarters of an hour a day, and Sundays.

My brother Frank and his wife Colleen brought Cindy and a horse for Alden. Cindy performed very well.

Frank brought up a car that dad gave me and took the truck and horses back home after the Little Royal.

We had used the horses as an excuse to go out at night. The horse barn loft was full of chopped feed, and we hid a couple of cases of beer in that feed. During final exams, I looked out the window and some farm workers were blowing all the food out of the barn. I thought, "That's it: I'm out of here."

We had three cases of beer hidden at that time, and I thought for sure it would be found and we would be caught and expelled.

After class, we rushed right over to the barn. It was completely cleaned out - the beer was gone. We sat on pins and needles for several days, worrying about our fate. Nothing was ever said. The farm workers simply got some free beer, and they used to grin at us every time we walked by.

Back to the farm in 1959

After graduation, I took Marj home to her family farm at Blackie, where I met her two brothers and her sister Judy, who was two years younger than Marj.

After high school Judy joined the navy, where she met Bob Dodyk whom she later married. We got along very well and had a lot of fun with them.

Marj had won an international trip through 4-H to Washington D.C. for a week that spring. After that she went back to their farm where I visited her a couple of times. Later that year she got a job as a bank teller in the BMO bank in Taber.

She moved into a basement apartment and did visit our farm quite often. We got engaged later that year.

When I got home from Olds, the field work was already under way. That spring we seeded a lot of barley, durum wheat and hard red spring wheat - over 2,400 acres in total.

Later that spring, I made arrangements to rent Herb Craft's 160 acres. It was very sandy soil and the top soil had drifted badly. It was also badly infested with wild oats, which took me over three years to get rid of.

I was also renting another 400 acres, 200 of which was very rocky. That meant I spent a lot of time picking rocks. I still had the pigs, but I got good crops that year on 200 acres.

I sold 4,000 bushels of malt barley and another 3,000 of feed barley. The next spring, I ordered a new Meteor car that I was able to pay cash for. That impressed Marj, I tell you.

Gerald and Jack went to England that winter. They drove my new car back from Oshawa, Ontario on the way home.

With Marj's job at the bank, we made many new friends in the district. One couple was a Mountie and his girlfriend. Another was a bank employee named Joe, and his girlfriend. He always wanted to hunt and came out several times to hunt pheasants.

The first time I took him, it wasn't a good experience. He was very excitable. Shooting pheasants was only allowed with a shotgun that had the capacity to hold no more than three shells without unloading. You could only shoot the cockerel pheasants and only in the air.

One evening we were walking up a lateral canal that supplied water to the reservoir - Joe on one bank and I on the other.

A hen pheasant popped up and started to run, about 25 feet in front of me. Joe began shooting at it on the ground. He had taken the plug out of the shotgun so it shot five shots. He shot the hell of the pheasant and scared the hell out of me, as dirt was flying only about 25 feet ahead of me.

I never took him hunting again.

Our ditch rider, Walter, always wanted me to take him goose hunting. I watched a flock of Canada geese for two days when they came in to feed. We dug and camouflaged our pits and got into them a half hour before the geese usually came to feed.

We could hear them coming about a mile away. We had all agreed to wait until they were within range, or about 300 feet away. They were in perfect formations, about an eighth of a mile away.

Walter jumped out of his pit and started shooting. running towards the geese. He scared them all away and scared the hell out of me.

Walter was not really welcome on many hunts after that.

We did take him once or twice more but made very clear the rules of the hunt.

Over the years. I organized many successful goose hunting adventures. On one hunt Gerald and I and two neighbours, and maybe Frank, shot 25 Canada geese in less than half an hour.

After Marj and I got married, her dad often came for hunting. My brother-in-law Bob Dodyk came for a visit and was excited about going on a hunt, but he didn't trust nobody. We went out after dark on night to dig our pits. He saw us digging and thought we were just having him on, and he would not dig his hole.

We finished ours and covered it up with camouflage – old straw, etc – and said we were going home. All of a sudden, he was swearing and digging like crazy while we sat in the truck enjoying coffee.

I had a strict rule that I wouldn't allow any liquor while we were hunting.

The increase in hayfields and better grain fields also resulted in an increase of wild rabbits. We spent many hours shooting them with 22s in the winter. One winter, Rod and I stored them in one of his steel grain bins so they would stay frozen.

In March, we loaded them up, filled two half-ton trucks and took them to a mink farm in Medicine Hat. We were paid 50 cents a rabbit, as long as they were not shot up with a shotgun. We had over 600 rabbits. It truly was a lot of fun hunting rabbit - it gave us something to do. We always had guns with us when we did the chores.

The rabbits would dig themselves into the snowbank and you would just see their ears and their eyes. We could walk up to within a couple hundred feet before they jumped up.

Rod and I did most of the feeding of the 350-cow herd; he and Louise had gotten married and lived in the same yard as I did. After feeding every day we would play three games of hockey on a hockey table. We got pretty competitive with that, and pretty good at it too.

Rod and I fed the cows for Dad and Jack for two or three years, using half ton trucks and square bales.

Gerald and I continued to haul and stack the hay and straw bales in the fall for the next four years; we also hired Natives to help with that.

Another hunting adventure we enjoyed was taking a friend or neighbour snipe hunting. We didn't get too many people to fall for it.

The longest wait I ever got, when I played that trick, was my nephew. He spent four hours shining the flashlight into the sack and got very cold. He walked up to the house and realized he'd been had.

It was again a very busy year, picking rocks and irrigating, helping Frank and Rod build their new houses. Marj would often come out to the farm – she enjoyed it and helped out wherever she could. Mom, Louise and Colleen readily accepted her.

We also had many friends in the District, including two of her best friends - Grant and Marilyn Fletcher. Marilyn had also gone to Olds School with Marj.

We got married in July 1960 at her local church at Gladys Ridge just up the road from her parents' farm, and the reception was held at the farm with a large crowd of friends and relatives

Our honeymoon was an eight-day trip by car to B.C. and Coeur d'Alene, Idaho. We traveled through B.C. by way of the Big Bend Road, as Rogers Pass was still being built. I remember that very windy, dusty road. We left Golden at 6:00pm, and it was 169 miles to Revelstoke. We got to Revelstoke at 1:30am.

Our motel was not very comfortable – we actually took the mattress off the bed and put it on the floor. There was lots of construction going on and we were lucky to get a room.

Our first house was an old two-storey on the Craft land I had bought. It had lots of rooms on each floor. There was a small living room and a pantry. We had to pump the water from the well, about 1,000' down a small hill. We had a wood cook stove and only a cooler for a refrigerator. We had a Volkswagen motor to power a small light plant.

It was not a great first home, but Marj accepted the challenge and dove right in to make it a home. She was at home a lot by herself, as I was in the field. She did keep her job at the bank for about eight months. Rod finished his house and moved into it just before Christmas, and Marj and I then moved into the small house in Dad's yard that Rod and Louise lived in.

We lived there for three and a half years. It was heated with a smelly old oil heater.

I still had my sows, and I remodeled an old building I could use for farrowing them. At that time, each sow raised six, or possibly up to 12 weanlings, and each one would sell for between $7-$12. We also raised 100 chickens and 20 turkeys to try to make extra income.

We bought our groceries from the Taber supermarket, owned by the Fong brothers. I was lucky as they allowed us to charge the groceries and only pay them twice a year.

Marj and I had an ongoing argument because she smoked quite heavily. We worked hard to try to get ahead and Marj helped out where she could; she hauled grain and helped with harvest.

A lot happened that changed our lives. Rod and Louise had gotten married and had two sons: Kevin and Kerry. Of course, we all spoiled them.

Frank and Colleen got married, too.

Some important dates as I remember them
- Eleanor left the farm and attended secretary school and started work in Calgary in 1956
- Her and Harry were married in 1957
- Gerald and Marg were married in 1962
- Marj and I were married in 1960
- Patty was born in 1961 and died in 1962
- Dad died in 1978 and Mother in 1988

Marj's mother and sister came to our home often after we got married, and helped us to settle in. We only had a cooler for a refrigerator so that could be a bit of a problem and we also had no phone.

I always got along with Marj's mother, Neva. She was a great lady - friendly, capable and a great cook.

Her dad was a bit bossy and a difficult man; he always interfered in the kitchen.

In my family, there was seldom any arguing or open hostility. When we visited Marj's family, there was often a lot of arguing with one another. Several evenings when we were visiting, I would go to bed early and they would argue for several more hours. It was usually Marj's dad and one of the brothers.

Marj's dad did give us 12 cows as a wedding present, which was a tremendous benefit to us. Gerald gave me a yearling registered palomino quarter horse that he helped me halter break that summer. Billy eventually became a remarkable saddle horse – worked cattle very well and was very durable. I think he taught every kid in the district how to ride.

He had a fantastic, quiet disposition and was with me for 32 years.

Changes in farming

Farming and ranching changed very much from 1948 to 1960 in our area. Cattle feeding alone evolved with the majority of the ranches wintering their cows on range, and not grazing on half of the grazing area in summer.

We kept it for the winter feed.

The area north of the Sweet Grass Hills and along the Milk River Ridge had low snow amounts and warm winters with many Chinooks, therefore making it supportive for winter grazing. Still, some years there were blizzards and deep snow resulting in huge cattle losses.

On our farm, up until 1948, most of our winter feed for the horses and sheep was stored around the farmyard. It was put up in stooks, or large stacks with a sloop, and loose hay.

We bought our first baler in 1948. It was a wire-tie, as were most of the balers. It had a large thirty-horse-power Briggs and Stratton motor.

The Taber irrigation district had started up in 1946, supplying irrigation water around Fin Castle, 10 miles west of us. Some of the farms started to grow and sell alfalfa bales. We did buy quite a lot of hay with wire around it.

In 1950 Dad bought our first twine-tie baler. It, too, had its own motor, but this allowed us to bale and store a lot more straw from the combines.

We bought our first PTO baler in 1956. We had planted our first alfalfa field in 1955. For several years, our hay was cut with a 7' wide sickle mower, left to dry for a couple of days, then raked and baled.

This was a slow process. In 1959 we bought our first swather.

Gerald, Frank, Rod, Eleanor and I had to work closely together, as there was so much to do. Any men we hired were usually put to work doing summer fallow.

We made arrangements to do Dad's farming in exchange for the use of his equipment in 1958.

Gerald did buy a grain drill and a Case 600 combine. Frank bought a three-ton grain truck and Rod bought a Massey tractor. That summer we decided to purchase a lot of our own equipment. I bought a new 14' grain drill with a fertilizer attachment, a 19' Viber shank cultivator and a 10' fertilizer spreader.

This meant we all owned pretty much the same amount of equipment dollar wise. We decided to take advantage of the farm credit lending policy for lending money to what they called farm syndicates.

We borrowed $37,500 for equipment. This bought us another three-ton grain truck, a 17' Case cultivator, a 6' V ditcher, a six-bottom plow, a 930 Case tractor, a 330 Case tractor with a front-end loader, a rock picker, a 14' swather, plus a large 1010 Case combine with a cab - all brand new.

We were on our way to being self efficient young farmers. We agreed to do Dad and Jack's farming in exchange for a land rental agreement. One parcel we rented was 800 acres of dry land, two-and-a-half miles from a graded road.

The access to it was a very rough ungraded road. It would take us three-quarters of an hour in a three-ton truck one way. Rod was actually the one who took on the parcel of land; he seeded it all to rye.

I rented 160 acres with 85 acres of it irrigated land, as did Frank. Gerald bought 329 acres of land. We took turns sharing equipment, usually rotating every third day.

We grew a lot of Betze barley for malting, and in order for it to pass the malting standards, we had to have less than 2% cracked kernels, no sprouting and no small seeds. Our harvest was a little demanding!

We had no hired men until 1965 when I hired a trainee from Norway named Erik.

Our wives did help haul grain at harvest, and usually brought lunches to the field. Dad and Jack usually hired natives from Saskatchewan to haul and stack the bales.

Jack was also supposed to watch the cows; usually if there was a problem one or two of us had to go help.

In 1959

1959 I also broke up 90 acres on section 24. It was quite level and could be irrigated without a lot of additional work. I surveyed and plowed in the required field ditches for water, and I machine-leveled another 40 acres and put in border dikes to facilitate easier irrigation.

This land, too, was extremely rocky, so many more hours were spent picking rocks. I made plans and a design to level 70 acres on the northeast of 13 for irrigation.

That fall and the next spring I worked with government surveyors to take readings by transit every 100 feet in both directions. A 70-acre area was mapped out for easy machine leveling.

I hired the Kambietz brothers in 1962 to level this portion with their large chain earth movers. This took them over two months. First, most of the topsoil was stripped off, then the land leveled, then four inches of topsoil was put back on.

Again, this was rocky land. I had a huge rock pile hauled away for irrigation dam construction that took four large rock trucks and a Cat loader eight days to haul 10 miles in 1964.

We also filled a large slough. This portion also required an eight-inch terrace for proper slope, but the water did flow evenly on the 70 acres.

I used canvas dams and a spade to set the water; this took an hour-and-a-half every six hours.

Pig barns

Marj and I both spent a lot of time building up a farmyard in a dry, sandy location. We planted trees, built fences and designed a farmstead. After Patty's death in 1961 I put my mind to planning and designing other buildings.

I applied for irrigation on the home quarter and had a drag line come in and dig a large 125' by 250' reservoir for water storage. It was large enough that there was a grant for 50% of the cost.

In 1963 I bought a house in Coaldale and hired carpenters from Taber to do the basement for me. They had to bring out their own power plant, as I did not have electricity.

But it was too wet and soft to put in the foundation, so it didn't get done until the following year, in 1964.

I did the septic tank and field drainage for the sewage into the pig lagoon. We worked on the house, installing water, propane, etc and moved in in 1964. We spent many years remodeling this house, putting in lawns, sidewalks, planting trees and a garden.

Pigs

In 1959 and for the following three years I was making plans and designing a confinement pig barn, as well as deciding what breed and type of pigs I should go into.

One of the big concerns was disease in pigs. Howard Freedeen and the research station at Lacombe had developed a breed of hogs which they called the Lacombe breed. I first met him when he visited the Olds college as a speaker.

For sure, the breed was superior to the typical Yorkshire breed common in Alberta.

As a cross-breed, it went to market on less feed. Doc Freedeen was a little concerned, though. He had kept a clean and pretty much disease-free facility at Lacombe. But as it was a government facility, it had to be open to everyone, so he was concerned about disease.

I decided to use the Lacombe breed, but in 1961 the pigs at Lacombe did develop atrophic arthritis pneumonia.

This caused me to consider and research S.P.F. hogs, and on a trip to Edmonton to visit Patty in the University Hospital I briefly met with Dr. Donahue with Alberta Agriculture. He felt I should be encouraged to consider the S.P.F. hogs. When we talked on the phone a month or two later, he looked into this further for me. He put me in touch with Stan Price (president), Lorne Stout (secretary) and Bud Boate, who were all involved in the S.P.F. Association.

On a trip down from Calgary, we stopped to see a pig farmer, Kjeld Nielson. He had one of the largest S.P.F. herds in Alberta. At that time, there were only 10 S.P.F. breeders in the province.

Kjeld was doing very well selling breeding sows and boars. He also had Danish Landrace pigs. The Norwegian Landrace were well-known as superior pigs world-wide, but Norway would not export pigs out of the country. The Danish Landrace had many of the same traits.

They were long, lean pigs with less fat, and had 14 nipples for nursing as opposed to 12 in most other breeds. That meant they could nurse more baby pigs. Denmark or Norway would not join the European common market for many years, as that would have meant they would have to allow other countries to buy their superior swine.

The Norwegian government, even today, only allows the export of approximately 100 gilt or sows a year. Most countries in the world developed a lard-type pig, but the Landrace was developed for bacon.

I researched hog breeds for quite some time, and eventually decided I would buy some Landrace bred gilts from Kjeld Nielson. The gestation period for a pig is three months, three weeks and three days, or 114 days.

I made plans to put up a confinement pig barn to go up in 1964. I planned to get Kjeld to breed me 16 gilts to farrow in February 1964.

Then I started to design a confinement barn, as well as facilities to house 60 sows and 150 feeder pigs. Many of these I would raise and sell as breeding stock.

I had toured Kjeld's pig barns and other confinement barns in the area – they all had problems I knew I had to avoid in my plan. At that time, there were only 10 confinement barns in Alberta.

Most were arched rib-type buildings which were hard to ventilate. Many were large and damp. I contacted Dennis Darby, who was with the Alberta Department of Agriculture, with some of my plans and ideas. Most of his buildings required very large automatic fans to draw out damp stale air, and by drawing the air in from open large windows or doors.

I came up with a gable style barn with only a 7' ceiling, which was well-ventilated, especially in the attic, complete with vapor barriers. There was a two-inch opening along the one wall just below the eaves, two small automatic fans, plus one large one on the opposite wall.

This meant the air would be drawn across the barn and along the low ceiling after coming through the attic. Two vents were on either end of the attic, keeping the barn dry with fresh air across every pen.

I also put in 10" by 12" doors every 16 feet that could be removed during a very hot day.

The barn was to be 36' by 100' long. I next talked to Wayne Ulrick, who had been assistant bank manager at CIBC in Taber. He had left Taber in 1961 and was managing a building company in Calgary.

He had built many farm buildings and was impressed with my design. He offered a few suggestion and asked to be considered as the building contractor as it moved forward.

footnotes

I did not have a telephone, but lived in the yard with Mother, so all my calls went through her. She was on a party line, same one as Rod and Gerald.

I made arrangements with Dennis Darby to call me if he came to Taber, and he said he would contact me through the district agriculturist. The D.A. had a very bad stutter.

One morning he phoned Mother to have her tell me a meeting had been set up. Rod was listening in on the call. Mother told me about the meeting at 7:00 pm. Rod and I were working together, so at 5:30 I said I'd better get ready. Rod started to laugh and said I still had lots of time.

This poor D.A. also talked real slow. He tried to tell Mother the meeting was at 7:30 but would get stuck on the 'sssssssseven.' He tried several times, but she kept saying, "Yes, 7:00," and he finally gave up.

Rod said this went on for several minutes. When I got to the meeting the D.A. was so glad I got the time right.

I hired Wayne Ulrick and his company, Marathon Construction, to build the barn. They were to begin construction in late 1963. First, I had to dig the lagoon, dig and put in the sewage drain pipes, and drill an artesian well. I also had to have the electric power installed at the site.

I applied for electricity from Calgary Power to be installed in early 1963, but I had not made the final land payment to Herb Craft at this time. They would not put the power in until the land was in my name.

So, I made the payment to Herb on April 1, but it took the lawyers four months to get the title transfer done. I had ordered the building materials for August 1963, but the delivery was not made until late October.

It was an early winter and we could not dig in the footings or pour any concrete until the spring of 1964. I also had a 24' by 40' pole frame shelter for the sows built in 1963, but it was out of square and so badly done I made Wayne tear it down and rebuild it. He then sent out a crew to build it properly - four men from Holland who had immigrated to Canada.

They would only work in my barn for four days a week, then they would be gone for three days. I found out it was because of Workman's Compensation. They worked under one name four days a week for me, and then build houses in Lethbridge three days a week.

They built the barn as I wanted. In a couple of months they had the whole thing done. Later, Dennis Darby put a patent on the barn and made money selling the design.

The things that did not work well in the barn
- Wayne had suggested I put a furnace in the barn, which turned out was not needed
- He also suggested I needed a large piston water pump and it was expensive; it only lasted one year and I replaced it with a jet pump at the quarter of the cost
- Also, the small loading chute to load out the pigs faced south, and it was difficult to load pigs out in the sun. That problem was solved when Erik from Norway came to work for me. I had 10 pigs in the loading chute ready to ship. I went to the house to get my wallet, and when I came back Erik already had the pigs in the truck. I asked him how he did that so fast. He grabbed a bucket, put it over the pig's head and it backed up wherever he wanted it to go. It was a pig trick that I used for many years

The barn would also have four farrowing pens in where the newborn piglets could lie away from their mothers to avoid getting laid on. These pens were equipped with infa-red heat lamps. The sow and new pigs were only left in them for four or five days, then moved out into a larger pen.

This worked very well. During the first or second day of birth, the newborn piglets were given iron by mouth. Also, their eyeteeth were cut out. If you did not do this, they sometimes bit or damaged their own mouth. I liked to castrate them by three weeks of age. This was always a problem in the winter, as I did not have a hired man.

Sometimes Marj would help me, but it was not a job that she liked. Rod often helped, and over the next two years I also sold Rod weaner pigs that he would feed to market.

He rented a big barn, too.

The pens inside the barn were constructed of two-by-six pressure treated tongue and groove lumber. Each pen was five-and-a-half feet wide and 16' long, with concrete floors throughout. Everyone had made them out of ordinary lumber, but the pigs would eat them. The pigs didn't bother the pressure treated lumber.

The gutters were four feet wide and covered with steel expanded metal, so the pigs trampled their own manure into the pits. I washed the pens down every third day, but the pigs were fed on the concrete floor.

Pigs are very clean animals, and if they have a choice they will not lay in their own manure. They love to wallow or lay in mud to keep cool, but not in their own manure.

Pigs do not sweat, except from their nose. Even when I had the barn full of a thousand weaners it would only take me about two hours to feed the whole barn - more if a sow was farrowing.

I fed a balanced ration once a day. The reason for that it was proven that if you only fed once a day as opposed to twice a day, your hogs would be lean with less fat on the bacon and ham.

A few other facts about pigs
- They have a layer of fat next their skin that has very few blood vessels in it. I had a special little instrument that I could measure the fat with. I used this to help me in selecting my replacements for breeding. I wanted that fat to be less than three quarters of an inch. I wanted my pigs to be at least 31 inches long and ship them at 219 lbs body weight, usually at less than six months of age
- Because of this layer of fat next to hide with very little blood movement, pigs are not susceptible to rattlesnake bites. In fact, hogs were utilized a lot in the Okanagan in the development of orchards - they would actually kill rattlesnakes

- The pig's organs and blood types are very similar to human's, and a lot of work has been done to develop pig's hearts, blood, lungs and kidneys for transplant to humans, especially the blood
- In 1991 Pat and I were invited to the national cattle convention in Phoenix, Arizona. The keynote speaker was a futurist who talked at length about pigs being used for human benefit in this type of research

I was successful in selling quite a few gilts and boars for breeding. The largest sale was to George Powell, who borrowed the blueprints for my barn and had Hutterites build him a barn. They did an excellent job. They made a few changes in the load-out chute area and put in automatic window openers. He bought 60 bred gilts from me, six to farrow every week for 10 weeks. His farrowing pens were in a separate barn attached by a walkway to his feeder barn.

Another good sale was to Courtney Carlson of Glasgow, Montana and his neighbour. The hogs in the U.S. were mostly Berkshire or Berkshire crosses. These were black pigs bred more for lard. The U.S. was just beginning to use the bacon type hog like I had.

Courtney and a friend drove up to my place, looked over my operation and decided to take some pigs back with them. I did not have any bred gilts for sale, so they bought 10 100lb pigs from me, as well as a boar.

But they had to be blood tested for tuberculosis before entering the U.S.

They were in a hurry. I got in touch with Health of Animals in Brooks, Alberta, and a government vet drove down the same day. He drew blood and took it to the diagnostic lab in Lethbridge, which is a highly monitored and secure facility located 15 miles west of Lethbridge in the Old Man River plateau.

You had to get prearranged security to enter that facility. Two days later I drove up to Lethbridge and got the result. I then had to take them to Brooks to get the Health of Animals vet to do the required paperwork to get the hogs into the U.S.

Most of this time, Courtney was with me and we got along very, very well. 45 years later I met him at the international room at the Calgary stampede. I also sold a lot of boars to the Hutterites and local farmers.

I guaranteed all my boars. One of my neighbours said one of mine did not breed, so I replaced it. The next year, he came to me and said the new one wasn't breeding, either. I mentioned this to one of his neighbours and he said, "Bullshit. There's little Landrace pigs running all over his yard."

I stopped in one day, and sure enough, there was. I told him I thought he owed me some money and he never said a word - went into his house and came out with cash.

I charged $125 for a bred gilt or $125 for a boar. This was about double what I could sell them for slaughter.

The black Berkshire hog had a black pigmentation for the hair root in the bacon rind: that was not appealing. Most of the U.S. hogs now have eliminated that, and they use a lot of red Duroc or the white breeds that do not show that black pigment.

Selling pigs to the U.S.
In 1968 Courtney Carlson put together six different farmers in northeast Montana who wanted breeding pigs from me, at various locations from Malta to Glasgow, Montana. They wanted a total of five bred gilts and 12 sixty-pound gilts and two young boars.

I was short on breeding stock and could only supply the younger pigs. I contacted Kjeld Neilson and made arrangement for him to supply the others, and also to have the book testing and paperwork down to ship the pigs across the border.

I put a false floor mid-point up on my wooden stock racks in my three-quarter-ton truck. The young pigs were confined to the top level. Kjeld agreed to bring his pigs as far as Lethbridge. We would meet and load his pigs on my truck. He wanted to follow me in his car to Glasgow, so made arrangement for his hired man to bring his pigs down.

When we met in Lethbridge he had more pigs on his truck than we had agreed to. He had six bred gilts and 10 young ones; he expected to leave some of mine behind so he could send more.

His hired man had to take his extras back home.

The U.S. veterinary inspection entering facility was at Sweetgrass, Montana. By going through Lethbridge, it was 360 miles from my place to Glasgow. All the pigs had to be unloaded and inspected at Sweetgrass and the paperwork done, and this took over three hours, so it was noon before we got on our way to Glasgow going through Havre.

Courtney had arranged to have each farmer meet us at their respective towns, but we had five different drop-offs. Kjeld was very afraid of getting lost, so he followed very close behind me. I stopped twice to ask him to back off a little. We finally got the last pigs unloaded in Glasgow at 1:00am.

The next day we did some sight seeing, went out to the Ft. Peck dam and irrigation diversion and hydro generators. The Ft. Peck dam is the longest and highest earth-built dam in the world.

On display were hundreds of Indian artifacts and dinosaur artifacts that they had found when constructing the dam, the roads and the irrigation canals.

That evening there was a meeting of hog producers, and I was asked to give a side presentation of my hog barn. Courtney told me that two farmers built similar barn the next year.

We went home via Opheim and visited with a large hog producer. All his hogs were raised 100% outside in large straw bales that they used for shelter. He had over 150 sows year-round.

We then crossed back into Saskatchewan at East Poplar port of entry. It was a one-man custom officer at the Canadian side and you would have to be there before 4:00pm or you waited until the next day.

He badly needed Canadian one-dollar bills. We only had 20 that we could spare.

The Cypress Hills area is very rough and has large amounts of snowfall in the winter. They used large track vehicles for school buses four months of the year - each seated about eight kids.

From there we went to a Assinaboin, Saskatchewan, Maple Creek and then home.

It was very dark by the time we got to Maple Creek, and we noticed the sky in the west was lit up. As we came over a small hill, we seen a large R.V. parking lot with a large field beside it full of campers. It was the day after the Calgary Stampede and many people were heading home.

We heard there were over 1,000 camped for the night at that centre. Maple Creek is in the heart of ranching in Saskatchewan, and south of Maple Creek is Ft. Walsh, established in 1875.

The fort has all been rebuilt and is a great place to visit. It is located on the Saskatchewan side of the Cypress inter-provincial park. On the Alberta side of the park is a town called Elk Water. The elevation there is approximately 1,250 metres. During the last ice age when glaciers were melting, they did not reach the Elk Water plateau. As a result, even today many plants were evident that are not growing in other areas of the western prairies.

I found Elk Water a real gem, and over the years have visited on several occasions.

The pigs did provide us the income we needed to expand our farm, and we were able to buy more land and increase our cattle herd. By 1968 we had built several new buildings, corrals and a large feed lot.

We erected some round grain bins, had storage for over 30,000 bushels of grain and had built a large 240' by 60' cattle shed. We had purchased another section of land along the Grassy Lake highway in partnership with my brother Frank.

Patty and the second year of our marriage

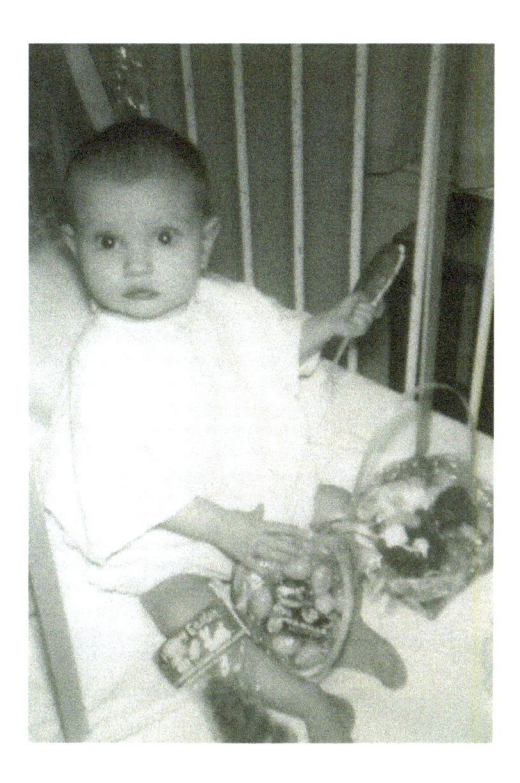

Patricia Elaine (Patty) Brewin passed away at 11 months of age from heart failure

Patty (Patricia Elaine) was born with a hole in her heart, lung issues and with occasional problems with her bowels. We had to insert glycerin suppositories to help her have bowel movements. She was considered a blue baby because of the lack of oxygen in her blood.

Dr. Enman, and Dr. Dick served her for the first 24 hours, and we were then advised that unless we got her to Doc Bannister at University Hospital in Edmonton, she would not survive. Arrangements were made, and an incubator was set up in my car. Myself, Mom and my brother Jack left at 2:00 am for the 10-hour drive to Edmonton. Mother got carsick often, but she rode in the back seat with Patty and took good care of her.

We arrived at University Hospital and they immediately took her in for examination. They did what they could for her but advised me she would have to stay with them for at least six weeks and told me to prepare for the worst.

Marj had remained in the hospital in Taber. Mother's brother, Jack Shenfield farmed at Spruce Grove, and we stayed with them for a few days, but spent most of our time in the hospital with Patty.

After five days, we were advised we may as well return home, as I should be at home with Marj. Mother helped me, and we made arrangements to christen Patty, and then returned home.

My cousin Jocelyn and his wife Stephanie visited with Patty every day and kept us informed how she was doing. After a month and a half, we were told we could take Patty home - her little body and heart were just too small to operate.

When Marj and I went to pick her up, we were told that the hole in her heart had to be repaired, but not until she was six years old, as it was just too small. We were told that at two years of age they would attempt some minor work.

Dr. Bannister was a world-known heart specialist, one of the first to do any open-heart surgery. He assisted with the first heart replacement, so we knew Patty had the best there was at the time.

She was placed on oxygen and we had to monitor breathing and bowel movements closely. Whenever she had a real problem with her stomach or bowel, we often had to take her to the hospital at Taber.

Everybody immediately fell in love with Patty. Most of the time she was so happy, with a smile that would melt your heart. It was truly a godsend to have Patty in our lives.

She became the darling of all my family's lives as well as the Newman's. A lot of our time and efforts were diverted to her care that year and farming took second.

Patty had a major attack the following spring. We tried to get her to the hospital, but she passed away in her mother's arms. This was her cousin Ricky's birthday (Rod and Louise's son). We had the funeral and buried Patty in the cemetery in Taber.

Her pallbearers were all nurses who took great care of her on our many visits to the hospital.

One of these pallbearers was boarding in town, and about three years later she was in her apartment and some guy came in and stabbed her four times. She lived through it but they never found out who did it.

Patty's death was very difficult for myself and Marj: we both cried a lot. When you lose a child you also lose part of yourself. I do know her death had a lasting effect on my life. I tried hard to overcome some of this loss by throwing myself into the farm, but there was always something missing.

Our farm did keep moving ahead and our daughter Beverly was born healthy and active in 1963 on her grandad's birthday, February 10.

Our son Daniel was born January 28 the following year. Marj's mother came and stayed with us for two weeks to help out and we really did appreciate her.

In the fall of 1963 I marked out the yard and the location of the lagoon and the barn, along with the pole frame barn. I hired a local contractor to dig a 100' by 125' lagoon to handle the hog manure. I arranged to have an artesian well dug, 180' deep with 6" steel casing.

The contractor for this work was from Foremost. His foreman was his own son and his two friends. They were to arrive on site 10am on a Monday morning and at noon they still hadn't arrived. I went looking for them. I stopped at a neighbour's farm six miles south of Grassy Lake and was told that three trucks had gone past his place by 8am on the way to Grassy Lake.

I went into the bar in Grassy Lake and even though it was early they were quite drunk. We agreed they would move their trucks out and start drilling the next day. They were not very experienced with the drill. I was told it would take them two weeks to drill the well but it took well over a month.

When they struck water, they were to place the well casing and cement it off around the outside so no water would surface, other than up the middle of the casing.

When it came time to cement it off with a mixture of cement and sand, etc, they found they had not cleaned the three-inch rubber hose and the cement nozzle from the previous drill.

They decided to free up this hose by applying air pressure to it. They told me this would probably take about 40lbs of air pressure.

One man crawled 20 feet up the derrick to direct the cement down the outside of the casing. Another directed the hose, and the boss got in the truck to regulate the RPM therefore the air and pressure on the hose.

On the first attempt it did not free the cement from the hose. They tried a second time. I got back about 100 feet. They revved it up and I watched the pressure gauges – they went all the way up to 150 lbs. Finally, it blew out the hardened cement that was inside the three-inch hose. The mixture of water and cement hit the guy on the derrick, peeling him off like a banana.

The hose swung around and hit me in the ear. I spent three weeks cleaning cement out of my ear. I ran over and turned off the truck, even though I couldn't hear.

I phoned the owner in Foremost and told him what had happened. He came up, fired his son on the spot, and completed the drill without anymore problems.

The well, continued

The well did flow 8.5 gallons per minute, which was pushed to the surface by natural gas pressure. There was also a small flow of natural gas that came up with the water, and in that area I had to vent it off.

I installed a 2,500-gallon cistern to store the water - a continuous flow. In southern Alberta, there is what is called the Milk River Sands, 150 feet below ground level, which contains water and natural gas.

At Brooks, it is 140 feet below surface, and at our location it was 120, and at the U.S. border it's 90 feet underground. This is also the source on natural gas in southern Alberta.

It is artesian water with a high salt level. It's fine for livestock, great for bathing and washing, but has a taste that is not appealing for drinking. I did dig in a separate water line into the house, and also built a separate cistern for drinking water, which I hauled in from Taber.

The manure gutters were 3.5 feet deep with inside wall built at a 45-degree slope to encourage clean drainage.

I also put up two large 400-bushel hopper bins for feed and purchased a portable feed mixer mill so I could also introduce hay into the ration. I used my own grain and purchased concentrate for extra protein.

I would grind 500 bushels every week.

I switched to growing a six-row barley called Keystone, which was a very high-yielding variety, but which was susceptible to lodging and wind damage.

I borrowed $125,000 from Farm Credit Corporation, repayable over 21 years at 6% interest. The hog operation was a wise decision; it set up my whole farm operation and development.

I would finish my slaughter hogs to 210 to 230 lbs, at under six months of age with an excellent feed conversion of 2.1 lbs of feed for every pound of gain.

Present Kennedy's assassination

In November 1963, the Newmans asked me to go up and help them with their harvest. On the way through Lethbridge I stopped at the U.F.A. Coop, where a Hutterite told me about John F Kennedy being assassinated.

SPF certification

To comply with S.P.F. program and keep certification, the Alberta government had their own vet that would visit each S.P.F. operation three times a year. I attended the meetings of the S.P.F. association and was elected as a delegate to Health of Animals of Alberta Agriculture.

All these meetings were held in Edmonton four times a year, under the direction of Dr. Jim O'Donahue. I was shy and unsure of myself, but was well-received as a delegate, and I became a friend of Dr. Donahue.

On one trip to Edmonton, I took Marj, Bev and Dan with me, and we spent a day at Al Oming's Wildlife Park. There were some twin orphan baby moose that Bev and Dan got to bottle feed.

Hunting on Dad's property

In 1961 I sold all my pigs on Dad's farm.

After the canal was filled with water, they introduced Ring-neck Pheasants into the wastelands that was created from seepage and leakage from the canal. This resulted in many hundreds of acres of great habitat for upland bird hunting.

It also resulted in an increase of predators such as hawks, foxes and coyotes, but the pheasant population expanded rapidly. The Taber and Brooks areas became famous for their bird hunting, and many dignitaries and famous people were sometimes seen in the area, such as Bing Crosby and Dan Blocker, who was seen almost every fall.

Doctors, lawyers, etc. suddenly made best friends with farmers.

Just a half mile north of Dad's farm was an area of about 110 acres that was too wet and boggy to farm. It soon became overgrown with cattails and weeds, so provided ideal shelter and cover for nesting.

Dad considered all these birds his, and was very selective about who could hunt. He would patrol using the municipal roads and the canal banks, and would stop any hunter and tell him, "Get the hell off my land!" He wasn't afraid of nobody.

He truly enjoyed the challenge of keeping hunters away and had many of them very afraid of him.

One day I we were out surveying, myself and three government surveyors: Ray, Dennis and DeLloyd.

Dad drove into the field and scared them to bits - Dennis and DeLloyd ran as fast as they could to their truck. It was a very hot day, and they were just plain scared.

Ray and I each enjoyed a cold pop Dad had brought for us before we called the other two over. I do think chasing hunters added at least 10 years of enjoyment to my dad's life.

In 1959 Dad bought a restaurant in Ft. McCloud. He would go to Ottawa or Toronto every year for the annual Restaurant Association meeting - always by train. Bus lived in Ottawa so Dad would spend a few days with him.

Dad also invested a lot of money in stock market and did very well at it.

One incident took place when I was going to Edmonton for a meeting for three days, taking Marj and the two kids with me. Mother asked if she could get a ride with us as far as Innisfail to visit her sister. Dad also asked if he could ride with us to Edmonton, as he wanted to visit with some government people regarding his position as chairman of the Taber hospital board.

Before we left at 6:30am, Dad phoned his stock broker in Lethbridge and found out that his Barons oil stock had taken a huge jump. Mother told him, "Sell some of them!"

Dad was on a high. We stopped at Lethbridge at his broker's and found that they had gone up some more.

Again, mother said, "Sell some!" but by then he was on cloud nine. When we got to my sister's in Calgary, he had her phone his broker, making out that she was his private secretary. Well, bad news: the stocks were down.

We continued on our way to Innisfail, Dad in the back seat by the door, mother in the middle and Bev by the other door. Mother kept telling him how bad a decision he had made not selling. It really was getting quite humorous.

Dad fell asleep. I heard the back door open, because as Dad woke up, he grabbed the door handle and unlatched the door. Mother reached across him and pulled the door shut.

Mother liked to play tricks. Dad woke up with a start, and asked her, "What the hell do you think you're doing?"

Mother never missed a beat. She said, "I'm trying to push you out the door, you old fool!"

Well, the fight was on. I pulled over and put Mother in the front seat. Dad shot glares at her all the rest of the way to Innisfail where she got out, I'm sure with an inside grin.

I spent the rest of the trip to Edmonton trying to convince Dad that she'd just played a trick on him, nothing more.

Dad always stayed at the McDonald Hotel in Edmonton, and for my 65th birthday my kids gave me tickets to the rodeo finals in Edmonton, booking rooms for me at the McDonald Hotel.

It was great to stay where my dad had always stayed, and during that visit our dad took us all to the legislative buildings and introduced us to some of the M.L.As.

Dad loved to get up early to irrigate some of the grassland, usually around 4am, and he always took his car. Early one Sunday morning Dad knocked on my door - he had driven across the prairie in his car and got hung up on rocks and needed help.

I grabbed a jack and shovel and was not in a very good mood as I headed out to help.

We had to walk the last 300 feet to his car, with Dad following behind me. All of a sudden, he started swearing and cussing, and I turned around just in time to see a large rattlesnake slithering down his hole. Apparently, I had missed stepping on it by about a foot. I was very lucky it didn't strike me.

Dad rolled and demolished three different cars on his way to see his broker; the neighbours were afraid to see him coming.

One of the surveyors who worked with me was Dennis Erickson. He won, I believe, close to $90,000 in the Irish sweepstakes. When you bought your tickets on the Irish you gave a nom de plume instead of your own name.

Dennis called himself 'the duck hunter.' When he came to work the morning after, it had been announced that the duck hunter from Taber had won. Dad congratulated him, but Dennis, of course, denied it was him.

A week later it came out that Dennis had won. He came to Dad and asked, "How did you know?" Dad said, "Dennis, you spend all your spare time duck hunting – of course you were the duck hunter!"

Leveling the land

The government surveyors and draftsmen designed the project to level my land. It took them over a month to do this. In the design was a head ditch at the end of the 70 acres. One terrace six inches high was put in halfway across, with a ditch down the west side.

A catch ditch at the quarter mile distance had an ideal slope of one inch for every hundred feet.

I hired Steve and Mike Kambietz, with their chain land movers, to do the leveling for me. It took them most of the summer, and it took me every spare minute picking rocks.

I usually grew malt barley or soft spring wheat. Later, I leveled 40 acres on the southwest of 24.

My home quarter on 22 was not assigned irrigation water when the main canal was built. I met with S.M.I.R.D. on many occasions to try and get irrigation water rights on this land.

My brother Jack was the chairman of the S.M.I.R.D. at the time, and he always discouraged my application, saying the land was too rocky and sandy - not suitable for irrigation.

There were many farmers applying for additional water rights, and Jack felt it would look like favouritism if I was granted water rights.

The problem was, he used his position to increase his own water rights. After two years it was finally decided I could be grated 40 acres of the water rights on the north end of my land.

But I had to pay 50% of the cost of the lateral canal construction, which no one else had had to do. This cost me $28,000; I got the approval in 1967

Harry Viener

My dad became friends with Harry Viener, mayor of Medicine Hat. He served as mayor for over 20 years, and six years in a row he had us take a horse to the Taber parade for him to ride.

The first year was 1956, and this began an involvement in the Taber parade for me, for many years. There were six years with the mayor, two with Bev and Dan on their bikes, 12 when I was leader of the Bon Ayr 4-H Beef Club, and four years as a member of the Taber Rodeo Committee.

Twice, I supplied horses to be used as flag bearers.

One year when we took a horse in for Mayor Viener, there was a rodeo performer and stunt man named Buddy Heaton with his buffalo that he rode.

He was a little late, and asked Gerald and I if we would help him get ready. He was a wild man who was about 6'5", with a buffalo he rode named Old Gunter. Buddy performed in many rodeos, parades and starred in many movies.

Once, John F. Kennedy had a parade in California, and Buddy Heaton entered the parade without permission, and just rode along.

Buddy either used chains or rawhide as reins, because the buffalo was so strong.

One stunt he did was in the arena: he would ride his buffalo toward his truck with the back door open and jump his buffalo into the truck at a lope. Buddy would roll over the top of the cab and land on his feet in front of the truck.

Old Gunter had to come to a quick stop inside the truck. Buddy had the truck well-padded, but it truly was act to watch.

He also became famous training, showing and performing with appaloosa horses – he did very well with them.

Mayor Viener had two large, two-storey hardware stores in Medicine Hat. You could find anything in those stores – we often shopped there.

The Cuban crisis

In 1962 Gerald, myself and five of our neighbours went to the mountains north of Coleman, Alberta to hunt elk, taking horses. On the second day in camp, the game warden told us of the Russian U.S. conflict in Cuba, and the real possibility of a war. He kept us informed all day and advised us that we may have trouble getting home if war broke out.

We spent all night packing up and headed out early that next morning. It was three days after we got home before tensions eased, and we could feel reasonably sure that this conflict was over. We did not go back up hunting that fall; instead, three of us went southwest of Pincher Creek and got one elk and three deer.

Khrushchev wrecked a well-planned hunting expedition.

Harvest in the 50s

The three number 55 John Deere combines Dad bought in 1951 and 1952 served us very well. There were easy to operate, efficient, and quite easy to set to facilitate proper thrashing.

Dad also bought the pick-up attachments to enable us to pick up swath grain. much of out crop, however, continued to be standing and straight cut. With more irrigation and improvement of the crops, we did slowly switch to the swathing harvest technique.

We got quite expert at converting a combine header from sickle and knife cutting with the reel, to the pick-up attachment in approximately three-quarters of an hour.

We took off the reel, pulled out the sickle, which was 14' long, removed six knife guards, installed the belt to the pickup pulley, set the chains on both ends of the pickup to determine the angle of the pickup. One of the problems with the straight cut method was the sway bar and pitman. To move the sickle back and forth, you had to be certain it was at the proper tension, well greased, and you monitored it closely.

The chain feeder house, when taking the grain into the concaves, also had to be checked every morning. Concaves were set with a three-quarter inch wrench, depending on the crop being thrashed.

The screens were easy to adjust to facilitate proper grain separation, and there was a large fan that blew air up into the screens to help separate chaff from grain. The screens and straw walkers did tend to plug up, so we carried laths to clean them, usually three or four times a day.

The grain that needed two cycles was returned by return elevator, back over the concaves, and the clean grain was carried by elevator into the hopper or grain tank.

We would determine if grain that was thrown over and wasted was blown out or thrown out by the setting of the fan.

There was a small door on the return elevator that you could open and inspect for proper cleaning.

You sat on a platform in the front of the hopper and had easy access to all the controls and steering wheel. There were no cabs on the combine; the hopper held approximately 50 bushels before we needed to unload it.

Jack's job in harvest was usually to do the baling, but one day he came out to drive my combine while I ate lunch. He asked me to set the fan and wind for thrashing the grain.

I got off to do it, and as I often did. I left the machine in motion. There was a small opening you could reach in to pull the lever to adjust the wind setting.

As I reached in, my hand got caught on a V-belt; it went around the pulley, cut my hand very badly and it took 16 stitches to sew it up. The bad part of that was that Mother wouldn't let me help with harvest for two or three days, and I had to go to school.

Gerald, Frank, Rod and I did all the harvest with these combines for over 10 years, with Gerald, Rod and I each on a combine and Frank hauling all the grain.

He would leave an empty truck at the end of the field and take the truck full of grain to unload while we did the combining and filled the empty truck.

This kept Frank very busy, as only one truck had a hoist to lift the box full of grain. The other truck, he had to shovel most of it out. The truck with the hoist held approximately 300 bushels, the other held about 250 bushels.

We grew a lot of barley, which was quite itchy to harvest. The wheat was not, but oats were the worst - the dust from oats was almost like little knives.

We also grew a lot of Durum wheat, which has a three-inch beard on it; this often plugged up the straw walkers.

When the grain tank got full, you take your hand or arm and level it out. Then, you could fit approximately another 10 bushels into the hopper. There were two ladders on the combine; one up to the motor, and the other up to the platform.

There was a fairly comfortable seat to sit on but often we just stood up. You had a view of the ground and the header in front to you.

But you could also access the platform over the top of the motor, and the hopper when it was full. We usually worked until about 10pm, as often the grain would get tough at night.

We also worked seven days a week.

In 1955 we combined for 32 days without taking a day off.

Late one night in 1954, I was the last one to come around the field Gerald and Rod had got to the truck and shut down for the night around 11:30pm.

The field was such a size that you would usually just make it around before your hopper was full and you had to level it out. This was easy to do without leaving the platform.

Rod walked out this night, partway up the field, crawled up above the motor into my hopper to level the grain. I had not seen him and put my arm back to level the hopper twice. The third time I reached back, I got a real fright - I actually grabbed his arm. What a shock that was! I was not aware he was even there; I let out a real scream and cussed him out and he laughed and laughed.

This kind of became a game we would try to pull on one another now and then.

When we bought the Case 10-10 combine with a cab, you entered the driver's platform, kind of from the back of the cab and to the left of the driver's seat.

The cab had a fan, but no air conditioner, so it could get quite hot. Often at night the cab door was open. Another trick of Rod's would be to crawl up the ladder, slowly bend down and place his face right up to mine in the dark. This would scare the britches off you. Rod loved to lay these kinds of tricks.

After he was married, though, I think I got even with him a bit. I had to talk to Rod, and stopped at his house, and Louise told me what field he was in. She also asked me to take his lunch out to him.

Rod loved Nanaimo bars, and Louise loved to make them. She sent about eight along with his lunch. I sat in the truck and visited with him while he ate his sandwiches and got to his Nanaimo bars.

Rod really hated uncooked eggs, or even the thought of a raw egg. As he took the first bite of his Nanaimo bar, I said, "Rod, don't you realize the white part of the bar has raw eggs in it?"

He threw it out the window and cussed Louise for using raw eggs.

I had no idea what Nanaimo bars were made of. For some reason he never asked Louise what Nanaimo bars were made of for quite some time, and I enjoyed lots of great Nanaimo bars at Rod's expense. By then Rod and Louise had two teenage boys who also loved Nanaimo bars.

Rod was 6'1" tall and solid muscle and was a bugger to work. I could beat most people at arm wrestling, but not Rod. I tried many, many times at stag parties, etc, but Rod was always the person to bet on.

When Rod was in the hospital shortly before he died, I mentioned this to him - that I always wanted to beat him. His reply was, "You never could, and you never will."

I think he was 100% right.

At that time, I was living in Williams Lake and Rod was in the hospital. Gerald phoned me and told me that Rod was not well, and I should get out to see him. I booked a flight to Calgary, borrowed a car from Bev, and drove down to see Rod. His room was in the ground floor in the care home and looked right out onto the row of parked cars.

Bev's car was one of those that, as long as you had the keys in your pocket, you were supposed to be able to unlock it and start it. After the third day, I had to head home. I also got to visit with Kevin, Rod's oldest son whom I had not seen for 30 years.

I walked out to the cars, to what I thought was Bev's car, and tried in vain to get into it. Finally, I heard a tap on Rod's room window – he had been watching me. One of Rod's favourites was, when someone messed up, he would call them a dummy. He was grinning, calling me a dummy, and pointing to a car up from the one I was trying to get into. It was exactly the same make and colour as Bev's.

The last time I seen Rod alive, he was laughing his head off as I drove away.

He ashes are spread on one of the large hills half a mile from his house.

Rod and I were very close. We were the two youngest boys and we worked together, played together and really enjoyed one another's company.

Combines versus threshing machines

I was recently asked about threshing machines and the switch to combines. I do not remember the threshing machines, although they were used up to and into the 1940s. The first combines I remember were pull-types with their own motors, which were needed to thresh the grain. The one we used was a model 36 McCormbick Dering, with a 24' header.

I believe this was a used machine when Dad bought it. I remember Gerald as operator of this combine, and Frank driving a Case L tractor pulling it. Another combine was a John Deere Number 17 pull type.

Dad bought this new in about 1946, with a 20' header.

This was a very good machine. I do not remember many problems with it. Most of the grain was piled in large piles on the ground. You pulled up tight to the pile and opened a slide chute that emptied the hopper.

Footnote: I do not know why the grain tank on a combine was called a hopper. I always wondered it if was because there were a lot of grasshoppers mixed in with the grain. I looked this up and could not find the answer.

On the Number 17 combine, there was a platform up top, in front of the grain tank, where Dad sat to control the height of the crop that was being cut, and to watch for rocks, etc.

There was a wooden seat he could sit on, but he seldom sat down. There was a large wheel he could turn to adjust the height of the platform.

The grain was cut off about six inches above the ground, and a canvas conveyor belt, reinforced with one-inch hardwood slats. This conveyor belt took the cut crop along the length of the header and deposited it onto a shorter 6' long canvas, that took it up and dropped it into the feeder house.

That in turn dropped it into the cylinder and concaves that started the threshing process. I usually sat or stood on the tractor fender so I could see Dad. The distance between Dad and me was about 15 feet. Most of his instructions were simply to tell me to go faster or slower.

If I did not pay attention, he would sometimes throw a hammer or wrench at the fender to get my attention. I tried to avoid that, as I had to always pull the hand clutch to stop the tractor and retrieve the tool.

Both Rod and I helped with the harvest, and we were allowed to miss a lot of school in September, to help out. We also had a self-propelled Massey combine. I remember Rod operating it.

Mother made sure we kept up on our learning, and our marks did not suffer.

During the war, most of the iron and metal was needed for the war effort. It was, however, recognized that food supplies were also vital. In this effort, Massey Harris Machines was given the go-ahead to build and market 650 self-propelled combines.

The first of these went on market in 1944, and the first John Deere self-propelled was built and sold in 1947. We did have both of these machines on the farm.

One of the big dangers was from fire. Air was drawn in to keep the radiator cool and came in from a large screen above the combine motor. A lot of chaff and dust was created through the threshing process. You had to watch the screens, and clean them regularly, if they started to get covered with debris.

Many acres of grain were destroyed on crop land in western Canada in ripened grain, because of fire. One that was often referred to was in the Skiff area, where I was told it burned a huge area 40 miles long.

Dad treated me like a man, helping with harvest. It was a time when we really bonded with him.

Pesticides and crop spraying

The farm experience had many different challenges with insects, pests and weeds. Many of these were not native to Canada but were introduced by European farmers.

The varieties of grain were all brought in from other countries, and were improved and developed for a hard, high quality bread wheat flour in Canada. Almost from the start, Canadian bread wheat was the top for bread in the world.

Varieties such as Red Bob's, Marquis, Thatcher and Canus all had high protein and excellent milling qualities.

These were susceptible to saw fly larvae that laid it egg in the hollow wheat stems. When the eggs hatched, the larvae ate out the soft plant stem, and the ripening grain would fall over. Hence the name – saw fly.

Rescue and Chinook wheat varieties were developed; they had a solid stem preventing the larvae from hatching. Most of our wheat that was grown, up until about 1962, was Chinook.

Cut worms were also a big problem some years. Your defense against them was using an insecticide spray. The cut worms went under the top inch of dirt, in the daytime and surfaced at night. Your best results were obtained by night spraying with D.D.T. and Dieldrin.

The cut worms were most active in newly-seeded crops. We would drive around the field in the daytime with the half-ton and mark out a track. Then, at night, we could follow the track with a tractor and sprayer attached to the tractor.

Grasshoppers were also a huge problem; they would lay their eggs on the head lands, and the young grasshoppers, as they hatched would move into the grain fields.

When I was about five or six, I remember going with Dad into Grassy Lake and loading up shavings that had arsenic mixed with it. We then drove along the headlands, scattering this mixture, which killed the grasshoppers, often in bare feet.

D.D.T. was also used for this.

In the 1960s we sprayed for grasshoppers with Dieldrin or Lindane. All of these pesticides were dangerous, and they were not controlled. Very little research had been done, or training for farmers.

Many farmers have suffered the after-effects of the pesticide sprays. I spent many days on the tractor with no cab, spraying, often with no protective clothing.

We also treated our grain seeds with Lindane for wire worm and root rot.

In the late 1970s safer products, such as Sevin, were developed as effective pesticides. Many herbicides were also used for weed control - 24D Ester were the most common.

During two different years, we had a beet webworm infestation. They ate the broadleaf plants, as they loved the succulent leaves. They did not eat wheat, oats or barley, but sure cleaned the weeds out of the crops.

They also liked aspen and caragana trees. Yes, farming had many challenges besides drought, wind and frost.

Frank and his pheasants

My brother Frank bought a load of post and lumber from B.C. and built a large pheasant containment pen approximately 800' by 500' and enclosed it all with 8'high chicken wire when he was about 18 years old.

He raised a variety of pheasants: ring-neck, silver and golden, and released a lot of the ring-neck pheasants, as well as bobwhite quail.

His son Roy developed a keen interest in raising these birds when he was 10 years old.

Remodeling our house in 1964 and 1965

We moved into the house I had moved to Coaldale onto its foundation in the late summer of 1964.

We went right to work making it suitable to live in. I installed a septic tank and drainage, which also emptied into the lagoon. I did all this work myself with the help of Marj.

We did not take much time off the next four or five years, but for the most part they were good years.

I was 75% hailed-out in 1968.

We took trips to Blackie to visit Marj's family two or three times a year. We also went to her family's cabin at Sylvan Lake each summer for three or four days. I remember the six-year-old boy next door at the cabin. He would come over whenever he seen me outside, and we would tease and kid each other.

One day he asked me what the hole in my cowboy hat was from, and I said of course it was from a bullet.

He was a little impressed – rolled his eyes and said, "Yeah, well, I have six toes on each foot."

I did not believe the little boy and told him to prove it. He took off his tennis shoes and sure enough: six toes.

We bought a new Meteor car in 1965, and a used Volkswagen half-ton. We continued to do a lot of Jack and Dad's farm work but did concentrate on our own farms.

We did all the branding and processing of calves for Dad and Jack. At first, Gerald did all the castrating, but by 1965 he had me doing most of that.

It was quite a gathering when we all got together at the main ranch corrals – 10 or 12 nieces and nephews, and four brothers and their wives.

The kids would often ride the calves.

Bev, Dan, Sandra and Dixie as babies

Bev was born on February 10, 1962, on Marj's Dad's birthday. It was a nice day for February – a Chinook had set in the day before. I remember throwing bales over the fence to feed the bulls and was not even wearing a coat. Marj's mother came out for about 10 days when Bev was born. Everyone was very excited about a baby girl – up until that date all my brothers had only had boys.

Bev was a quick learner, and everyone loved to hold her. Louise and Colleen were also pleased to finally have a baby girl that they could dress up, change diapers and spoil. Bev was a good baby.

The next year she wanted slippers for her birthday. We were able to get her a pair of pink slippers but left them with Rod and Louise. I remember plowing through a snow bank with the tractor to make sure she got her slippers on her birthday.

For several years, she had the nickname 'Pinkie'. She loved to colour and draw as she grew up, did great at school and always had lots of friends.

Dan was born on January 28, 1963 – a very cold day. From day one he was a husky, tough little guy who loved to be outside. When he was six months old Marj did up eight bottles of formula for him and I took him in the cab of the truck to feed the cows with me.

He got into the diaper bag and devoured all eight bottles in just over an hour.

As he got older, he loved to hang out with the trainees. They always liked to tease him and have him around. The one time I remember being any different was when Helge from Denmark was with us. I was expanding our corrals and feedlot. Dan, who was about three years old, was out with Helge, asking questions and being a nuisance.

I went out to get Helge to come in for dinner, and could not see Dan. I asked Helge where he was, and he grunted, "Oh, he's around."

Finally, I seen Dan's little head inside a post hole. Helge had stood him in the hole Dan wouldn't bug him.

I was using 8' posts to put in the ground about two and a half feet, and Dan was almost full in.

All the holes were dug by hand, and the posts set and tamped in. A lot of holes were dug that fall and corrals put up. I nailed most of the planks on myself, and a lot of that was not done until December.

When Dan was two, a friend, Marg Hopkins, brought over several little dresses for Bev, as her daughter had grown out of them. Dan cried and was really mad because he never got anything. Marg and Marj put a cute little dress on him and he was happy. He was quite a sight in a dress with his broad husky shoulders and skinny little legs.

Sandra was born April 4, 1969 – a warm, windy day. Bev and Dan liked to go with me to check the cows. They were a lot of company.

The day Sandra was born we had a set of black twin calves born too. These calves were sold at six months of age, and we opened a bank account for the three kids in their own names.

Sandra also was a quick learner, and she loved to colour and draw and to read, very early in age. She was also independent and always said, "I can do it myself."

She would often read to Gerald and became a favourite of his. At 11 months of age Sandra developed pneumonia, with a very high temperature. We took her into the hospital and they put her in cold water to bring her temperature down.

She was in the hospital for almost two weeks and got the cold water treatment a couple of times a day. When she was in the hospital, I got my hand caught in the P.T.O. when hooking up my grinder mill. Most of my thumb was tore off - it was only holding on by tendons, a couple of veins and small amount of skin. This was March 13, 1970.

The doc told me there was an 85% chance I would lose my thumb. Doc Weibe was an excellent surgeon, and he did three separate operations on my thumb. All the time I was afraid it would turn black and have to be amputated.

I was hospitalized for 12 days. Gerald fed my pigs during that time. They did save my thumb but even today I have very little use of it, it has very poor circulation and gets cold very easily.

At that time, there were three other men in the same hospital who had had similar accidents; they all had to have their thumbs amputated.

I had to take therapy on the thumb twice a week for a year, and it usually involved hot wax treatments.

I was in one wing of the hospital and Sandra in another. Every time we went to see her, she always had her blanket in her arms and wanted to go home.

Dixie was born on June 7, 1971 and when she was six months old she skinned her forehead, and for a long time had a round scar on her forehead. She had club feet, so at six months of age she had both legs put into a cast. She was also in the hospital with pneumonia at a young age.

The cast had to be changed every four months, but Dixie soon learned how to use her little casts as weapons to kick her brothers and sister to get attention. She was also a very quick learner, liked to colour and draw, and her and Sandra were very close.

Dan's lagoon experience

The lagoon had a spot where the sewage ran into it, that never froze. Or froze very lightly. When Dan was two years old, he had a serious accident. The Fletcher girls and their mother were over for a visit, and the four kids, Bev, Dan, Janene and Judy, were playing outside.

I was putting shingles on the new back porch, and Marilyn had told the kids to play close to the house and not go near the barns. This was a mistake: it was like a dare for the four small kids. Suddenly I heard Bev yelling, and her and Janene running and hollering that Dan had fallen through the ice.

I jumped down and ran to the lagoon, expecting the worst. I found Dan up to his neck in the cold lagoon. Little Judy was lying on her stomach holding Danny by his little red parka hood.

I was able to crawl out and grab Dan and rush him to the house. Marj met me at the door and got him right into warm water in the bathtub. He did not smell too good for a few days because of the lagoon, and it took several hours for him to really get warmed up.

His biggest concern was because he had lost his little gum boots. There is no doubt that Judy saved him from drowning, and we will be forever grateful to her.

Kids growing up

One of the most memorable things for me was all the kids growing up. We were often together with their cousins. Marj, Colleen and Louise helped with the harvest, and the 10 cousins were always together at one another's place.

They loved to play in the dirt and build their little irrigation systems. Often little Mark was used as a dam. "You lay down there and stop the water."

Bev was the only girl but was always included and protected by her cousins. Roy and Bev were very close, and he always looked after her.

Marj's brother, Dick and his wife Hazel and their kids came down a few times each year, so there was quite a bunch of them. This was especially true when Eleanor's three boys also came to the farm.

We got along well with Eleanor's husband, Harry. He came to the farm three or four times a year and we always got together for Christmases.

The favourite pastime of these cousins was exploring and making their little farms among the trees. They also liked to drown out and snare gophers, a practice that one cousin, Greg Wagner, did not like.

Sandra was an active and cute little girl and was a favourite baby in the district. My brothers Frank and Rod only had sons, so they really spoiled both Bev and Sandra.

Bev and Dan started school at the Kinniburgh school which was quite small, with four classrooms for Grades 1-9. They had a very small gym and played no organized sports.

Harold Peterson was the principal of the school, and he knew I had played a lot of basketball. He kept after me to come coach the kids in Grades 7-9, and I finally agreed. There were no basketballs or hoops, so out of my own pocket I bought two basketballs and two nets, and myself and the janitor put them up in the gym.

I gave the bill to the parent teacher association, but it was over two years until they paid me back.

For the first two winters, we just practiced at the school. And then Mr. Peterson informed me he had arranged some games with Enchant School. We went up for the first game, and got beat really badly: 50 to 4, but we kept at it. One family, the Bekkerings in our school, were quite good. Their uncles, dads, etc, all played a lot of ball.

One of their sons, Harry, was on my boys' team and their daughter Irene was on the girls' team. They often played around with their dad. We soon felt we had improved a lot and joined a league with eight other schools in the district.

We did quite well. My cousin, Kerry, was in high school in Grassy Lake and often did the refereeing. One time he threw the principal of his school out of the gym for arguing. Kerry really enjoyed that – he had authority over that principal and used it.

The next time we played Enchant, we lost by only two points. About three months later, I found out Enchant had won the provincial championships for schools of that age.

Harry went on to play basketball at a very high level, on high school and university teams.

Frank, Rod and a neighbour started at Boy Scout troop at the Sherburne Hall. Dan attended as a Cub, and Marj was the leader for the Brownies. Bev was a member of that troop for three years.

When Dan was 12 I agreed to coach the boys' hockey team. I was never really involved with playing hockey, but I did coach that team for three years, as I had to drive Dan in to hockey anyway.

Marj's brother Gordie fell off a shed they were building and broke his back when he was 25 years old and was in a wheelchair for the rest of his life. Gordie and his wife Peggy raised sheep, and Peggy became well-known as a quality sheep judge. She did a lot of judging at shows all over Canada and the U.S.

Eleanor's husband used to go pheasant and goose hunting with us; he was a very good shot and a responsible hunter. We had a lot of fun.

One of the first times Frank and I took him hunting pheasants, we were walking along a small irrigation canal in late October. It had no water in it and was covered with long grass. It was very windy, perhaps 80 mph. I looked up and seen about 25 Canada geese flying right toward us. Because of the wind, they were having some difficulty flying, and were only about 50 feet off the ground, coming straight at us.

We crouched down in a ditch, and it was a very easy hunt. Both Frank and I had double barrel shotguns and fired at this flock of geese.

I said, "I think I got two," and Frank said, "I think I got two," because four geese had fallen.

We asked Harry, "Did you get any?" and he replied, "No, they looked like big bombers coming in and I was afraid to shoot."

We had many good hunts with Harry – both geese and pheasants.

Harry was the one who taught me how to play crib. I was not very good at it, and he said he would only count the points I missed. After four or five games of that format, I soon caught on.

Bev started Grade one in the Kinniburgh School, with nine in her class. She had lots of friends to play with and was top of her class.

Dan started school the following year, at the same school, with one boy and one girl in his class. Both of Dan's classmates left the school, so Dan was the only one in his class. He, too, was a good student, but it was boring for him. His teacher did not pay a lot of attention to him.

I was elected president of the Kinniburgh Home and School Association and held that position for five years.

We had good crops in the 1960s and early 1970s. Frank and I bought some grassland together in 1967. That was the year Rod was in the hospital and I was in charge of his farm work. Louise, Kevin and Kerry did his chores and Rod hired a trainee by the name of Hakon. Rod wanted to pay me, but I made a deal with him where he did my income tax.

We got our first colour TV in 1966. I had it delivered for Christmas. They brought it out at 5pm Christmas Eve and plugged it in. It was still cold, and immediately blew the picture tube, so we did not have colour TV for Christmas morning. They did, however, bring one out on Christmas Day. It was a 16-inch; I had bought a 21-inch and it was a week before they got the correct one in.

Accidents I had

Three accidents happened to me at the farm at Purple Springs, and I was lucky they didn't have more serious results.

My pig barn had a three-and-a-half-foot gutter on either side of the barn that the manure drained into. There was a large plug in the bottom of that gutter, which was pulled once a week for the effluent to drain out into the lagoon.

One morning I came into the barn and there were three pigs in one of the gutters. I pulled the plug and opened the door – more for light than anything else. I crawled down in the gutter and lifted the pigs out on the barn floor.

Each pig weighed about 100 lbs, so it took some effort to lift those bloody pigs out. It took me perhaps 20 minutes. I crawled out myself and made it about halfway to the open door when I passed out.

When I woke up I was very weak and sick and realize that it was from the methane gas. It took me a few days to feel right again, but I had no help and had to do the chores myself.

Second accident: I had a small gravel pit on my property, approximately six feet deep. There was approximately six inches of dirt, or overburden, on top of the gravel. I was up on the top, cleaning this off with my tractor and front-end loader. I got too close to the edge of the pit, the tractor had no cab or roll-over protection and I went over the bank and the tractor started to roll.

I could not jump to the high side, so I just kind of threw myself over the lower fender, realizing that I was jumping under where the tractor would likely roll.

I landed on my side, looked up and could see the one large wheel and fender above me. I kept rolling a couple times more. I was very lucky the tractor did not complete another roll, as I would have been under it. The tractor kind of teetered for a few seconds, then settled back the other way.

The tractor was still running; I got up and shut it off, and luckily, there was no fire.

Third accident: we were living in Dad's yard and I was doing a lot of the chores with a hired man. Jack was in charge of feeding the bulls. He had put them in a 40-acre pasture half a mile from the yards and main corrals, as we had a very open fall.

The forecast was for a storm and a blizzard, and I told Jack he should bring the bulls home the day before the storm. He thought, however, that they would be fine. In the middle of the night a north wind came up with blowing snow, and it dropped to -35 degrees.

When I walked up to the feed lot and corrals the next morning, I realised that the bulls had not been brought in. There was no shelter in the pasture they were in, the tractor would not start, and the snow was too deep for the half-ton.

I decided to walk to get the bulls. I was able to follow the fence for the first quarter mile, then walk along the canal for the last quarter mile to the bridge and the bull pasture. All 11 bulls were huddled together with their backs to the north wind. I was unable to drive them to the gate, so I kicked the wires off the fence in the corner, to access an approach that led up the bridge.

I fought with them for some time, and finally got two to go out and over the bridge. The others followed close behind, and took a short cut home to the corrals, but broke a trail for me to follow close behind. They went right into a large Quonset and huddled there.

I realized that the right side of my face was frozen. We were out of the wind in the hut, and it allowed me and bulls to get a rest. One of the bulls laid down and would not get up, and he died. Of the other 10 bulls, four had badly frozen testicles that, when they thawed out, bled badly.

We had to replace those four bulls, as they were unable to breed. I stayed in the hut for a couple of hours to warm up. The wind was at my back as I walked among the grain bins and buildings to the house. My face blistered a little as it thawed and was very sore for a couple of weeks.

My sister, Marjorie asked me to buy a four-year-old mare from her. She worked a lot with horses. This horse was called Jingles, and he was sired by Gerald's stud, Davey and out of a registered mare. I gave her $1,700 for the horse, and Jingles turned out to be an excellent saddle horse – lots of cattle smarts and tremendous endurance. She was no quitter on any task we did.

My horse Billy got his leg caught in a barbed wire fence when he was about 18 years old; he had a bad limp and I had to use padded horse shoes on him after that.

Billy loved kids. All my kids and many neighborhood children learned to ride on Billy. He had a tremendous disposition. Dan used him as his horse in the 4-H horse club. Billy lived to be 33 years old.

I was given three other saddle horses when looking after Darwin Lund's horse, when he went to Zambia and Australia to rodeo. These were all good ranch horses, named Chief, Cheery and Blaze.

Ranch at Skiff

In 1971 Frank and I bought the ranch two miles north of Skiff in the Chin Coulee, and Gerald bought the one across the road. It had several draws with small trees, Saskatoon bushes, etc.

At one time, it was owned by Charlie Furman, and prior to that by Mr. Sicks, who founded the Sicks Lethbridge Brewery. On Gerald's side of the ranch we found part of an old still, such as copper pipe, etc.

Frank and I also took an artificial insemination course at Pincher Creek in November of 1971. We caught on real quick. One of our instructors was Alex Mills from the American Breeder Service, and for the next four years he would sometimes phone and get me to help out at one of his schools.

My pay for this was a hotel room and meals. It also helped when we started selling semen from our bulls, as I got to do some free promotion.

For several years, the A.B.S. delivery truck stopped once a month at Purple Springs, so it was handy for us to get semen and supplies.

Rod also took an A.I. course the next year. It is difficult to successfully breed a horse by A.I. with frozen semen, largely because the duration of heat in a horse may vary from two days to 20 days and it may also vary from cycle to cycle.

Rod was successful in breeding one of his mares through A.I.; this was the first horse successfully bred through A.I. in western Canada. Rod's mare was Crackers, and he called the little filly Ritz.

I mentioned earlier that we often went to the mountains to get lumber. It was a long, hard trip and we always loaded the trucks to the hilt.

One time we were coming home through Blairmore, where the highway was right above the houses and stores of downtown.

Frank hit a small bump in the road, and it was enough that the wheels came right off the road. He had a hard time steering, and it scared the hell out of both of us. It settled, however, before we went over the edge.

We had to go through the Piegian Indian Reserve, and one time we seen this wagon pulled by one horse coming toward us. It was missing a back wheel, and had a drunk Indian sitting in the driver's seat. We laughed, and Frank made the comment that we would see his wheel up the road a-ways. Sure enough, about two miles further along there was this wheel right in the middle of the driveway.

We had many incidents on those trips. We always stayed at Elko, in some log cabins. I got a nickname in Ft. MacLeod on one trip. We had ruined a tire in Elko, so money was tight. I was 13 years old, and when we stopped for supper everyone else ordered something cheap, but I ordered a T-bone steak. I had the nickname T-bone from that day on.

Remodeling the house in '64 and '65

We moved the house onto the foundation in late summer of 1964, and went right to work making it suitable to live in. I installed a septic tank and sewer line in to the lagoon.

In 1965 I hired an agriculture trainee from Norway named Erik Holde, who spoke no English except for 'yes' and 'no.' The translation book was an important part of every conversation.

I hired him because I had the biggest work load with the pigs, but Erik worked for all four brothers. He actually lived a half mile down the road at Gerald's place. He was a great kid. Marj and I visited with him when we went to Norway in 1972.

The next summer I got a trainee from New Zealand, Hugh Sutherland. His sister and brother-in-law came to Lethbridge to work for one year and were often at our farm.

I got a trainee every year after that for 26 years – sometimes two. I got two trainees in 2010 while at the Fraser River Ranch and had 31 in total over the years.

We got trainees from many countries: Norway, Denmark, Sweden, England, Germany, New Zealand and Australia. Many became, and still are, great friends.

Most memorable and cherished of those are the Ruddlenklaus from New Zealand. They're family now.

In April of 1966 it was the start of a severe blizzard, lasting on and off for 10 days. We received over six feet of snow. Rod had already seeded most of his crop, and we were also in the middle of calving.

We got all the cows to the corrals, five miles north of the buildings we could only travel back and forth by tractor. Frank kept one tractor, Jack kept one, between Gerald and I we had one, and Rod had one.

Rod made more than one trip to Purple Springs to get groceries for us all. We took shifts but averaged less than three hours sleep a day.

When the storm finally stopped, I could not even find my car for about a week. It took them over a week to plow the road to my place. Rod and Jack were plowed out the first few days.

The worst part came when the sun came out and shined on the snow. The cows' bags all chapped from the hot sun rays reflecting off the white snow crust, and they would not let their calves suck.

We had three Indians working for us, one a young guy from Saskatchewan. He spent all day bottle-feeding calves, mostly with powdered milk. That winter when he went back to Saskatchewan, there was a fire in the house where he lived. He and his young family all died in the fire.

Luckily, our losses were not real big – about 5%. The following year, Rod had to have a back operation. He had crushed vertebrae for many years, and it was beginning to affect his legs. He spent two and a half months in the hospital in Calgary on a Stryker bed, where he would lie face down for three hours, then on his back for three hours.

The operation was a success, but he could not do much for a year. He hired a trainee, Hakon Borve, from Norway. I looked after Rod's farm with the help of Hakon.

Chianina calves bred in Montana

In 1971 we found our we could not buy Chianina semen in the U.S. but could get three ampules in Canada. We were not able to take it to the U.S., but if we got it there we could breed the cows and bring bred cows back to Canada. This was a loop hole in the regulations; if we could somehow get the semen into the U.S., we could import those cows with the embryos back into Canada.

It paid to have vets in our group who knew how to research and get around the regulations. We bought six open cows at Conrad, Montana, and made a deal with retired rancher Bill Miller to keep them and watch them when they came into heat.

He was a very neat old guy that loved to have us just come down and visit.

He would phone us when a cow came into heat, and we would take the semen samples across the border in a Thermos. I went down once to breed a cow, I think Frank went down a time or two, and we split the semen, so we actually bred five cows.

We had four confirmed pregnancies; and brought the cows back across the border before they calved. Frank kept them at his place when they were due to calf, and Bill Miller came to see what we had. We got three heifers and one bull calf.

Even though the mature Chianina animal is white, all the calves were born black. The calves were long – we commented that they were a length of rope. I'm still not quite sure how all this worked, but I do know we had the first cross-bred Chianina calves born legally in Canada.

We later sold these calves to a breeder in England. It was a real hassle exporting them. We worked through John Rudiger, who had set up a procedure to work with the government to export some of his Charolais cows. We hired him as our agent.

I know the calves had to be 15 months of age to clear quarantine into England. We sold these calves for $2,500 each.

We do have the distinction of having the first calves born in Canada with Chianina genetics.

Dogs

During my time at Purple Springs I had a variety of dogs. Marj's sister and brother in law had a dachshund that they could not keep in their apartment in Vancouver, so they put it on an airplane and sent it to us. His name was Rex – he became our pet and we had him for about 10 years.

He eventually got an ear infection and we had to have him put down. Our next dog was a very smart Lab cross who liked to ride in the truck with me and try to worm his way behind me on the driver's seat.

They were building up the roads south of my farm, and during that time is was very rough – you could only go about 10mph. One morning I was going to Gerald's, and I seen Jack driving toward me. Jack had a bad habit of always looking around, and only looking at the road occasionally. The dog wormed his way behind me on the seat, and I slumped down so I could just see the road through the steering wheel.

The dog moved forward, and actually put his feet up on the steering wheel. When Jack went by he glanced over at us. I could just see his face out of the corner of my eye – his mouth fell open and his eyes were as big as saucers.

He thought the dog was alone, driving the truck. I continued on for about an eighth of a mile and turned into Gerald's yard. Jack backed up as fast as he could and was surprised to see me get out of the truck, too. He did not appreciate my little trick.

We gave this dog to Marj's brother, Gordie, as we never really had room for the two dogs.

When Dan was five years old he wanted a dog. I let him and Bev pick out what they wanted by studying different breeds. They decided on a Norwegian Elkhound – a very pretty and active dog – and named him Kody. The kids were very good about feeding him and loved to play with him when he was a pup.

Norwegian Elkhounds were bred in Norway to herd reindeer. Really, this was their only purpose. It was a natural instinct for them to herd reindeer. They are not very smart dogs: they can only learn 27 commands, as opposed to the average border collie that can learn over 100.

Kody had the instinct to go in front of the cows whenever I was driving them. He would frustrate me, as he always turned the cows back towards me. Kody was with us for 10 years. He developed a large cancerous lesion on his side and lost a lot of weight. One morning, we could not find him. I found his body in my dugout, which was right full, and we wondered if he had gone in for a drink, but I think he was hurting so badly that he actually drowned himself.

When my daughter, Naomi, was young we got a border collie pup. It was a very smart dog that we got to be a companion for Naomi, but I was just getting it trained to work cattle when Rod came to my door one morning, saying he had found the dog dead on our driveway.

What had happened was that I had allowed a local honey producer to put some beehives in my trees. A skunk had gotten in the hives, so he put some poison in eggs to get the skunk, and the dog got into the eggs. The fellow who owned the bees had not told me he was going to put poison out.

When I approached him, he more or less told me that his bees were more valuable than my dog. I told him to remove his beehives, but when he came out to get them his truck would not start.

He hooked his other half-ton up with jumper cables. When he started the truck, the battery blew up and actually started his truck on fire. I had a water hose about 200 feet away, so we were able to put out the fire and wash his struck down.

He was very fortunate – he did not get any acid on him when the battery exploded.

A week or so later, we got a border collie that was good with the cows and was also a great pet.

The farmyard and the kids

In 1965 and 1966 I hauled in a lot of top soil and good dirt and put in a good, quite-large lawn area all around the house. By the summer of 1966 we had a very nice green lawn. We also planted a lot of trees and shelter belts, as well as three rows of trees 150 feet from the house for a wind break.

I put in concrete sidewalks on the south and east ends of the lawn. One led to the yard and the other to a large garden. We soon had a good area where we would play our own version of soccer.

We built up about four feet around the house, so we had a nice hill on the east and north sides. The trainees also liked to play soccer. By age three, Dan loved to play ball hockey in the basement part of our house. He and I spent many hours and he got quite good – he was very competitive. I bought a Case 12hp riding lawn mower with a rotary cultivator attachment.

By the time Dan was six years old, that little tractor was constantly on the go. It was their enjoyment vehicle around the yard. They hooked up a wagon to it, and it went round and round giving rides, often to little Dixie and Sandra.

I also seeded a large grassy area of about two acres in the yard. I had installed irrigation with 2" hand pipe that was 30' feet long, that I used to water the trees, lawn, grass and garden.

There was also lots of green grass and water puddles in the yard. We had a border collie puppy that chased the sprinkler nozzles. I changed those pipes three times a day. The kids really enjoyed playing outside, and they were also good at helping out.

In the winter, I fed the cows with the half-ton. I would load up 52 bales on it, go to the pasture, put the truck in gear, jump down and throw the bales off, then stop the truck and take the strings off the bales.

By the time Bev and Dan were seven and eight, they would come with me and drive the truck on weekends and holidays. They really were a lot of help. Marj was often busy with Sandra, Dixie and the housework.

But Bev and Danny really did pitch in feeding the cow herd. I also fed a lot of my calves and a pen or two of feeder steers, along the feed banks that I had installed.

This usually took about two hours and lots of bales of grain. I stacked the small square bales nine bales high, next to the feed bins. This was both for shelter and easy access to the bunk feeders.

I did not hire any help in the winter. The worst time I had was the three months after I tore off my thumb, as I basically only had one arm.

Bev and Dan caught the school bus about 300 yards from the house. They could see the bus coming two miles away, so they were seldom kept waiting on their school bus. One driver was quite old, and not in very good shape. Everyone along the route watched out for him, and really had concerns for their kids' safety.

After he picked up Bev and Dan, he would go around a corner on the way down to Gerald's, and on at least three occasions Gerald and Marg phoned me to ask why he had not shown up. I would go look for him and he would be stuck in a snowbank waiting for someone to come find him.

On two occasions, a neighbour finished the route for him. He was at least four years past the safety age, and past his ability.

When Gerald and Marg's kids were small, and before they started school, Gerald would take his family to California for a month every winter. I would do his chores during that time, as I lived close by.

One winter, we got a storm out of the southeast. We called these storms the Manyberries chinook, as Manyberries was 50 miles to the southeast. These were the storms we dreaded the most. They often brought strong winds, and often lots of snow.

I had bought my 830 tractor with a front end loader that year. It blew hard all Christmas and the day after. The snow drifts also had a lot of dirt in them and were hard and high.

I had about 20 replacement heifers in a corral with a slab fence. About eight of these were buried in the snow next to the slab fence, and I had to dig them out by hand – the snow was so hard.

And I wasn't about to use the tractor. I hooked onto a small wagon and put bales on it to feed my cows.

It was only a half mile from my place to Gerald's, but the road was plugged solid. I walked down to Gerald's to do his chores the day after Christmas. The snow was hard and easy enough to walk on. At Gerald's, I had to feed about 30 bales which I hauled into his corrals by hand. He had one automotive waterer which froze up, and I had to thaw it out with a small propane torch.

They lived in a small house which was heated with oil. His water lines come in through his back porch, and they also were frozen. I ended up walking home in the dark. The next day the roads were plowed out going north and south one mile west of my place.

I was able to get my truck out and get on the east/west road by weaving around snow banks. Later that day I plowed it out, somewhat, with the tractor.

I went one mile west, one and a half mile south to the irrigation canal. The road along the canal was blown clear, so I went one mile east and then one mile north, back to Gerald's. That part of the road was open because of the deep draining ditch on the east side of it.

This got me to Gerald's yard, but I had to shovel out a big snowdrift in order to turn around.

Joe and Nellie Kinniburgh lived along that part of the road. They had spent Christmas in town but got as far as my place on December 28. They followed me to their driveway which was also hard to dig out. It was three weeks before they plowed the road between my place and Gerald's, and in places the snow piles were 15' high.

There was a concern about rabies that winter and spring, and we were advised to stay away from any skunks. A few days before Gerald got home in March, I drove into Gerald's yard, and his dog had a dead skunk on the lawn.

I got some large garbage bags and put the skunk inside two of them doubled together. The skunk was already starting to rot and was quite smelly – still pretty much frozen, but stinking and rotting.

I tied the garbage up tight and put the package in the trunk of my car. It warmed up some, and with the sun on the trunk of the car, it got quite warm in the trunk. I took it into the vet's to have it examined. When I took it out of the trunk, the warm air had caused the bag to swell up like a balloon.

When I took it into the vet's, the back door was closed, so I took it in the front where two ladies were on staff. I explained what was in the bag, and the last thing I told them was, "Do not open it up – either put it outside or in a freezer."

Well, guess what? It wouldn't fit in the freezer, so one of the ladies took a scalpel and cut the bag open. Just as I was getting into my car outside, I heard screams, and them hollering, "Tim, you son of a bitch!"

The ladies burst out the outside door with Kleenex over their faces. I had a major laughing fit.

I believe these ladies and the wives of the two vets were determined they had to get even with me a hundred times over. They played many, many tricks – some not nice – on me.

My vet friends

I cherished my friendship with Dr. Don Hamilton, the vet and his wife Marian, as well as Dr. Darwin (DC) Lund and his wife Patty. Don and Darwin purchased the Taber vet clinic from Dr. Stu Little in 1960, and we used their clinic for veterinary supplies and their services for the health of our cattle herd.

Don and Darwin and their wives were very active in Taber and were highly respected. They served on many committees and volunteered with many organizations.

The Brewin families soon became friends as well as clients. Gerald and I often visited with them, and soon found ourselves serving on many of the same organizations, such as the rodeo committee, and exhibition boards.

When Bev and Dan attended high school in Taber, Don and Marian's home was like a home away from home if they needed a place to hang out, in the event of a storm. The Hamiltons always made them welcome.

I often made a point of visiting with them at their animal clinic. All four of them were great practical jokers and loved to play jokes and tricks, particularly on their friends. I attended several cattle shows and various events and could always be assured an entertaining time.

One year, at 10 days of Agribition in Regina, it was non-stop with Marian and Patty playing tricks on everyone they knew.

Often, when I visited with them at the vet clinic, they would have some way of playing a trick on me. I tried to get them back, but usually was no match for their tomfoolery. I could mention many tricks, but the one everyone still talks about is a streaking incident.

One evening my phone started ringing, and when I would answer it the person on the other end would be laughing, wanting to hire me. Finally, I found out that Marian and Patty had put an ad in the paper that read, "Streaker for hire," and listed my phone number.

A lot of fun was had with that, especially when one of their friends would phone and try to set me up. I finally started saying I didn't do the streaking myself, but hired Don and Darwin to do it, but they were unable to do it because their uniform had shrunk.

One of Patty's friends phoned me three times one night, and I really had a lot of fun with that. I could go on and on about their tricks; even today when I meet them I have to be on guard.

Don and Darwin were highly respected vets; both also worked as meat inspectors, and both spent time in the Artic.

Don was a federal meat inspector for the muskox meat that was being exported to Taiwan. I did get to eat muskox at a meal one night at Don and Marian's.

I served seven years on the Taber rodeo committee, alongside Don and Darwin, as well as several years as director on the Taber Exhibition board.

During that time, we were responsible for the design, fundraising and building of the large Taber Agriplex building. Patty had the distinction of being the Canadian Ladies Barrel Racing Champion, as well as being Miss Rodeo Canada.

Darwin was also a professional rodeo cowboy and competed at rodeos all across the U.S. and Canada, winning many championships. He competed at both ends of the arena but was best known as a steer wrestler.

He competed at rodeos in both Australia and Africa. I sometimes took care of his horses while he was away, and he paid me by giving me three good saddle horses.

In 1969 we formed a company to import and raise Chianina and Romanola cattle, with partners and shareholders. This included five Brewin brothers, Dad, a brother-in-law, Don and Darwin.

Darwin and Patty's three kids joined both the 4-H Beef Club and the Taber Light Horse Club that I was leader of. Darwin and Patty's oldest son, Corb Lund, has become a well-known country and western singer. He is a good friend and acquaintance of mine, and is really looked up to by my family, particularly some of my grandkids.

He treats them like his own family. Corb sang a few songs and entertained at my brother Gerald's funeral. Marian and Patty even tried to play tricks on me at that time.

TIM'S FAMILY TREE

Tim Brewin born Lethbridge Alberta 1940
Married Marj Newman (first marriage)
Daughter Patty died after 11 months

Daughter Bev married Keith Jones
Sons: Greg, Michael and Carson

Son Dan married Georgie Cassidy
Son Conner
Daughters Sarah and Mackenzie

Daughter Sandra married Dean Reimer
Daughters Megan and Caitlin
Son Adam (died at one day old)

Daughter Dixie married Steve Roberts
Daughter Camille
Sons Jack, Ryan and Will

Tim married Sherylene Magyar (second marriage)
Daughter Naomi married Pete Weibe
Son Alexander
Daughter Aurora

(See Brewin family tree for dates)

Tim married Pat Bak (third marriage 1994; Past passed away 2012)
Tim and Linda married 2013
Linda's daughter Denise Plante-McGregor
Daughter Austin
Son Dylan
Son Colin
Colin's son Raine
Austin's daughter Jolene McGregor

Also Ruddenklaus from New Zealand (very close family friends for 35 years – chosen family)
Owen and Judith (three children)
Daughter Kate married Ian
Kate and Ian's son Liam and daughter Eloise

Son Paul married Tracy
Paul and Tracy's sons Josh and Charlie

Daughter Rachel married Chris
Rachel and Chris' daughter Jennifer and son Matthew

Ina Stobik from Norway
Worked for Tim and Pat at the Fraser River Ranch and became very close to Pat
She did not have any grandparents, so chose Tim and Pat as her chosen grandparents
Linda and Tim are very close to her as grandparents

Chianina cattle

The first permits to import Chianina cattle from Italy were awarded in 1970: there were seven in total. Two of these were awarded to people who worked for the federal government doing research work at experimental stations.

This was considered not right, and they were to cancel or release their allotments, and in both cases they got together with others, mostly with inside connections, and companies were formed that they were shareholders in.

Only Chianina bulls were imported that year. There was a lot of excitement around bringing this breed in, particularly among cattle research specialists and geneticists.

The breed was very different from any cattle in North America, and it was felt it would help advance genetics and research by 30 years.

The first importers did very well financially. We had also applied for permits but were not successful. That fall we arranged a meeting with the Minister of Agriculture, Bud Olson, who was passing through Taber. He gave us some advice and direction about how we could stand a better chance of getting permits.

My brother, Rod had got one the year before, to import a Maine Anjou bull from France. He traveled to France and selected a bull named Eden and imported him. He placed him in the American Breeders A.I. Stud at Bragg Creek, west of Calgary.

They collected semen and marketed for Rod. Eden was a very good bull, performance-wise. I bred some of my cows to Eden, and Rod's son, Kerry bought a calf from me, out of Eden, and won the Taber and District 4-H grand championship.

In the fall of 1971, when we formed the company called Purple Springs Cattle Company, we agreed to apply for permits to import cattle from Italy and share in any successes we had.

Gerald was elected president and Dr. Hamilton the secretary treasurer. Each shareholder had to invest $12,000 initially, and we met with Dr. Woodward from the American Breeders Services to get his suggestions about other Italian breeds that may have a benefit or impact on Canadian cattle.

He suggested the Romanola breed. Frank and I each applied for a permit for Romanola, and each got one that we used to bring in bulls. The other shareholders all applied for Chianina and were successful in getting a total of two permits. Our company all shared in the importation of two Chianina heifers and two Romanola bulls.

The next year we got two more Romanola permits and imported heifers.

Our bulls' names were Marco and Monelo, and our heifers were Patricia and Penelope. We took these heifers to several shows and exhibitions.

Also in 1971, there was a meeting at the Chateau Lacombe Hotel in Edmonton to form a Chianina association, attended by over 200 cattlemen and research specialists.

I never understood why they chose such a fancy hotel; three of us did not wear a jacket and had to get one before we could enter the hotel.

Jonathon Fox from Lloydminister was elected president, and a friend of mine from Olds, Bob Richmond, was secretary. I was put in as director, along with two brothers from the Berg family and Tony Perlich from Lethbridge.

At that meeting it was decided to be aggressive in promoting the breed. It was decided to hold a barbeque, and to do this the manager of the research station in Lethbridge offered the lawns at that facility to hold the event.

Tony Perlich and myself were asked to arrange the event – I was the chairman. We had a barbeque on the lawn of the research station, and a large banquet and dance at the El Rancho Hotel.

More than 500 people attended. We were able to get all the meat donated, and approached the Sicks Lethbridge Brewery, who donated 200 cases of beer and a refrigerated truck, as well as two bartenders to serve the beer.

One of the conditions of this donation was that we had to pick it up at the brewery at 31 degrees Fahrenheit, keep it at that temperature and serve it at that temperature. By the way, it was all Pilsner beer.

There was also an auction sale of some semen, and a half-blood Chianina heifer.

This event raised a lot of money, and really set up the Chianina Association on a sound footing for promotion of the breed.

In September of 1972 we got a telegram from the Health of Animals, letting us know that we had been successful in getting four permits to import cattle from Italy – two Chianinas and two Romanolas.

We had three weeks to get to Italy and make our selection. Each shareholder borrowed $25,000 from the bank to import these cattle and to buy and breed some domestic cattle for upgrading.

It was decided that I should go to Italy to pick out these cattle. We knew absolutely zero about how to do this, so we retained Lavonne Sumption and Wes Coombs to help us, as they knew what areas to go to.

Both of them had been involved in the importation of cattle, and within two weeks Marj and I were on our way to Italy.

We left Sandra with Gerald and Marg, and Dixie with Rod and Louise.

On our way, we spent three days in England, and visited with my three aunts (dad's sisters). We also watched the changing of the guards at Buckingham Palace, visited Trafalgar Square, Piccadilly Circus, and did a lot of sightseeing.

Earlier, Rod and Louise had been in London two times, and were able to direct us how to travel and where to stay. Our hotel was actually a large, six-unit home redone as a bed and breakfast.

On the third day, when I checked out our flights, we found out that a lot of the civil servants were on strike in Italy. We were advised to fly to Rome as soon as possible. The next morning, we left via Air Italia for Rome. All the other passengers were from Malta. The plane was very crowded and dirty.

We flew over the Matterhorn and were able to see the top of the mountains above the clouds.

It was a six-hour flight to Rome. We landed and had quite a shock. There were fully-armed soldiers and guards everywhere. It took us about four hours to clear customs.

We had a hotel booked, but I'm sure the taxi driver took us on a long trip to one owned by his cousin.

In order to register at the hotel, we had to give the clerk our passports, which were not released until we checked out three days later.

We toured around Rome: went to the Colosseum, the Palatine Hill and the Roman Forum, the Trevi fountain and many other sites. We were told we had to register at the Canadian consulate, and it was about a two-hour walk to get to it.

We were also we had to make sure we visited the VIA Venato, a sidewalk café, but were told not to sit in either the front two rows, or at any of the tables. They were for the men trying to hook up with prostitutes and call girls. Those front two rows were very busy. We sat in the back row and found everything at the café to be very interesting.

We boarded the train from Rome the next morning to go to Chianchano, which is in the center of the Chianina cattle area, in Tuscany.

The cattle breeds in Italy have been kept more or less separate for hundreds of years, in their own valleys or areas. The large white breeds, like the Chianina and Romanola, have not been crossed with other breeds, although a little crossing was starting to be done with the Friesian, which is bred for meat.

When we went to the train station, we got a real shock. The train station was huge, and all of the trains came right inside the station to load and unload. There were perhaps 25 tracks, and it was a beehive of activity.

When we got on the train, we had been told that there was a dining car, but what you did was order your meals. They brought them to you in your seat. It was a five-hour trip to Chianche, and we never got our meal for three hours. I'm sure it was just brought on board at one of the train stops.

Going north from Rome, the country really changes. More and more farms were evident. The southern part of Italy is quite poor, with a lot of unemployment. As you went north, you could see how the people's lives improved, and by the time we got to Arezzo, there were some very nice homes and farms.

I was very surprised at the large amount of fruit and olives rotting and falling onto the ground. I found out that, because of the strike, they could not get or afford the labour to pick it.

We arrived at our hotel in the early evening. They served the evening meal at two different sittings – at 5:30 and 6:30pm. We booked for the 5:30 sitting, and that's the time we ate every night.

The first night when we were on the elevator to the restaurant, two Italians tried to speak to me, and were really quite friendly. I could not understand a word they were saying, however, and they seemed to get quite annoyed.

I told Lavonne about it the next day, and found out that what they were saying was, "Bon appetit." I guess they were quite annoyed with me.

The next morning, Lavonne picked me up and we drove around looking at different farms that had purebred Chianina.

We had also hired a university student as an interpreter.

Many areas we could not go into because of Foot and Mouth Disease.

The farm actually had to be free of Foot and Mouth for 10 years, which limited our selection to about 25 operations in Tuscany.

We were only interested in selecting females, as too many bulls were already coming to Canada. They had to be under five months of age.

We traveled around a good deal, and finally selected five. We had three permits, but were advised to select two extra, as there was a very good chance some would not pass quarantine.

The main highway was what is called the Autobahn, which goes through Switzerland, France, part of Germany and all the way down into Italy. There was no speed limit, so they drive like crazy. We seen two or three accidents where the car was completely demolished – the death rate on the road was very high.

We went to see Siena and watched a festival with horses racing in a courtyard, where there were teams dressed alike, from various parts of the city – it was fiercely competitive.

They raced around a large city square, with huge crowds watching them, that apparently could get quite violent.

We met some other Canadians, who were also selecting cattle in Siena, and enjoyed some of the local sights.

Lavonne was an American. On the way home from Siena, we stopped at a high-class restaurant that I understood was a favourite of many Italian celebrities. We were made very welcome when they found out that Marj and I were Canadian.

But as the evening went on, Lavonne started getting loud and drunk. When he went up to pay his bill with U.S. dollars, he was not very welcome anymore.

We found the food in Italy to be truly fantastic, particularly their pasta and meat dishes. We used fresh olive oil on almost everything.

One day, we went out visiting farms looking at cattle, and at every stop we made they gave us a glass of wine.

In the late evening, one farm gave us a large tumbler that looked like wine but was homemade liquor. It hit me like a brick and I could not drink it all. Lavonne also got extremely drunk. I don't even remember how we got home that night from Tuscany.

Lavonne drove us to Bologna and Ravina – the area that was the center for the Romanola breed. There were only nine farms that we could select cattle from.

The origin of the Romanola breed goes back at least 5,000 years. Their bloodlines have been kept clean.

It is a beautiful area, and the farms seem to be prosperous. We stayed in the small town of Forli, which has canals running through it that they use for transportation.

We selected three young bulls. One of my selections made it to Canada, but my first choice was the bull called Marco, on Frank's permit. The bull sent to me was Monelo, which was a gentle bull, but not the same quality as Marco.

We also selected from another herd that had some young heifers that were only two and tree months old. Later, Frank and I each got another permit, and took our heifers from that herd.

The head of the Romanola Association was Dr. MCuri, who was very nice and efficient.

It took me almost four hours to complete the paper work needed to arrange shipment of these young bulls. I had to put down a 50% deposit for the Chianina cattle. It all went through Lavonne and his export agency. With the Romanolas, Dr. Macuri preferred to deal much closer with me and the Canadian importers.

From Bologna, Lavonne drove us to Florence, where we were on our own in a large city, where we became tourists. We visited many palaces and gardens, and it seemed that every statue was supposed to have been made by Michelangelo, and there were thousands of them. I believe it was just the style of the artwork.

In Rome, we visited the Vatican, and were shocked at all the gold, satin and riches. We were not allowed to go into much of them – not being Catholics.

In Florence there is also a huge cathedral called the Duomo. We went all the way to the top. There is also painting on the ceiling, just like the Sistine Chapel. There are stairs right to the top of it – it is very beautiful.

We were asked by friends in Taber, Norm and Alice Long (he was our insurance agent) to look up their son, Tim, while we were in Florence. It took a lot of walking in very narrow streets, but we finally found him in a very small apartment. He was very glad to see someone from home. He had been in Italy for two years studying art.

The city of Florence had been flooded in late 1800, and many signs of that were evident. The Duomo had water stains 9' up on its front doors, but the water had not made it inside the church. Tim took us out for pistachio ice cream – the best ice cream I ever had.

When we left Sandra with Gerald and Marg, we asked her what she wanted us to bring her, and she said, "Ice cream." We really wished we could have taken some home to her.

There was so much to see in Florence: beautiful gardens and palaces. We had reserved a room at the very fancy Grand Hotel. They never appreciated me dressed in jeans and cowboy boots. They told me to go wash my boots, and I cleaned them in the bidet.

The Arno River runs through Florence. It is quite large, but really is a big water of sewage. The oldest bridge is the Ponti Vecchio; it's the only bridge not destroyed by Mussolini when the troops captured that part of Italy.

Today it is lined with shops. The bridge itself is not in shape to allow traffic across it. We spent a half day shopping along that bridge, and three days total in Florence. Then we caught a flight to Copenhagen, Denmark, touching down for two hours in Milano.

Milano is in northern Italy and appeared very clean and modern – it definitely showed more signs of being a prosperous part of the country.

We were met at the airport in Copenhagen by Helge and his brother. Helge had been a trainee in 1968. We spent four days with him and his family. They lived about 45 miles north of Copenhagen, where the closest town was Jyderup.

They lived on a typical Danish farm with beef cows, pigs and various crops, even sugar beets. We visited the local church, built in 1492, which had a tree growing in the church yard. Church records show that it was planted in 1492.

Helge's dad could not speak any English, but he could drink beer and say, "Skol!" We had a good time.

One afternoon Helge and his brother took us into Copenhagen, where we did a little shopping and sightseeing Bicycles were everywhere. Helge wanted to show me some very beautiful Danish ladies. We stopped and talked to two who were very attractive. Helge took many pictures of us, always grinning and having a good time.

Finally, he told me those attractive ladies weren't ladies – they were dykes. Those pictures made the rounds at home.

From Copenhagen, we flew to Norway, with a brief touchdown in Sweden. We spotted where they make Volvo cars and trucks in Sweden.

From there we spent a day in Oslo, Norway, then flew to Tronkein, Norway where our first trainee, Erik Holde met us. He was from a small town called Sparbu, and was in the reserve army, but had a few days relieve while we were there.

They were doing maneuvers, and his division was playing war games against another division.

He realized he had got behind the so-called enemy lines, and when we were driving back to his farm, he jumped out, got his gun out of his truck and captured some of the 'opposing' army.

Erik's family came to visit – there were over 20 people and none could speak English. We were put in a room upstairs with very little heat but slept under a goose down quilt that was about 8" thick.

Erik worked with his dad but had his own pigs and land. They had found many Viking artifacts when working their fields.

A big union rush was on while we were there, and no one was supposed to work more than eight hours a day. Even on the farm, Erik would not go along with that, and was constantly in conflict with the union.

We really enjoyed Erik and his family, who were very modern. In Norway, there are seven different dialects. I asked Erik to phone another friend, Hakon, in Bergen. They could not understand each other, so I spoke English to Hakon.

We flew to Bergen, where Hakon Brove (trainee in 1967) met us. We visited Hakon, his wife Helegeuien, daughter Sev and son Einer for five days. Einer told his grandparents I was "really stupid" because I couldn't "talk right."

Hakon worked away from home, across a fiord where you could see glaciers, etc and low mountains - very beautiful.

His dad kept eight milk cows four miles up the mountain and walked up every day to milk them in the summer time. He brought down some of the cream on a cart, but he also made cheese at the summer farm. We also got along very well with them.

There was a restriction in Norway on how much liquor you could buy, so Hakon made his own very good whiskey and beer.

Two weeks before we arrived, someone broke into his place and stole 12 gallons of his whiskey.

Hakon and Helegeuien drove us to the train – about 120 miles away from their farm – for the trip back to Oslo.

Little Sev sat on my knee, and just as we pulled into the train station, she peed herself, so I got on the train with wet pants.

We stayed in Oslo overnight, and got up at 5:00am to a very foggy, closed-in sky. We got to the airport but had a two-hour delay to catch the Scandinavian Air flight to London.

When we finally boarded and the plane took off, and flew through the fog, the sky was blue, but there were many, many airplanes circling, waiting to land. How they kept track of them all, I don't know.

Scandinavian Air was a fantastic airline. We landed at the Gatwick airport, then took a bus to Heathrow to catch our Air Canada flight back to Canada. We just made our flights by a few minutes, all the way along.

Often the perception was that farming in Canada was advanced, and many of our practices were more modern and advanced compared to Europe. Yes, we seen some older farms and backward practices, particularly in southern Italy. However, in Denmark and Norway their farms were very efficient; we seen one 800-head Herringbone dairy, where they were using tram lines in their grain fields (pre-worked tracks to avoid damage by the tractors.)

Crop yields were very good, and marketing seemed to be well-planned, although some grain was stored for three or four years.

Home from Italy

I grew some corn for my feeder cattle for eight years. I used Jack's planter, and his brother-in-law Francis did the harvest for me.

Corn is an excellent cattle feed. One year, my corn grew to 11'6" tall. For two years, I grew a multi-tiller corn to get more grain and higher protein. I just piled my sileage on top of the ground and packed it with a small front-end tractor and loader.

So, I had too much spoilage. I did not cover it but did put barley and oats on top so that it sprouted and grew - this prevented some spoilage.

This provided a canopy and sealed the sileage pile.

For the first two years, I used hand-moved sprinklers, and then installed a pivot, which provided better irrigation with far less work.

My field did not have proper drainage, so I experienced some flooding.

The breeding of exotic cattle by AI expanded rapidly. With cross-breeding you achieve better rate of gain and feed conversion.

Many of the new breeds also had better cut-ability, better marbling and carcass results. Within two years many new associations were formed. I joined six of them. Almost all of these associations allowed you to start with half-blood animals and breed up to where your animals contained 15/15ths of the breed, and they were then considered full bloods.

I bred cows to most new breeds and had cross-bred heifers. In 1975, there was an exotic cattle sale in Edmonton. I had a Murray Grey heifer and two Maine Anjou heifers that I entered in this sale.

Frank entered four heifers, Gerald entered one, and Rod had eight. The commission was supposed to be 8% to cover the cost of the catalogue advertising, etc.

The sale went very well - we averaged about $2,500 for each animal. However, the director and organizer of the sale decided to charge 15% commission instead. Most contributors were darn mad. We decided we would never contribute to a sale at the Northlands in Edmonton again.

Bronchitis

I developed a cough, and an unusual amount of mucous discharge in the 1970s. I had several x-rays, etc, and eventually Dr. Weibe informed me that it was bronchitis. I was told if I did not take steps to alleviate it, I would eventually develop chronic bronchitis.

I was advised to get out of the pig barn and the fine dust particles from the feed and switched to palletted feed that I purchased from Maple Leaf Feeds in Medicine Hat.

This greatly increased the cost of feeding my pigs, to the extent that they were barely profitable. It was a difficult decision, but in 1974 I slowly closed down my hog operation due to health problems. Some of the coughing continued, and I also developed sinus problems. In the late 1980s I was referred to a specialist Medicine Hat, and it was also found that I had an issue with polyps in my nostrils.

I went in for surgery to correct both problems. The doctor simply referred to it that he was going to do a rotor rooter on my nose and sinuses. It was a four-hour operation, and the next day they removed a very blood-soaked long length of gauze out of my nose.

I remained in the hospital for five days, and twice more the gauze was replaced. That definitely resolved the problem with the polyps, and most of the issue with my sinuses, but I was advised to avoid grain dust as much as possible.

This was difficult, being a grain farmer. I was very grateful for the trainees, as they could do most of my combining.

When my son Dan turned 17, he operated the combine as often as he could. My bronchitis and sinus problems definitely had a large impact on my decision to quit farming and concentrate on ranching.

Beacon and pilot training

Growing up, there was a beacon of light that would shine to the west of us. I remember it at night, as it would shine in my window every few minutes. It was a warning signal at the Taber airport for pilots and weather signals.

This beacon remained long after the war, for at least for or five years.

During the war, RAF pilots from many countries were often trained in southern Alberta. They were stationed at Claresholm, and their training was Claresholm to Brooks, to Medicine Hat, to Taber and back to Claresholm.

Most potential pilots were stationed there for six to nine months. This location was selected because it was similar to the terrain and weather in Germany.

The dads of two of the New Zealand trainees I had were trained at this location – John Bishop's dad and Hugh Sutherland's dad both trained at Claresholm.

They all had experiences and memories that they shared with their sons.

When I was laying out my farmyard in 1965 and 1966, large B52 bombers would fly over at a very low altitude, often only 5 or 600 feet off the ground. I was told it was for pilot training for the Vietnam war, but I researched this and that's only partly right.

It was far more involved that just pilot training. Boeing was the main manufacturer of the B52 bombers, but many companies and airline manufacturers were involved in building and supplying aircraft for the U.S. Air Force in the Vietnam war.

Canada was not at war with Vietnam, but because of NORAD, Fairbanks, Alaska and Goose Bay, Labrador were two of the main training and testing facilities.

Smaller Air Force bases such as Penhold, Alberta and Cold Lake, Alberta were also important, and had close proximity to the large Great Falls, Montana Air Force base. Some pilots were trained to fly the B52 bombers at these bases, but the route was also important to test the bombers after they were retro-fitted, and alterations were made, such as new radar.

One of the design changes was when the standard B52 was altered to what was called the Big Belly B52, allowing larger cargo and bomb storage capabilities.

This also meant alterations to the wing design, more powerful motors, new radar technology and many upgrades to the plane.

These alterations required extensive testing, and some of this was done over southern Alberta.

And my farm, as it was on the fly path between Cold Lake and Great Falls, often had these planes fly over it.

Much of this work was and still is classified, but I was able to find some information. I found a map of the flyway; and it showed major pin points where the simulated bomb drops were at Brooks from 20,000 ft., then low altitude flying to avoid radar detection, after rapid descent to below 1,500 feet above ground level

Then they would increase power and altitude to 20,000 ft. as they crossed the international boundary.

The map shows the following:
1. Cold Lake, Alberta as a base and departure
2. Red Deer River
3. Brooks, Alberta and Lake Newel as the bomb drops at various altitudes
4. The descent to 1,000 feet to avoid radar
5. The Grassy Lake reservoir where they were to be at an altitude of 1,000 ft. My farm was a a quarter of a mile from that body of water
6. They were then to increase power and altitude to 20,000 ft. at the border; this meant very large noise levels just over my farm; Great Falls air base by air was only 50 miles from the border; these planes were large and very noisy as they went over my farm

A lot of this happened at night between 2am and 8am and again in the afternoon between 3-8pm; sometimes up to 40 flights a day.

A few flights I remember in particular:
1. I was driving south from my place and one of these planes flew right along the road over me; my truck started to shake, I looked up and above me at about 800 feet was a huge plane, pouring on the power and scaring the hell out of me
2. I was in the combine when one went right over me; I thought the combine was blowing up; I opened the door and looked out - again a large plane
3. I was coming home from my brother Frank's, and ahead of me about a quarter mile was a huge plane at about 300 feet altitude; I actually thought it was going to crash; all of a sudden it turned on the power
4. About midnight one night, we were coming home from Alden and Millie's as we come up over a hill, we seen one of these big planes coming at us at about 500 feet
5. I was installing the water lines in my yard; I had a 6' deep trench for my garage to my corrals, about 700 feet long. It ended up under the cement pad in the corrals, so it was straight up back; at the other end the dirt sloped up to a hydrant. We were in bed about 3am and we heard one these planes coming right over our yard, very noisy; after it passed we heard a lot of noise from foxes; what had happened was that the fox family had come into our yard, likely to eat mice out of the bale pile. The plane scared them and they ran and fell into the trench. I went out with a flashlight and drove them back along the trench where they could get out. The mother fox sure kept her eye on me as they crawled out of the trench - they all ran in different directions

The planes did these maneuvers for five-and-a-half years.

It was not easy trying to get to get information on these B52 bomber flights and numbers that flew over my farm.

But I was able to add up what I could; some were to test structural strength on the new designs and some tests were after radar and equipment were added for navigation. Some were after the planes were loaded up with technical and radar equipment for surveillance, and equipment for locating enemy locations.

648 flights were made out of Cold Lake, with simulated bomb drops and low level flying to avoid enemy detection. 36 similar flights were out of Penhold and 34 of these flights were out of

Fairbanks, Alaska. The flights were all along the same path, and the ones from Fairbanks took place after large fuel storage was added to enable longer air time.

All these flights terminated at the Great Falls Air Force base, and after the Vietnam war many of these planes went to Europe and were used in Bosnia.

This testing was done in Canada rather than the U.S. and it appears that was for two reasons. Number one was the terrain, and the second was that the U.S. did not want communist countries to know what they were doing and how they were testing their planes.

This reminds me of another incident in 1976. I was using an automatic bale wagon to haul and stack our bales, and sometimes some of the bales would fall over. Bev, Dan and their cousins would make tunnels out of these bales. They had tunnels and little side pens scattered for several hundred feet. They loved to play games in them, like hide and seek. They could crawl along just fine, but it was hard for an adult.

Owen was a trainee working for me, and they talked him into trying to find them inside. There as just enough light to see in some areas. Owen followed the kids in but could not find them. He made his way out and complained that it was really stinky in there.

I took a few of the bales off, and sure enough, you could tell there was a skunk in there. Owen and I took off more of the bales until we seen the little black and white fellow right about the spot where Owen had turned back inside the bale tunnel. He was one lucky fellow.

During my time on the farm, I had several encounters with skunks and porcupines, but the worst small animal I got caught in my mower conditioner was a large raccoon. It wedged between the rollers and actually plugged them.

Billy at Manyberries

In 1966, I was asked if I could provide saddle horses to go to help out at the Manyberries community pasture. Two people I knew had the contract to do the artificial breeding at this pasture. I needed more riding time on my horse Billy, so I drew up an agreement and sent him.

He was one of 12 horses the four riders needed. The Manyberries pasture is a huge area with over 2,500 cows to be bred by A.I.

Some of the horses were too soft and were sent home soon after the program started. By the end of the second week they were down to only eight horses instead of the 12, so instead of getting used every third day, they were used every other day. It was to be a 42-day breeding program. On the last eight days Billy and a black gelding were being ridden two out of three days.

The riders were all young, and in their early 20s. They lived in a small camper and did their own cooking, etc. One night it got cold, and they turned on the propane burners for heat at about 3am but did not open any vents for exhaust. The A.I. technician came at 6:15am and found only two of the boys awake. He got them all outside, but they could not wake up one of the boys. It was almost a two-hour drive by road to the nearest farm, but only four miles on horseback.

One of the boys got on the black gelding and another on Billy and took off across country. The black gelding played out before they reached the farm. Billy made it all the way. They phoned and a small plane was brought up. They flew the sick boy to the Medicine Hat hospital, where they were able to save his life. He spent over two weeks in the hospital.

I did not know about this until four years later, when I hired one of these boys to work for me. When he seen Billy, he went over and gave him a big hug and told me the story about Billy and said there was no doubt - because of Billy's stamina, they were able to save the kid.

When Billy came home from the pasture, he was in very poor shape; I never let him go from my place again.

Sherburne Hall

The community we lived in decided they needed a community hall for various functions, and around 1954 an abandoned school named Surburne was moved to a central location where we had the ball diamonds, etc.

It was placed on a basement and the building added on to. So, we had an approximately 100' long dance floor. A kitchen was built and bench seating was built along each wall. For many years it was used for dances, badminton, suppers the gun club, card parties, etc.

They also held turkey shoots there every November. Marj and I were put on the social committee in about 1965, and I was also elected president of the hall board. There was not any running water to the kitchen or any indoor bathrooms. We got a grant from the municipal government every year, and also raised other funds.

It was decided we should put in bathrooms and hot and cold water to the kitchen. We planned this, along with a large cistern and sewage disposal. Three people were against it, and we had many very heavily contested meetings for over a year. Finally, though, we did install the bathrooms, sewage and remodeled a decent kitchen.

All of my brothers served on the hall board at various times, and my brother Rod, along with John Fettig and Walt Rombough, did most of the work on the cupboards.

The hall always had a good amount of money, largely due to grants for hall societies. For a few years, I was also a member of the Taber pistol club. We could not get a permit to shoot pistols in our own hall but did shoot at the cadet hall in Taber.

Coaching hockey

We enrolled Dan in hockey and he was put on one of the regular house teams in Taber. There was also a provincial team.

I am not a fan of these selected provincial teams in the early fall, making kids wait to play exhibition games until playoffs in the spring.

All the costs for each boy was the same, but the boys selected for the provincial team got far more ice time and big advantages to become better players.

Often the more elite families in a town had their boys picked for the special teams. Dan practiced once a week and had one game on the weekend. I had to drive him into town, so I volunteered to coach his team. Besides playing against the other three teams in Taber, I also arranged for his team to play against teams in Coaldale. I coached for three years, and our team was quite competitive. We had a wrap-up banquet and awards ceremony every year. I was asked to select players for the different awards each year, but the awards were usually predetermined by the 'Who's Who' in town.

I did have some very good players that played hard. The second year, Dan's team won the most games. I was promised two players from the Juniors A team to help me coach, but they seldom showed up.

The third year, a boy from west of town was put on my team. He could hardly skate but worked hard and was a tall boy for his age. By Christmas time he was one of my better players; he was still not a great skater but had a lot of hockey smarts.

In February I was told they were moving him up to the provincial team. The boy told me he wanted to stay with the team he was on. The minor hockey executive told him if he didn't move up, he would not be allowed to play in Taber. His mother, myself and other coaches went to the executive and convinced them this was not right. After three meetings and threats to take his stance to the provincial level, he was allowed to stay and play with his team.

He quit hockey at the end of that season, but not until he came to me and thanked me for sticking up for him.

I did enjoy coaching the boys. We did have a lot of fun, and I hoped I helped some of these boys. The thing that bothered me the most was the large number of dads that would drive their boys to the door of the arena, make the boys take out their own equipment, then the dads would head to the beer parlor until practice was over.

Many of the dads did not come in to watch their sons play. The last year myself and Doug Henry, a coach on another team, kept track of how many dads never went to any of their son's' games. Only about 20% of the dads came to watch their sons play, and about 30% of the others did.

A couple of Dan's good friends were on his team, as was his cousin Mark. Mark's mother came to all his games and was the loudest supporter for the team.

In 2015, I went for coffee with my nephew, Roy Brewin. With him was Ron Smith, one of the players on my team all three years I coached. Ron thanked me for all the time I put into coaching hockey, and also for being his 4-H leader.

Many of my grandsons play or have played minor hockey. Two of my granddaughters play Ringette and are very good at it – they have won provincial championships and have been on national teams in Manitoba and in Alberta.

Farming in 1972 and the cattle industry

These were exciting times, and we have a few profitable years. We remodeled the house – put up wallboard in the basement, and built a downstairs bedroom for Dan, who did not want to share a bedroom with any of his sisters.

We also built a large back porch with a sink and a floor drain so it was a good mudroom. In calving, this was very valuable to warm up newborn calves when they were brought in from the cold.

My brothers and I continued to farm together, sharing machinery. Our wives often hauled grain, etc, and we went to many livestock events, field days and so on.

One of these was to the government research farm at One Four Alberta, where they were testing new techniques for grazing, grass seeds and breeds of cattle. They were eventually successful in crossing buffalo with beef cattle.

This research station was very interesting. They had a tremendous corral system, much of it made of 4" thick planks, because they handled the buffalo. The One Four station is located 60 miles outside of Manyberries, Alberta. It was an extremely dry area of open grassland, miles from any river.

They did have a small creek where trees were planted.

It was like a little oasis when you drove into the yard at One Four they put on a field day every other year, and we went three or four times. On the way there, you drive though an old river bed - they call it Lost River. It extends for miles with very few trees and is like the badlands.

It was said there were cattle in that area that were wild – impossible to round up. Years later I got to ride in this area with the manager of the Pinhorn community pasture. We did see about six cattle up a draw - all had long horns. When they seen us, they spooked and run like crazy. I don't know if these were some of the wild cattle they talked about.

Separating our cattle from Dad's and Jack's

Frank, Rod and Gerald decided to take their cows out of Dad's herd and run them on their own places. Dad and Jack asked me to continue to look after their A.I. breeding, branding and processing of their calves. In exchange, I got to run about 60 head with Dad's herd. This helped me a lot as I did not have much pasture of my own.

We did purchase and rent pasture land, and by 1978 I had a herd of 160, eventually building up to 300 head.

We took cattle to the Regina Agribition for the first time in 1973, and we took Chianina. Jerry Beaton did the grooming and fitting for us; he was a professional showman, and we did well at these sales.

Rod was quite successful with his Maine Anjou. When Bev was 12, she led my heifer into the ring at Agribition, and for two or three years Bev and Dan went to Agribition with us for the week.

You had to keep your animals in for the entire week. In 1974, we took some Chianina heifers; every breed was assigned a barn, or an area in a barn. That year we had a metal outside Quonset-type building with over 100 head of various consigners.

It got very cold, -30, and the Agribition decided to heat these outside barns. Soon many of them were sweating and wet. We went down to feed them every morning at 6am.

Don Hamilton, our vet partner was with me, and he noticed that several of the animals were coughing - some had pneumonia. We opened the door and convinced the Agribition officials to turn down the heat.

Fortunately, none of our animals got very sick, but many did. If I remember right, the Bergs brothers from Duchess lost a very valuable heifer.

Dan and Bev really got to know their way around. One year several neighbours and their families went with us. Along with the Brewin kids, there was about 15 kids from Purple Springs, taking in all the sights, and got to be quite well known.

A trainee named Jeff Smith, who had come back to work for me a couple of years, did chores while we were at Agribition. My nephews, Kerry and Kevin, also sometimes stayed home, and along with Marj and Louise, helped with the chores.

Trainees

An important part of our farming experience over the years were the I.A.E.A. trainees that came to work for us. Most were on six-and-a-half-month work visa. My family has many fond memories of most of them. We only had problems with two or three in total, that asked to be moved.

Two also asked to be placed with another host family. I have visited with 11 of these in their home countries. Twelve have come back to Canada to visit, and three have immigrated to Canada.

I could write a story about every one of the trainees. Almost all have done very well, many with their own farms. We also had two females that helped out in the house and garden.

One of these girls has returned to visit me, and we have kept close contact with her, and visited with her and her family in New Zealand.

Besides the trainees that worked for me, I also became good friends with some that worked either for my brothers or neighbours. Three of them are Sam Pye and Bill Roland in New Zealand and Lindsay Malcam from Australia.

These three would often stop at my place for a cold beer. I developed a close friendship with them, and their families also became close to one another. Another plus was how very close some of the trainees became with one another.

I still do have the placement lists for all but three years from IAEA, as well as many letters from trainees.

I also have a red address book that Marj and I kept. with all the trainees' addresses, birthdays, etc, up to 1973. It also has a list of dates and improvement to the house, along with the cost of the cupboards.

Many lifelong friendships have flourished between these trainees over the years. The IAEA exchange program was well-organised and well-run and is still in existence today.

I did have a few minor problems that I will mention. One was that the trainees were too young at 18 years of age. If they needed to return home, they had to pay their own way home.

One boy named Anthony from Australia was placed with me in July, and three weeks later he got word his mother was very sick, and that he should go home. The program did not provide any insurance or offer help in this type of emergency.

Anthony was on the phone trying to work it out, and one evening he was told he should get home as soon as possible.

Because his dad was at the hospital, Anthony could not contact him, and he did not have the money to get a plane ticket, and IAEA would not help him. It was a $2,100 fare, and Anthony promised me he would repay me if I would advance him the money. I phoned Air Canada and arranged for a flight, drove him to Calgary and he got to go home in time to see his mom.

I did worry some about getting my money back, but Anthony's dad wired the money to me the day after he got home.

I got two married couples that became family with us, and as my kids grew up they became very close friends. Dan developed good friendships as he worked alongside the trainees. Our closest friendship was with Owen and Judith Ruddenklaus – a newly married couple who came in 1976.

Another married couple, Peter and Mary Schuttle from Switzerland, were with us in 1977. They later immigrated to Ontario and Sandra stayed with them on a 4-H award trip for a few days.

We have kept in contact with them, and Peter has come to visit me twice.

In 1966, we got our first New Zealand trainee, Hugh Sutherland. Hugh became very close to us, as he was more interested in being with our family than being with the other trainees. He did take a weekend trip to a trainee party in Bassanno. They rolled a car and he received a cracked skull and ended up in the hospital in Brooks.

I went up to see him as he was having a difficult time. They kept him in the hospital for four days. I then went up and brought him home. I phoned his dad while he was in the hospital and kept him informed how Hugh was doing.

They were afraid of concussion. He had been helping me tear down the old Kraft house that was next to our yard when he got hurt. It was a two-storey house and he was told not to climb ladders, etc. for almost two weeks.

I was using lumber from this old house to build the garage - two-dimension rough lumber. The weekend Hugh got hurt we had the forms ready to pour the footings in the garage.

I had killed a rattlesnake on my way home from my first visit to Brooks. We coiled it up outside our back door and little Dan stood beside it and called his mother out. She got quite excited about what looked like a live rattlesnake.

That snake is well-preserved in the garage footings.

Hugh always wore shorts, and I will always remember him operating a combine on a very cold day in his bare legs at 35 degrees Fahrenheit.

A trainee from Sweden named Bjorn caused a crash at a yield sign when we were away on the Sun Road in Montana. He received a large fine and his license was suspended.

Another New Zealand boy was doing some fencing one day when I was painting the roof on the Surburne Hall. The boy lifted the barbed wire up to nail it to the post with his bare hand. The wire broke and cut his hand bad. It required 21 stitches.

Marj brought him down to me at the Sherbune Hall and we took him to the hospital, and he could not use his bandaged hand for two weeks. His name was John Bishop, and he has visited us several times through the years, as he had a Canadian girlfriend.

A similar wire-stretching accident I remember was when we had a trainee from Australia. He and Dan were putting new wire on a fence when it broke and cut Dan's leg bad. We were fortunate that we did not have more accidents with the 31 trainees.

Most of the trainees were farm kids. We had a girl, Carol Gardener from New Zealand. Vernei was from Switzerland – very capable and a hard worker.

She did eventually complain, as she usually got up early and made breakfast. She worked all day, then cleaned up after supper in the evenings. Her wages were less than the boys, and when this was brought to my attention, I was glad to work out a fair settlement for her.

She was a good friend who has also visited us in later years.

One of the girl trainees was the girlfriend of a Danish trainee that worked for a potato farmer eight miles from my place. They had decided to stay in Canada. The year I hurt my ankle they come over and helped feed the cows. Her and her boyfriend got a job in Lethbridge and later that fall, I visited them sometimes. They eventually got married and bought a farm in Manitoba.

Besides the trainees, we had several other young people work for us. One was Terry McKintyre from Ontario. He was Marion Hamilton's nephew. He worked for us for three summers, and several of Dan's friends also worked for us at various times. I truly enjoyed having these young people around. Bev had a good friend named Bonita that came out, too.

Dixie had a friend that came to the farm a few times when Dixie was living in Lethbridge. This girl was really allergic to cats, but she loved them. Often, we took her home with swollen, running eyes.

These young people will always be remembered and have a special place in our family.

Another I have to mention was a boy named Karl from Sweden, who had a bit of a drinking problem. One weekend two carloads of trainees took a three-day trip to Banff. They rented rooms in one of the big hotels and had quite a party.

Karl got quite drunk, I understand. He woke up the next morning, downstairs, with no clothes on. They had put him in the elevator buck-naked and pushed the button to the lobby.

He could not remember his room number, so he spent the night in the laundry room.

Cupboards

Alden and Millie Fletcher were our best friends in the 1960s and 1970s - we spent a lot of time together.

When they were married, Alden moved a house in that he remodeled. He hired Bud Gillespie from Bow Island. Our house needed a lot of improvements - we had drafty windows, and the cupboards and bathrooms needed to be remodeled.

So, I also hired Bud Gillespie. In late 1967 he roughed in three windows and did some work to renovate the bedroom into the living room. The trainee Hakon insulated and sealed the windows. He had done a lot of this in Norway, and used oakum, which is normally used in plumbing. There certainly was no draft from the windows that Hakon sealed.

I set aside $5,000 for renovations in 1967, and $10,000 in 1968, and new drapes were added, too.

In 1974 cattle prices took a huge plunge; bred cows dropped from $750 per head to less than $400. This was due to over supply.

Oil wells and seismic work

For four years in a row starting in 1971, there was a lot of seismic exploration done on my land. They paid me well to cross my land and drill every 200 feet in both directions.

They would drill a hole 250 feet deep, put a charge of dynamite down, and the blast would give them a reading of what was underground. This was often down in the winter, so did not affect my farming. I was paid $10,500 for each 160 acres that they did these tests on.

There would be three large trucks for drilling, three trucks for the dynamite crew and about six men to lay out the wires.

A lot of university students worked at this job, and a lot of them were females. In 1970 alone they did seismic work on four of my parcels of land. In 1976 they drilled an oil well on my property, and as they had to put in roads for access, I was paid $14,000 for this oil well for the damage and disturbance of my soil. They would scrape back all the top soil on about six acres but replaced it when they left the site.

But they also scraped up a lot of rocks and piled them for me to pick. On one site they did not pull the drill pipe when they left; it was capped off 15' below the surface. They had hit natural gas.

Several years later they revisited the site. I could not tell what they were doing, but it appeared they dug down, removed the pipe and cemented off the hole.

In 1971, they drilled another oil well on my property, but I was only paid $10,000 because it was considered much poorer land.

On one well they drilled on section 13, I came along just as they were dismantling the derrick. They had dug a large hole that they used for waste and were going to dump a large tank of diesel in the soil. The fuel dealer would not take it back. I asked for this diesel, and they gave me about 3,500 gallons of good diesel fuel This saved me from buying diesel for most of my seedlings that spring.

This was not the only good deal I got on diesel while farming. In 1984 we were using liquid fertilizer and had large storage tanks we only used from February to June. My fuel supplier came to me and he had a chance to bring diesel in from Kevin, Montana at one cent per litre.

He hauled in more than 8,000 gallons for me. I never found out why it was so cheap. I scrubbed out the liquid fertilizer tanks and put the diesel in them. At that time, we were farming quite a lot of land, but this diesel was enough for the first six months of the year. These were breaks for me that really did help out.

In 1976 I was informed by Revenue Canada that they were going to do an audit on me. I was doing my own income tax and was confident that I was OK. What triggered the audit was that I sold one load of barley, that I had forgot to claim; for $525.

They came out and took all my records, and I did not hear anything from them for over two months. The bank manager did tell me that they'd been into the bank to get all my bank records. The head auditor had left me his card, so I phoned him. He was very rude and told me I would have to pay over $26,000 and that he'd be out within a week.

I could not understand it, but I sure worried until he came out. When he did, he was much friendlier. It turned out I had borrowed money to buy some grassland, and the auditors originally thought this was income. I did have to pay tax on the $525.

But they also found a $700 expense I had not claimed, so it was a wash.

We had coffee with this auditor. I asked him what percentage of audits showed mistakes, and people had to pay back tax, and he said about 25%. He went on to say they caught the majority of these by the person making a slip of the tongue over coffee.

Once such one was the week before in Del Bonita. They knew something was wrong but could not find it. They finished the audit, and over coffee the fellow started to brag that he put a lot of income into his mother's name, as they did not have the same last name.

I think this auditor hoped that I wold reveal some scam I had.

Ketchup and Chinese Food

Sometimes several of us would get together and go to Lethbridge for Chinese food. This would be 10 or 12 of us that would really enjoy Chinese food. I remember one time in particular, when Frank was part of our group. We were served by one of the owners who brought us the meal and was very proud that we always seemed to enjoy it, when Frank asked if he would please bring some ketchup.

Boy, did he get a lecture! "Not put ketchup on Chinese food!"

He was really offended – jabbered fast and furious. I think he did bring the ketchup, but for years, whenever we had Chinese food someone always asked for ketchup.

Pivot

By the early 1970s my brothers and I were expanding and going out on our own, buying our equipment and expanding our irrigation. Rod brought his own CCIL combine, and the next year he traded it off and bought a New Holland. Gerald stepped back some from farming; I bought 640 acres of grassland from him and broke up about 400 acres of that.

I also installed a towable pivot on it to irrigate my home quarter, as well as his home quarter. I installed a Sergeant solid state pivot, which I had never seen. Being solid state meant that the electrical alignment components were on a card, much like an iPad today. It was all a small computer, and very susceptible to moisture and dust, and it was a constant battle to keep in line and operate correctly.

Also, my source of electricity was a generator on a propane motor. The pivot had to operate at exactly 60 hertz of electricity, and fluctuation up or down of one or two hertz would cause the pivot to shut down.

I was like a monkey, climbing and resetting those cards on top of each pivot tower. The dealer and his service tech were out almost every day. It was all at 440 watts. One day when I went to town, the service tech came out but did not shut off the electricity. When he climbed the tower to re-align the pivot, he may have misjudged the wires, and got a shock that knocked him off the tower, unconscious.

When I came home, he had come around, and was up on his hands and knees. I got him to hospital, where he spent five days. We estimated he must have been unconscious for more than two hours because of the distance the pivot had moved from where he had climbed the tower and I found him.

Eventually I spent $16,000 and changed the alignment system to a Reinke system, which was all fuses. That was much less sophisticated and could be reset. The Sergeant pivot dealer would not cover any of that cost.

My Combines

I can't remember exactly when I bought my first combine - it too was a New Holland. I think I may have bought it together with Frank, but I'm not sure. I do remember it was made in Belgium, and all the bearings, shafts, etc., were of a higher standard than the combines made in the U.S.

In 1974, the motor on my combine gave out on me.

It was in October and I still had two weeks of harvest left. I lifted the motor out, which was not an easy task, as it was right on top of the combine. I took it to a place in Lethbridge to rebuild it, which took 10 days and cost me $8,000.

I installed it and it only ran two hours. They had not properly installed the intake manifold and it sucked dust right inside. I made sure it was there when they took it apart, and the problem was easy to see. I had a real go-round with them to rebuild it, and they would not let me take it out of their shop till I paid another $9,000.

It was getting late in the year, so I had no choice. Frank did bring his combine over to help me finish harvest. He had just bought a New Holland. I took this outfit in Lethbridge to court to cover some of my costs. The judge ordered them to repay me $10,000, but nothing for my downtime and labour.

They appealed this ruling, and he gave them 24 hours to repay me, or he was going to make them pay crop loss as well. I think it was the next fall I also bought another New Holland.

In 1984 I bought a Rotary TR85. It really chewed up the straw so the straw was difficult to bale. For four or five years before that, I had done a lot of Jack's harvesting on his grain in exchange for him doing my corn sileage.

For three years in a row I used a New Holland baler at no charge. It was a machine being tested by New Holland, and they wanted a million bales baled with the baler every year. This started in Florida in April and May, and with a crew of two they provided the baler to various farmers all the way up to the Peace River. It was good for me, as if something went wrong there were two mechanics right there to get the baler going.

Cattle feeding

For several years, I fattened all my steer calves and sold them straight to the slaughter house. Many times they were sold to Lakeside packers in Brooks. I would take sealed bids from different buyers and accept the highest bid. Usually this was Ed Lang from Lakeside Packers.

Jack leveling land

In 1973 Jack had 140 acres on section 23 machine leveled. The northwest of 23 contained 123 acres of native grass with a large ravine through it.

In order for me to trail my cattle over to my land on 24, this was my only access. Jack also had a quarter section that was known as Old John's machine-leveled. He wanted these two parcels border diked, but first they needed the rocks picked. Jack bought a large land leveler and asked me to help him border dike these two parcels and seed them to grain and grass.

Because I had a 14' grain seeder, and as the dikes were 28' apart, it worked well. I agreed to do this with Jack on the condition that the 123 acres of grass be put in joint title for Jack and myself, and this was done. I also did the harvest for two years on this land for Jack.

In 1974 Jack had 90 acres across the road from my place machine leveled at a very high cost, it as very rocky with huge rocks. He also expected me to border dike this land, but that was not part of the agreement, and I wasn't about to wreck my machinery on it. Luckily, Dad agreed that it was not in the original agreement.

Buying the ranch and equipment

In 1970 we bought a 103 New Holland automatic bale wagon. I bought an 830 Case tractor with a front-end loader, to equal out each brother's investment. This tractor was needed for the front-end loader, as well as an extra tractor for the farm work.

It had the advantage of an automatic transmission and was ideal for hauling bales as it would travel over 25mph on the road. It was also a great tractor for cleaning snow and for use around the yard. That same year Frank and I bought ranch land at Skiff Alberta that we could each pasture 70 head on.

The bank

In 1979 I worked on a plan with the BMO we both thought would be profitable, and lessen the grain farming for me. It involved purchasing four sections of grassland at three different locations and buying 200 cows. It would require an investment of $550,000, but because I was already tied in the CIBC the BMO was not interested in lending me the money. The agriculturist with the CIBC did look it over, and felt my proposal was very solid, and something his bank would get involved with.

The bank manager in Taber also looked at it, and suggested we forward it to Toronto. In Toronto they turned it down, but readily agreed to lend me $450,000 to expand my grain farming, both for land and equipment.

In grain farming it was difficult to show a profitable return, and I just kept borrowing more money at high interest. I did closely follow the cattle program we had proposed.

Cattle prices increased. If the bank had lent me more money for the cattle venture, I would have been able to make all the payments on the land and the cattle and be free of debt within six years.

Separation and divorce

In 1975 Marj and I separated. Bev and Dan stayed with me on the farm, and Sandra and Dixie went to live with their mother. It was a traumatic and difficult time for Marj, me and the kids - both emotionally and financially. Marj's dad made arrangements for a house in Vulcan for her to live in.

He put a small amount of money on it for a down payment, and I was told I had to pay monthly support payments, etc.

That went toward the payment of the house and child support for Dixie and Sandra.

There were several disagreements and ill feelings, but we both had visiting rights for all the children. I'm not going into details about the divorce, as it would just be a one-sided description, and that is perhaps not fair to Marj. The divorce was more my fault than hers.

Peggy Newman, Marj's sister-in-law came to the farm, and her and Marj loaded up what she felt was fair for her to take to Vulcan with her. This included some of the furnishings, etc; it was agreed what she could take.

I had payments due to the CIBC for two farm improvement loans for a total of $5,600. I went to the bank the next morning and told the bank manager I wouldn't be able to make those payments, as I needed the money for furniture and living expenses.

The bank gave me a six-month extension on the payments. I bought furniture that was needed in the short term. To meet the obligations of the payment to Marj, I sold six cows every month for five months. I met with the bank and made arrangements how best to move forward.

Five months after the separation, I took out a $55,000 loan at the CIBC to pay support, lawyers fees and farming expenses. I secured this loan with a personal guarantee and 10% interest. Later, the final settlement was awarded by my accountant, and a court assigned accountant. I borrowed another $75,000 on my personal guarantee; this was added to the original $55,000

Over the next 10 years, I was able to pay off some of this, but it was all floating interest and fluctuated as high as 18% in the mid 1980s. It was always the first loan the bank would refer to whenever I needed to borrow money.

The judge made it very clear that he would not grant the divorce until the final financial issues were settled.

The final agreement was that Marj was to receive cash - I would have no interest in anything she had in Vulcan; and she would have no interest in the farm.

We all moved forward as best we could with the children; and Dixie and Sandra visited me just about every other weekend.

Dan continued with his hockey, and Bev with 4-H, basketball and school. Dan and Bev worked very hard on the farm helping out as we moved forward. The next summer Judith and Owen came to work for me, and they truly were a godsend. They both worked very hard - Judith did the inside work and Owen did a lot of the cropping.

We were fortunate to have some good crops in the following year.

I continued on with the A.I. program for Dad and Jack, and I was able to meet all my obligations and payments, and the year after the divorce I actually made $127 profit!

Owen and Judith were great role models for all my kids. Judith often drove Dan to ball practice. Dan also became very fond of Owen, and Bev of Judith. I had made arrangements with the small grocery store in Purple Springs to charge groceries and pay them once a month.

The following year I was fortunate to have Peter and Bonnie as trainees. I was renting Gerald's home quarter, and Harold Brown's quarter, which was mostly hay. I was also renting 320 acres from the CPR.

This land was close to Purple Springs.

In 1978 Min Urano had seeded 329 acres to alfalfa along the Grassy Lake highway. He had grown potatoes on this land for several years, and because of the Black Leg, he switched to alfalfa for three years.

I made a 60/40 share agreement with him, as he did not have any hay equipment. He did the irrigation, and we did all the swathing, baling and stacking of the bales. we put up over 24,000 small square bales, 16,000 of which were my share. It was all good hay, and I sold most of it to a dairy. These sales allowed me to set more aside for Bev and Dan to buy a half-ton truck they shared together the year Dan turned 16.

We were able to put money into each kid's account for further education. The money we made on calves that were owned by the kids, was divided evenly depending on their age.

Dan really helped out for a kid of his age with the field work, and Bev was a big help in the house, particularly in the winter with laundry and meals.

She also drove the tractor and did a lot of the baling; they both helped feed the cows.

A.I.

In 1968 we made the decision to A.I. our cattle. This was done for three reasons:

1. To lessen the exposure to the bulls, as BANGS disease was not fully controlled in Alberta.
2. To use better genetics
3. To reduce the high cost of bulls

We made the improvements through dad's corrals and did the A.I. there. Two A.I. technicians who owned the business in Taber and did the breeding. We supplied the A.I. riders (cowboys) and either Gerald or I would often ride once a day.

The cows in heat were brought into the corral and bred 24 hours later. Jack selected Hereford bulls he wanted us to use. We all chose the bulls we wanted, including Angus and Herefords.

Darwin convinced me to try a new breed that was relatively unknown. The semen was not readily available and had to be brought in from Mexico, so I had 30 head bred to Charlois that year.

They were from a bull named Bevon, who proved to be a difficult calving bull. Frank did stay breeding a few Charlois the following year. In 1970 I bred 40 cows to a new breed, developed by Senator Harry Hays from Calgary.

This breed was bred up using Hereford, Jersey, Angus and Holstein, and they were, in fact, excellent cattle. They were easy calvers, had a great weight of gain, and proved to be fantastic mothers.

But their calves resembled cross-bred Holsteins too closely.

I really liked this breed but went out of them because they discounted the calves in the sale ring because of the Holstein factor.

At that time, we were selling all our calves to Herb Christie's market auction in Taber. Our calves usually brought a two or three cent premium.

Many were bought by Ontario buyers, and were sent by rail to Ontario. They had to be tested for TB, so after each sale we helped the vet and the auction market staff until about 3am putting a needle under the base of the tail.

Usually Gerald and Frank would go home and do everyone's chores while Rod and I helped the vet. Three days later you had to run them all through the chute again, and check if the tail had a swelling that meant the animal had TB.

Jack and Dad and the hired men would usually go out for supper after the sale while we did the dirty work. The next day Jack and Dad would pick up all our cheques. This sometimes led to disagreements, as sometimes the numbers never matched.

In 1968 the McKinnon Ranches at Bassanno had a problem with BANGS disease, and they decided the best way to clean up the herd was to go to AI breeding. They worked with the American Breeders (A.B.S.) and decided to breed most of their herds to some of the new breeds.

This really paid off for them, and in the fall of 1969, they held a large sale at the ranch in Bassanno. A.B.S. put on a field day, and those cows that were bred to what was called the 'new exotic breeds' sold at two or three times the going market.

This started the importation of many more new breeds. In 1971 Frank and I attended at A.I. school in Pincher Creek. We caught on to the A.I. procedure very easily, and by the end of the week were in fact assisting many of the other ranchers and farmers.

Alex Mills and Jim Clark were our instructors, and they really appreciated how well we caught on, and helped out. For a few years after, Alex would get me to work with him at some of the A.I. schools.

Farrowing barn

Rod rented a barn two miles from his place. He only wanted to raise feeder pigs and not have sows. I made an arrangement with him to supply him with 25 weaner pigs every two weeks. To do this, I built a farrowing barn 24' by 60'. I did not put gutters in that barn.

I used straw for bedding. I added four more farrowing crates to this barn and portioned off an area in each pen so that the baby pigs could sleep away from the sows. It was all cleaned by hand.

I had two trainees that year. One was on a four-month program – he came in July and left in November, and his name was Vaughn.

The day before he left in November, we finished shingling the barn and had it all closed in, but no cement or anything done inside except for electricity. So, I did have heat.

I would shovel enough gravel in every fourth day, so it warmed up and I could use it in the concrete and had the cement mixer inside. I would pour 10' of floor every third day, and in between I would build the pens. I poured the last 10' on Christmas Eve.

The first sow farrowed Christmas Day. This agreement worked out well for both Rod and I; he went out of pigs in 1974. The barn belonged to Marathon Investment. They moved the barn away and paid me to clean up the yard, etc.

I hired Gord Weibe to bring in his large D8 with rock ripper spikes on it. He straddled the gutter and one track fell in, which was enough to high-center the D8. He had to bring in a crane truck to lift the one side up.

I also built a large 240' by 36' partly-enclosed cattle shelter. It was a pole frame structure, and the poles were placed 12' apart. It had a metal exterior. I used pressure-treated lumber 6' up the inside because of the manure. We dug the holes for these poles, put them in, but did not tamp them in solid.

Then I put up the 12' long 2x6s for the frame structure; the poles then could be moved to accommodate the 2x6s. Once they were all in place, we put up some of them in to square it all up. The last thing we did was tamp the poles solid. This shelter worked very well in a winter storm for the cow herd.

In 1979 and 1980 I remodelled this farrowing barn into a calving barn.

Vaughn and I corresponded for 12 or 13 years. The last letter I got from him, he said, "Don't write for a while because I'm moving."

I never heard from him again, and other Danish trainees tried to find him. All they could tell me was that he had moved from Copenhagen.

Romanola Association and Canadian Livestock National Records

In 1969 and forward to 1974, 14 new cattle breeds were introduced to Canada. All of these formed their own associations and drew up their own constitutions and bylaws, which set out how the cattle would be registered.

C.L.N.R.'s head office was in Ottawa, and they were aggressive in soliciting the new breeds to use their business. They charged a fee for each animal recorded; this was not a government department, but in fact, was a well-organized business.

They recorded perhaps 80% of all livestock registrations in Canada. It was not cheap to use their service, and it had some drawbacks. For instance, they did not have a good system to record of performance on their certificates, and for this reason some cattle associations (for example, Charlois) designed their own record system.

The C.L.N.R. was concerned that other breeds would also set up their own systems. When we formed the Romanola Association in 1973, we had to decide how we would register our cattle. We, along with several other breeder associations, were sort of wined and dined by the C.L.N.R. to use their system.

Many of the new associations were formed in western Canada. The head office for the C.L.N.R. was in Ottawa, where all the records were located.

They invited representatives from all these new breeds to go to Ottawa in March of 1973. I was president of the Romanola Association, so I went down to represent our breed.

I got together with Ken Olinger from the Maine Anjou Association and Gordon Petersen from the Chianina Association, and we flew to Ottawa together. We met with other breed delegates from Alberta to have a bit of a plan on what some of our expectations and requirements would be, if we used the C.L.N.R.

Over 200 livestock, poultry, rabbits, dogs, etc, breeds were using C.L.N.R., and most had at least one, and some had two delegates at this meeting.

Two of the things presented were the fees that were being charged, and the fact that all the records were kept in Ottawa, and all the meetings were held in Ottawa. Our group was represented by a very well-spoken person, and we selected him to present our concerns for 19 different associations. There were over 500 delegates, so our voice was very small, but we did get a motion passed that one annual meeting every four years would be held in Calgary.

That afternoon we were given a tour of their office, and the space they needed to handle all the records. It took up four whole floors in a downtown Ottawa office complex.

That evening at the banquet I was sitting at a table in the center of the room, and Prince Charles attended the banquet. He walked up the center to the head table and shook hands as he went – I got to shake his hand.

I did not fly home with any of the delegates from Calgary but stayed in Ottawa to visit with my brother Bus for two extra days.

A few of the things I remember from that visit were his gold-plated R.C.M.P. rifles and a gold-plated sword he had. When he drove me around, we crossed into Gatineau, and he cussed as he went by the mint, as it was on the Quebec side. He returned a couple of shirts to a department store, and the clerk claimed she could not speak any English. She sure remembered it fast after a few choice words from Bus.

Enclosed is a copy of the fees for the registrations for the Romanola association. My sister Eleanor was of the Romanola Association, and my brother Frank was a director. We spent a lot of time on those bylaws.

The wheat board, the exhibition board and 4-H

The Canadian Wheat Board regulated the sale of most grains, except for feed grain. That was often sold directly to livestock producers, for most of the time I was farming.

The Canadian Wheat Board was established in 1921 and was dissolved in approximately 2001.

They would issue permit books and determine when you could sell your grain, usually based on a per acre; for example, two bushels per acre in your permit book.

We would then deliver our grain to the elevator, whenever the elevator had room. You could also get a special permit to grow certain grains. In the early 1960s we started growing malting barley.

If your sample passed, the malting company would order a railway car and give you four or five days to deliver it. Most of these cars held 4,000 bushels. Once the permit was issued, you dropped everything else and rushed to fill your rail car.

In order for a sample of malting barley to pass, it needed to pass certain standards, which mainly pertained to the ability of the grain to sprout quickly and uniformly.

It had to germinate and sprout at least 96% of the kernels, and therefore, cracked seeds or damaged seeds lessened the chance of your sample being accepted.

Most of the malting barley were of a two-row variety, because they contained a protein level of less than 12%, compared to the six-row barley which were 13 of 14%.

I was also quite successful in getting my barley accepted for malt, and often had two or three railway cars shipped each year. The premium for this malt barley was usually about .50 per bushel. One year I had stored my malt barley in one of the wooden bins on Dad's farm.

It was a hard bin to shovel out because of all the inside cross-bracing. I was called at 7am on a Monday morning that a rail car had been spotted in Purple Springs and I had 18 hours to fil it or it would be pulled. My grain truck held approximately 290 bushels, and I needed 4,000 bushels to fill the car.

My hand and thumb were still a large mitt from where my thumb was torn off, so it was difficult to shovel. It took me 13 loads to fill that rail car. The elevator agent left the doors open for me late that night.

I did meet the deadline, and it was one of only six rail cars full of malt barley shipped from Purple Springs that year.

I had a small feed lot on my farm for several years, feeding approximately 60-80 head. This was quite profitable. The fat steers were sold at one of three packing houses in Lethbridge.

In later years, I sold many to Lakeside Packers in Brooks; I always started my steers on feed by hand with a bucket, and at times this was 65 five-gallon pails. I got quite good at carrying two full pails in my left hand when my thumb was injured.

I was also loading and feeding out up to 60 bales of hay and straw to the cow herd.

I did not have a real good system to separate any sick or inured animals that needed treatment, so I usually roped the animals. Sometimes I had to treat two or three in one day, and when the steers reached over 1,000 lbs this took some skill with one hand. After this injury to my thumb, it never did heal properly to allow me to be good at roping again. Even today, I have very poor circulation in my thumb on my right hand. It gets cold long before the fingers and thumb on my other hand.

Another difficulty I had for a few years was welding. I was thankful that most of the trainees could weld and do repairs.

I enrolled Bev in the beef 4-H when she was 13 years old. We chose the Bon Ayr 4-H club, as we knew most of the families. Most of the other Brewins enrolled their kids in the Grassy Lake beef club.

The Bon Ayr club had 49 members and was too large for one club to show and display their animals on achievement day.

The parents all met and it was decided to split the club in two. We formed a junior club and a senior club, giving each club approximately 25 members. I was asked to assist as the leader of the junior club. We had excellent parents and perhaps the best 4-H leader in southern Alberta - Brian Anderson who oversaw both clubs.

My assistant was Steve Casbay, and Matt Perin and Loui Turcato were the leaders of the senior club. We all assisted Brian as the overall club leader. Our club got along very well together and all the families became like one large family.

Milo Barfus was the region's 4-H specialist. The entry fee for each member was $24, plus $25 if they wanted insurance. Our club decided we could provide better insurance at a lower cost if we did it within the club. The 4-H branch insurance only covered the cost of the calf, but nothing for the feed if the calf died.

We asked the parents to have each member pay $20 for insurance on each calf to cover the full cost of both calf and feed. The parents all agreed to try this insurance scheme within the club. We also decided the club should feed a spare calf that a member could use if their calf died. This calf, if not used, was sold at the district sale and the proceeds went to the club.

Luckily, we didn't lose a calf for the first three years after adopting our own club insurance.

So, soon we had a good reserve in our insurance fund. We invested this money and with the interest and savings we built up over $40,000 in the account. We eventually helped some of our members with a $1,000 fund toward their secondary education.

Our Bon Ayr members did very well at the regional show and sales, winning in all classes over the years. My daughter Bev won district reserve champion one year.

Our district included nine clubs, and the sale usually had over 200 calves.

After three years, I was elected as the president of the Taber 4-H beef club and put in charge of the show and sale. Originally our sales were held at the Taber auction market, but when it burned down, we moved indoors to the hockey arena, and eventually to the exhibition building.

I was elected to represent Taber on the southern Alberta 4-H council. I was eventually elected to the provincial 4-H council as president for two years and served four years on the Alberta 4-H foundation.

My nephew Kerry bought one of my first calves sired by his dad's Maine Anjou bull, and won the district championship with that calf. For several years we alternated the show and sale between Taber and Vauxhall. 4-H was always well-supported in the Taber area.

It also included a sugar beet club, sewing club, sheep club and a swine club as well as a Taber light horse club. Myself, Alden Fletcher and John Enns started the horse club. I was either the leader or assistant leader of that club for nine years.

I found the horse club most difficult to lead. The parents did not support the club that well. Many wanted the club to operate more like a professional horse show. I made it clear that we were only involved to assist the members. At the beginning of each year, the club would declare the goal they wanted to achieve that year. Some got very involved, but some kept it simple.

It ranged from just learning to put on a saddle, to roping calves.

We also had several fun activities each year - went to the mountains to trail ride and had several rail rides around southern Alberta.

I chaperoned 14 senior 4-H members to Ontario for eight days under the open house Canada program. The Ontario members stayed with our Alberta members for eight days on a return trip.

All of the members had to be at least 15 years of age. One of the members was De Anna Stober from Hays. Shortly after our trip she was killed in a car accident. I felt very honoured when her family asked me to sit with them at the funeral.

Many of our members went on in life and did very well in their chosen vocations. Some were even in politics One of my members who became quite famous was Corb Lund – his family and the Brewins were good friends.

Much of the credit for the development and success of 4-H in Taber has to be credited to Kay and Scotty Ferguson and their daughter Brenda, and the Turcato families and the Anderson Families. These people worked very hard to bring 4-H to Taber, lead 4-H, and were responsible for its development.

Exhibition board

In 1976, I was asked to help raise money and get donations for a new indoor exhibition building. Frank Fletcher and I were given a list of 29 people to approach for donations. 15 of those people lived in town, and the other 10 were in the Purple Springs or Kinniburgh area. The average donation in town was $10, and the average in the rural areas was over $950. The funds in total was far too short to proceed with the building. I was put on the board of directors to help spearhead the building and funding.

We held many events and raffles, and we also got a grant from the provincial government, the town of Taber and the old rodeo committee.

A site was chosen for the new arena and recreation facilities. In 1978 construction was started which at first involved leveling the site. We needed hundreds of yards of gravel, and a work bee was called for this.

I brought in two trucks and eight other farmers brought in trucks. I put a lot of time into helping to get this building up and running. 4-H also had many fundraising events. Darwin Lund asked Gerald and I to help out on the rodeo committee, as only six or eight people had been doing all the work. The Taber rodeo was the largest attended event in Taber at that time. For years, it had been organized by a group of volunteers, with only marginal support from the town.

Yet it brought in more people and more money to Taber than any other single event.

In the mid 1960s I was also a member of the Elks Club. The Elks helped with a lot of the work needed to put on the rodeo. It was very disappointing to see the lack of support, and often even negative support from the town itself, as the town merchants truly did benefit from the Taber rodeo.

Our committee consisted of Don and Darwin, Walt Rombough, Clair Jensen, Darcy Wills, George Reti and two or three others. The town merchants and the stock contractor were actually the big benefactors of the rodeo.

We worked every evening for two weeks, setting up the chutes and pens for the rodeo. I was fortunate that Kerry Brewin worked for me, and did a great deal of my seeding and spring work. I was also the rodeo committee's delegate to the exhibition board, and was asked to represent 4-H on the exhibition board.

I was very surprised, at the presentation of the first financial statement I seen for the exhibition board, to find out that the exhibition board had been applying for and receiving a grant from the provincial government for 4-H show and sales. The yearly grant had been for $2,000. I got the support from our 4-H beef leaders to write letters to the exhibition board and get back four years of this grant. I had several very heated arguments with the secretary treasurer of the exhibition board about this.

When the exhibition building was finally finished, Matt Perin and I arranged for a solid bean scale to be installed to weigh the 4-H animals. We worked many hours pouring cement, building pens so we would have it ready for the first show and sale held in the new building.

A retired employee from Weights and Measures came and helped make sure the scale was correctly installed and legal. 4-H beef clubs raised over $4,000 for the scale and pens.

Many other events were held in this new building: gymkhanas, roping clubs, car shows, cattle shows, bull sales and many social events. Trade shows were also held twice a year. The building truly was a huge asset to Taber – it worked very well.

Eventually a manager was hired, and it became a well-operated business. I truly did enjoy many years as a 4-H volunteer, a hockey and basketball coach, a 4-H leader and a member of the exhibition board and the rodeo committee.

Crop circles, UFOs and cattle mutilations

In the late 1970s and early 1980s, there were reports of people sighting UFOs, etc, in southern Alberta. Most reports were phony, but some perhaps not so phony.

There was, in fact, a passenger plane flying from Winnipeg to Calgary, where the pilot and co-pilot both swore a UFO flew right alongside them. We had some neighbours that said one flew right over them. Their car stopped and they were very spooked, and spent eight hours while the car would not start. They believed it was drawing electricity from their car.

They would not drive after dark after that.

Their started to be reports of cattle mutilations. The first one was of a purebred bull at Nanton, Alberta. After that, there were others. In most cases, tongues were missing from the animals, sometimes the eyes, usually the scrotums, penises and the anuses.

I did have two deaths I could not explain. One was a cow that had calved a month previously. The whole back end – anus and vagina and all reproductive organs, including right into her uterus were missing, and her ears, one eye, tongue and nose but not the stomach were gone.

The vet said at first it was possibly coyotes.

On the other animal, a steer, it was the tongue, nose, ears, scrotum, anus, etc, were missing. It was examined by the vet – we felt the cuts were all too precise to have been ripped out by a coyote. This one was very odd, as none of my cows would go within 500' of that carcass. They all formed a circle quite a distance from it. Even after I buried it, they would not go near the grave.

One of my neighbours lost a cow, and he asked the vet to have a look at it. The vet was on his way home from a call in Foremost that night, so he got directions and started to examine it using his headlights.

The owner seen him and walked over to help. The poor vet got a hell of a scare when he looked in his headlights, and seen this silhouette coming toward him.

That one was proven to be coyotes. After about five years the reports just seemed to stop.

Reports are given by R.C.M.P., government vets, etc., and in the papers, deaths were never explained. Most were put down as coyotes, but it was also clearly stated that they had a concern about a panic situation if it surfaced that these deaths were unknown, so every effort was made to cover up these unknown mutilations.

10 miles east of my farm, some farmers reported crop circles in their grain fields. This was at the same time as the cattle mutilations. I had three of these in my wheat fields one year, and two the next year.

They were about 120' across. All the grain was tamped down at ground level in the nearly-ripe crops. We could not find any path of entry into these circles, and they were quite a distance from any road. All the grain lay one way in the circles, and each circle was almost perfectly round.

Some of the farmers claimed the soil was almost burnt, but yet the grain was not burned. On the circles the crop did not grow well the following year. They were put down as being caused by small whirlwinds or tornados, but there were just too many of them. And they were too perfectly round. They did range in size – one at Burdette was over 500 feet across, and part of it was in fact in a sugar beet crop.

One night I was coming home with a truck full of grain from the combine at about 1am. I was very tired and I seen what appeared to be three bright lights just a few hundred feet off the ground. All of a sudden, two of them seemed to just shoot off rapidly. The others I could see for a few minutes. I could not judge how far it was away, and actually worried if it was, in fact, a helicopter.

I stopped the truck and could not hear anything. The lights were not flashing lights, just sort of a blue light. It did scare me. I was three miles from home, and I do not remember starting the truck, driving home or going to bed.

I had put the tarp on the truck before I left the field, and I always parked the full grain truck by the grain bins when I came in late at night like that.

The next morning, the truck was parked in the middle of the yard. The tarp was neatly rolled up and the lights were still on. I can't to this day explain that encounter.

People ask me if I believe in UFOs. I do, and even have a theory where they're from. I believe they're coming from the future.

Kids and the separation

Marj and I both tried to keep the kids close to one another after we separated. Bev and Dan visited her in Vulcan once a month. Usually, I took them to Lethbridge and they took the bus to Vulcan. I brought Sandra and Dixie to the farm once a month, also usually on holidays. I kept Bev and Dan involved in 4-H and school sports, etc.

Sandra and Dixie soon made new friends, and they took swimming lessons in Vulcan.

One of the positive things was the love and affection that all my family showed all the kids. Frank and Gerald had a sincere love for all kids, and Gerald in particular. He always cherished any time he could with Dixie and Sandra.

Many times, Gerald expressed his admiration and pride for Sandra. We did a lot of downhill skiing, and often went as a family - all of the kids became very good skiers.

Dixie was also admired as a small tyke on the ski hill. For a long time, she refused to use the poles. We went to Fernie, Kimberly and White Fish Mountain.

In White Fish, we often rented a condo right on the ski hill, where the kids could ski right up to the door. Sandra and Dixie loved to find a run where I could not follow them, because my skis were too long. On one trip to White Fish, Frank and Colleen, Gerald and Marg and a few neighbours rented a condo.

A few of the neighbour kids were older and enjoyed a few beers. The ski patrol stopped me once and said Sandra had been hurt. I caught up with them as they were bringing her off the ski hill. Her leg was broken.

At the time she was going to school in Lethbridge later, she also broke her arm roughhousing with Danny on the lawn.

Shortly after this we took a week's holiday to Anaconda, Montana. I took along a lot of plastic sleeves that I used for A.I. – we kept her cast as dry as we could, so that she could swim.

Marj and the two girls lived in Vulcan for two or three years. They then moved to Lethbridge and lived with Louise for a short time. After that they lived on Lakeside Drive in Lethbridge for a couple of years.

Eventually, she bought a house in north Lethbridge so most of their schooling, up to Grade 11, was in Lethbridge. She enrolled the girls in sewing in 4-H. Sandra won an awards trip to Ontario.

In Grade 12 Sandra went to live with Bev and Keith and graduated in Airdre, Alberta.

Dixie and Marj moved to Red Deer, and Dixie graduated from high school in Red Deer.

When they were living in Lethbridge it had been much more convenient to get to the farm. They four kids remained very close to one another. Many, many miles were put on the lawn mower when Dan and Bev pulled the girls in their wagon.

All the kids were a great help to me. When Naomi was born in 1980, they readily accepted her, and all five kids became very close.

The four older kids actually picked out Naomi's name when she was born. We took Sandra and Dixie to Disneyland for two days. On one trip to Yellowstone Park, we stopped at Kalispel where the motel had a swimming pool. Dixie fell and broke her front tooth on the edge of the pool – almost half the tooth.

Expanding the farm

I went pretty much on my own in 1976 and 1977. My brothers and I still did help one another out, and traded some machinery back and forth, etc; I rented land from Gerald and another 160 acres from my mother. My dad passed away in 1978.

I continued to expand both my grain and the cattle operation. Money was easy to borrow at low interest rates - the banks were almost pushing it on you. Also in 1978, I incorporated and put everything into a company that I named Tim Brewin Ranching Ltd.

Class A shares were issued to all the kids. These were for an interest in the company, in case something happened to me. Those shares did not pay dividends. All the Class B shares were issued to myself, and whenever profit was made, they did pay dividends.

Frank and I purchased a large manure spreader and a self-propelled bale wagon that hauled 160 bales. In 1979, I was hired by the Alberta Department of Agriculture as a field auditor for various farm support programs. One was a bred cow support program, and another was a feed grain program for all livestock. This job really helped me out a great deal.

I leased the half ton. My area was out of the Medicine Hat office. Every Monday morning, I would receive a list of 10 farms I was to visit and audit, including the amount of feed grain for the livestock and poultry numbers in farms in the county of Foremost, and the Cypress improvement district.

The job paid me very well - $18 an hour and all travel expenses. I had to get up very early, though, and try to get the chores done by 10am, and then leave, usually doing audits on two or three farms, and would be home by 4:30pm.

I only did this job in the late fall and winter, and after three years I was also given the Municipal district of Taber as my territory.

I really enjoyed that job as most of the farmers were very honest; the farmers in the Hays and Vauxhall areas were the best ones to work with. They often did not even enter all the cows, pigs or whatever, just in case one died before the audit was done. They were honest to the extreme.

However, there was a group of farmers, northeast of Taber, that I had a real challenge with. It was for the Bred Cow Assistance program, where the farmers were paid $50 for every bred cow. These farmers basically ran feed lots, often feeding yearling heifers.

They put a few bulls with their heifers, and claimed they were all bred. There were upwards of 2,400 head in their feedlot. The bad part is they would move the heifers between their different feed lots.

The auditor from east of Medicine Hat phoned me and asked questions about these farmers. I was concerned too, as I had inspected them the day before, and questioned their claim on my reports. He also questioned their claims.

Inspectors were brought in from Edmonton, and these farmers had to pay back a lot of money between them. One case was more than $20,000.

The biggest fraud I was involved with was a provincial government employee at Medicine Hat. He put in a claim and was paid for 600 head of bred heifers. When I did the inspection, he took me to an empty feed lot that was not even his own. He claimed he had moved his heifers out the day before. I phoned Edmonton, and they sent in the R.C.M.P. He was eventually charged with fraud.

The biggest challenge was doing inspections of poultry – chickens, turkey and ducks. You had to measure the size of the barn, walk through and determine if you felt it was full – 50% full or whatever. That would determine how many birds were in it. This was a formula that was used to determine the amount of grain the birds were eating.

The feed grain program paid $13 per ton of feed grain, whether the farmers bought it, or it was their own grain. I had an interesting audit with a diary farmer in Lethbridge. They would buy spent malt barley grain, take it to the feed mill, mix it with other barley oats and use it in the dairy ration. They put in a claim on the grain from the brewery.

I had to get a ruling from Edmonton that it was eligible, and because it was high moisture only 50% of it could be used. I was told to get all the records from the feed mill going back two years, to work out the amount of their payment. That took me over three days going over past weigh scale tickets.

In the end, everyone was satisfied that they were compensated fairly for the feed grain they fed to their dairy cows.

At the end of the third year as a field auditor, and when those programs ended, I was asked by Dennis Laycraft if I would work for the Alberta Cattle Association to determine cattle numbers in the province.

They wanted someone full time on a five-year contract, so it was not something I could do.

My ankle injury

In November of 1976, after Owen and Judith went home, my cows were still on my grass, six miles north of my farm. One night it had snowed a little, then melted, so the top ¼ inch of ground was very slippery.

I was driving my cows home riding Billy and turned back quickly to stop a calf from breaking away. Billy's feet went out from under him, and he ended up flat on his side with my right leg under the saddle. It hurt like hell, and after he got up I was able to move over to a rock where I could get back on. The cows knew their own way home as it was only about a mile to go, and I had set the gates so they could go around and into the pasture south of my house.

I stopped at my main driveway and was lucky to see Dan by the garage. I was able to get him to walk out and open the gate for me. I rode Billy close to the house, and Dan put him away for me.

I soaked my leg in Epsom's salt that night and was able to drive to the hospital for x-rays the next morning. The x-rays showed crushed bones. There was a lot of bruising and the doctor said it looked like the ankle itself was perhaps crushed a little. I wore a leather ankle support all that winter and most of the next year. While I was in the hospital, a Danish trainee named Orin Sigurson was also in the waiting room. He had stayed in Canada and was working for Tony Birch, a potato farmer. He had a Norwegian girlfriend, Bridget Olson, who stayed with him but was not working.

She came over for a couple of weeks and helped me do chores when Bev and Danny were in school. Bev and Dan were great helping me, particularly on weekends.

Oren and Bridget moved to Lethbridge in December – they eventually bought a farm in Manitoba and immigrated.

The following summer in 1977, Peter and Bonnie, a married couple from Switzerland, worked for me and did a lot of the farm work as my leg slowly improved.

The doctor warned me that it was likely it would bother me in later years, which it did. I eventually got arthritis and had to have the ankle completely reconstructed in 2013.

Lightning

In 1969, I insured all my bulls for unnatural death loss. I had a two-year-old bull that I had raised myself, registered, and I was keeping him for breeding. One morning in June I found this bull dead in about six inches of water that drained from an irrigation pond.

There was a young vet at the vet clinic by the name of Dr. Gilchrist. Before vet school he had worked as a butcher, so he had a good set of knives. He did an autopsy on the bull, and at first he could not find a cause of death, but he kept saying "I'll find it, I'll find it."

When he came to the liver he found several burst blood vessels; he was quite certain it was from a lightning strike. He sent the liver into the diagnostic lab and his cause of death was confirmed, so my insurance company paid out the $2,500 claim.

At the time, I was using Saunders Insurance as my agent; they had a farm policy where you could ensure all your livestock as long as you paid the premium on 75% of all the cattle on your farm.

I had them include this on my policy. Two years later I went out on a Sunday morning to check my cattle eight miles north of my building. There had been a lightning storm the night before. I found four dead cows and two dead calves on the downside of a hill close to a four-wire barbed fence.

The wire showed obvious signs of lightning, as it was burnt for 200 yards and broke in several places. The vet confirmed they had all been killed by lightning and this claim was also paid out.

Lloyd Knibbs

I had a very neat neighbour named Lloyd Knibbs, who had a herd of about 50 good Charlois cows. Lloyd and his wife lived close to me. Their daughter had actually babysat for us. Lloyd also coached our ball team for four or five years, was very athletic and very well liked.

Attending school at Grassy Lake, we were very fortunate to have Lloyd Knibbs help us. He and his nine siblings had grown up three miles south of Grassy Lake. They were very sports minded and won many awards and championships. They were well known in southern Alberta for their contribution to sports.

Lloyd was often available to coach young people, and also as a referee or umpire. We truly appreciated his involvement. He later was the coach on our district baseball team. He gave me a lot of instruction as a pitcher and a ball player. He seemed to always have extra time for me. I later farmer next to Lloyd's farm, and often enjoyed his visits and stories.

We shared a common lateral irrigation ditch, when we flood-irrigated and later when I used sprinkler irrigation.

Sometimes when I relaxed over a beer in the bar, I would have a drink and enjoy time with Lloyd and his wife, Ruth. I always really enjoyed Lloyd's stories.

I sometimes hauled bales and helped Lloyd. For sure, he had a positive influence in my life.

Another one of my ball umpires was Butch O'Donnell. A friend of mine wanted me to play golf with him one day. I had the clubs in my car in town. Butch came out of the grocery store, seen me, and came over to talk.

He seen the golf clubs and I got a 10-minute lecture about how the hell a baseball player could hit a ball and chase the damn thing himself.

Jim Noble

The Noble family farmed just south of us for several years. We became good friends with all of them. Rod, Jim and I even took up golf. Jim was also a good friend of Frank's. His wife, Elaine, grew up in Purple Springs. I first met her in high school in Grassy Lake.

When Marj and I got married and had kids we often visited with Jim and Elaine. They also had three kids of a similar age: Linda, Perry and Scott.

Linda sometimes babysat our younger children. We enjoyed Jim and Elaine's company, played a lot of cards together and hunted, etc.

Breaking land

In 1977, I decided to break up 320 acres on Section 1. It was all native grass and had never been cultivated. It had 160 acres of water rights on it with good drainage; it was rocky but had very good soil. It was a very mild winter, and on the 6th of February I took my 17 cultivator out, put spikes on the shanks and started to break up the sod.

My brother Gerald had backed off from farming some, and was working part time for a friend, so he was able to help me do this. He agreed to come and run one of my tractors for me, as I could only put in about five hours a day on the tractor myself.

I was still feeding some of the company cows plus my own herd, and within 10 days and with Gerald's help we had been over the field with the spikes three times and twice with the 12' double disc.

Gerald was downsizing his farm, and sold me 160 acres on Section 2, that also had potential for irrigation. We moved onto that field, and by April 15 had both parcels ready to seed.

Dan also ran the tractor and cultivator after school sometimes as he grew older, but he was on the school volleyball team which often practiced after school. I seeded both parcels to barley, and under-seeded Section 1 to grass and alfalfa.

I did get a good yield off both parcels, and I was successful in getting water rights on Section 2 the next year.

I put a Rienke corner pivot on it, which covered 139 acres, and the second year I grew soft white wheat on it. Soft white wheat is used for making pastry, and I grew it under contract. It didn't sell for quite as much per bushel as hard white wheat, but yielded about 30% more, so was more profitable.

It requires irrigation and good fertile land, and they prefer it to be very low in protein.

I began using liquid fertilizer from Cascade Fertilizer in Tempest, Alberta. They were just getting started in business and offered me a very good deal. They put up large 5,000-gallon tanks at my place, and I bought a 2,000-gallon nurse tank to take the liquid product to the field.

They supplied the cultivator and applicator which was 42' wide, so you could cover a lot of ground in a short time.

They also gave me six months to pay, so I usually could sell the crop before I had to pay for the fertilizer. I used this company for 12 years without any problems – some fuel and fertilizer outlets in southern Alberta were not as good.

I also used one in Taber to supply me with Anhydrous ammonia for nitrogen. I eventually had to launch a lawsuit against them, as their applicator supplied far less fertilizer than I was charged for; also, it was a very erratic application that burnt some of my crop.

Gerald used them to supply fuel to his farm, and eventually found they were delivering less fuel than he was being charged for.

Roy Peterson in Grassy Lake was my fuel dealer for over 30 years. A fuel dealer in Coaldale was eventually charged because he was not supplying the fuel he charged for. He did this for over eight years. What he would do is take the hose and nozzle off his truck and put fuel in the farmer's tank, about ¾ full, then put the nozzle and hose into the top of his truck and pump two or three hundred gallons back into his own tank.

It took some time to catch him, as all the fuel went through the meter, which printed out the amount of fuel pumped.

Getting back to the land I broke up, the new irrigated hay supplied me with several thousand tons of cattle feed each year. On Section 2 we grew various crops over the years - soft wheat, malt barley and sunflowers. I eventually rented it out to potato farmers - they paid me $200 per acre, cash, which was more than I could make growing grain.

When my dad died, he left me 300 acres of native grass, a quarter of it known as Murphy land. It was only suitable for cattle grazing, but on one parcel was a very large gravel pit that had supplied the gravel for the CPR railway when they came out west. Apparently, Chinese laborers were used on this section of the railway.

Dad said he seen camps of over 1,000 Chinese men as they built and maintained the railway and Highway Number 3.

Another interesting thing on that land was when my brothers Gerald and Jack were teenagers - they dug a dugout. Dad ran up to 3,000 sheep at that time but had poor water holes for them.

Gerald and Jack took the draft horses and a Fressnole and would work digging a hole. It was hard work. The horses were used to drag the Fressnole and fill it up with about a quarter yard of dirt. They would then drag it to where it was dumped by hand – literally grabbed on to the pipe, lifted at the back of the bucket, tipped it up, and the horses would empty it and return to make another scoop.

They got the dugout done about eight feet and hit a very hard clay layer. Jack took a bar and a shovel and dug down about another two feet. He hit water that shot up about three feet in the air, and barely scrambled out before he got soaked. This dugout supplied water for sheep and cattle, and as far as I know, it still does. It never did run dry.

The corner pivot I installed had a type of sprinkler on it that supplied accurate, even water to every inch of the field. I could set it to supply anywhere from a 10th of an inch, to once inch of water in any one spot. The corner pivot has a large arm on wheels that, in fact, followed a tracer wire around the filed that had a small electric charge in it.

There was a sensor arm on that arm that followed over the top of the sensor wire, so the arm would swing out, and instead of only irrigating a round field of 121 acres, it irrigated more of a larger field of 151 acres.

I borrowed the money for this system from the Bank of Hong Kong. It cost me $85,000, and I was able to pay that loan off in five years.

Eventually, I had three pivots on my farm and ranch at Purple Springs, and a total of four and three-quarters of wheel line irrigation.

Dan had another two miles of wheel line irrigation, and we also had four miles of 8" mainline and two miles of 6" mainline.

The wheel lines self-drained, but the mainline had to be picked up, drained and stored each fall.

Kids

All of my kids continued to do well in school. Bev and Dan played a lot of sports, had many friends and were very involved in 4-H. Sandra and Dixie eventually moved to Lethbridge with their mother, and joined the 4-H sewing club. Bev and Dan both attended 4-H Club Week at Olds, and many new friendships were cultivated. They won other 4-H awards and trips, too.

It was always special when Sandra and Dixie were at the farm, and a close bond continued with the kids and myself. I was very proud of them all. Bev graduated from high school in Taber, and I paid for a trip for her to New Zealand as her graduation present. She went over and stayed with Judith and Owen on their farm in Omaru, New Zealand.

She fit in well with them and was there for three months – Owen and Judith played a big part in her life. They had three young kids, and their family became Bev's family.

When she came back from New Zealand, she enrolled in the university at Edmonton, taking economics and agriculture.

We had put enough money aside for her for her first year, and the next summer she got a job doing research, etc., for the Wheat Board.

Along with that, and student loans, she put herself through university. She also herded 3,000 sheep at the Hays community pasture for one summer.

The fourth summer, she worked with her husband-to-be, Keith Jones, on a computer and accounting business they set up. He was also enrolled at the university, and was from Balzac, Alberta.

They were married in 1984. At the university, Bev roomed with a girl from Taber named Terri Calloway. Sadly, Terri was killed in a car accident, I believe the third year they roomed together.

I had bought Bev a yellow Camaro car to use at university. One day I got a phone call from the Calgary police, telling me the car was impounded and I could come and claim it.

I phoned Bev and asked what was going on. She was quite surprised and assured me her car was parked in the parking lot by her apartment. I phoned the police back and they were quite adamant that they had the car, and I should come get it.

They said the car, in fact, had been involved in a robbery in Montreal, and had been found in Calgary.

It took me three days to straighten this out, and only after I sent the police the copy of the registration with the VIN number, and it showed that one letter was different – mine was a J and the one they had was an F.

The police told me I would probably have been given the car if I had claimed it.

Bev and Keith settled down, ranching and farming, and have done very well.

They gave me my first grandsons – Greg, Michael and Carston. These boys, and all my other grandkids are a source of pride for me.

These three boys all fight forest fires in the summer, Greg in B.C. and the other two in Alberta – all crew chiefs. Greg is also in charge of one of the companies and crews that build the ice roads to the diamond mines in the N.W. Territories.

Dan continued on in high school in Taber, helping me on the farm. He got along great with all the trainees, and also had very many friends who worked for us from time to time. He often operated the combine in harvest. We had bought a New Holland #1,400 combine. I had two grain trucks and harvest was a big deal.

One of these trucks burned up in harvest. We had a very good crop of barley and were saving the straw to bale. A trainee by the name of Andrew Royce from Australia was operating the combine, and I was hauling the grain.

I was at home emptying the truck, when I noticed a huge amount of smoke coming from my field two miles away. I raced over and the truck and part of the field were on fire.

Several neighbours showed up, and we got the fire out in the field. The Grassy Lake Fire Department came out and, in all their wisdom, extinguished the fire in the truck. I kept telling them, "Let the damn thing burn – I've got insurance in it."

But they did put it out. It was more or less just the shell left, but the insurance company took $5,000 off the payment for what they claimed I could salvage. If they had let it burn, I'd have got full coverage on another truck.

Dan bought his own 160 acres of land in 1982. It had irrigation, and he put wheel move sprinkler on it. He grew lentils that first year, which were sold to a distributor in Lethbridge and were exported to India.

He brought a tractor of his own. He had also graduated from high school in Taber, and also went to New Zealand, and traveled with his cousin Brian Brewin. They also stayed with Owen and Judith, and raveled throughout New Zealand and Australia, often visiting past trainees.

In the fall and winter of 1982, Dan got a job doing construction on the main irrigation canal that run by our farm. They were increasing the flowing capacity of the canal by 50%. Dan moved into Taber and roomed with his friend Tony Casabay.

In 1983, Dan worked for Dowel for six months, which was a large company that did work on oil well production.

Dan went to university in Saskatoon in 1983 and 1984.

Dan was also very proud and took good care of the machinery, etc. He and Bev bought a truck together when he was 16. He also bought a motor bike that he was very proud of. It was a pretty classy-looking bike. It was stolen right out of our shop one night, and was recovered in Brooks, Alberta.

They had spray-painted it an awful purple colour.

He also bought a very nice grey-coloured half ton – I believe he was 18 years old.

Dixie was going out to pick him up in the field one day. She hit some loose gravel and rolled the truck. She was hurt a little, and had many scrapes on her legs, and glass particles in her head and scalp, probably for several weeks. Dan felt bad that his truck was wrecked, and he felt really bad for Dixie.

She felt very bad for wrecking Dan's truck.

4-H councils

In 1980, I was elected to represent the Taber 4-H district on the southern Alberta regional council. The Bonayr club membership continued to be over 40 members, so we were very involved in all 4-H regional events.

Highway cleanup was a big event and money-raiser each spring.

I was able to keep the 13-mile distance from Taber and Chin Lakes. This was a lower traffic area than was Highway Number 3, and I always felt it was fair for our members.

Our club members continued to do well at the show and sale. I was also the president of the Taber beef show and sale where the clubs were very competitive.

We held our three-day event in the Taber agriplex. We used a lot of shavings, and it took half a day to clean up after the sale. But I always got good support and help from most of the parents.

Brenda Engleson was a beef sale secretary treasurer and was in charge of collecting the money from all the buyers. She paid all the clubs, which in turn paid out each member for the calf.

We were able to get a lot of donated resources, such as auctioneers and truckers.

The clubs were very competitive, to the point is sometimes became very heated. One I remember was when the new Hays club was involved for their first year. We had set out a schedule for the three-day event. We set Thursday afternoon as a time the clubs could come in and set up their stalls and displays.

The clubs went all out, with a lot of effort for this. Terry Unruh, the Hays club leader, was not aware of how much work each club put into their stall displays. On Thursday afternoon when he seen what went on, he got his members together, and overnight they made some very neat stall decorations.

They got to the agriplex at 5:30 the next morning and set up.

When I came in at 7am, a group of about 20 leaders and parents were very angry with Terry, because he had not set up the afternoon before, in what they thought was the designated time.

Terry was so angry, he was going to pull his club out. I quickly called a meeting and pointed out what a terrible example this was being set for our members. I made a ruling that because Terry and his club had not interfered with anyone by coming in early and setting up as they had, it was fine. Some parents were not happy, but eventually I got support from all but two of the other club leaders.

Another thing I remember was one of the calves in the Enchant club had been born without a tail. The girl loved this calf, and entered it in 4-H. At the show and sale her dad went to the slaughter house, got a tail and glued it on.

Very few people could tell it was not the real tail – quite ingenious, I thought.

Nothing was said until the calf won Grand Champion, and some leaders wanted it withdrawn from the sale. Andy Brown, the judge, had judged cattle all over the world. We met with him, and he said, "I was judging the animal for its beef carcass. You don't eat the tail."

Andy had judged at the Royal European show in England several times.

The sale of the 4-H calves was very important to our club members. Many used this money to go on for post-secondary education. Our club always had a big wrap-up event in August at the Legion park, complete with corn on the cob – a real family event.

The members' cheques were handed out at this event. We played ball and horseshoes. Many of the members in my club I remember for special reasons.

One girl, whose dad could speak very little English, was in our club for three years. Her mother was very sick. The girl knew very little about how to raise a calf. Brian Anderson asked me if I would help her out. I went out to her place several times and showed her now to clip her calf and groom it. I also helped her halter-break it.

Every member had to give a speech each year, and in their third year this girl's speech was about the death of her mother the year before. She talked about how her older sister was expecting a baby, and how her mother hung on until she could hold the new baby before she died.

Her speech had everyone in tears. After the sale that year, her dad came to me and sincerely thanked me because 4-H meant so much to the girl.

Over the years, I have ran into many of my 4-H members. A lot of them have done well, and I am proud I could play a part in their lives.

In 1983, I stepped down as leader of the 4-H horse club.

The regional council elected me as a delegate to the provincial council, and all of our meetings were held in the 4-H centre west of Wetaskiwin four times a year.

The centre had its own dorms and facilities. The first year I went, Ted Youck, the director of the 4-H branch in Alberta, asked me to room together with him. He said that he snored a little, but I did not think that it would matter.

When other delegates asked who I was rooming with, they all grinned when I said, "Ted."

Another delegate, Vern asked if he could also room with us. I said, "Yes, but I understand Ted snores."

Vern's answer was, "Well, I'll give him a go."

I spent that night with Ted on the upside of the snore, and Vern on the downside. I never slept hardly at all. They were loud! Many good laughs were had at my expense about Ted's snoring, but I made some great friends on the provincial councils and was elected president in 1989.

Malon Weir was the secretary director of the council. It came up that there was no constitution for the council, and I was asked to work on that. It was well-debated for over three years.

While I was on council, there was a girl killed in Medicine Hat while training her horse. She wrapped a lead rope around her wrist, and the horse spooked and she could not get free.

Working on the council, I discovered that the council paid for an insurance policy. When I questioned Malon, asking if there was insurance for this girl, he said no. He said that the insurance was simply, only for council members.

When I brought this up at a meeting, it turned out that she was killed at a 4-H event, and she was in fact covered.

The Alberta government really supported 4-H. We had a 4-H leader's conference every year. There were nine regions, and each region took turns hosting this conference.

In 1985, it was our turn. We had a tremendous amout of help to put on a very successful conference.

Workshops were put on for leaders for all over the province, and 150 leaders attended. One speaker we had was a teacher and 4-H leader for Arizona. She was from a very remote area, and her school class consisted of 18 kids, who she enrolled in 4-H.

Most of these kids were from troubled parents. She had her members doing gardens, etc. She, in fact, won the award in the U.S. as the most influential teacher. She was a great speaker and motivator.

The 4-H branch spared no expense to bring in very qualified resource people.

Open House Canada

When I was president of the Taber 4-H council, one of my priorities was to arrange trips for my members. Through Open House Canada, we were successful in getting funding for three trips in five years. One of these trips was to New Brunswick, one was to Quebec and one to Ontario.

I chaperoned the trip to Smith Falls, Ontario in 1984.

I took Cher, Dixie and Naomi with me. Our host family was Margaret Kelk. Her daughter, Susan, was 15 and her son, Hugh, was 13. Margaret worked full time, but she was a great host and made us feel right at home. They were in haying season, so I helped Hugh cut and bale hay. I also helped Susan halter-break her 4-H calf, cleaned out the barn and built a small corral.

We rented a car one day and went to Canada's Wonderland, outside Toronto. The club and our host district took us on a tour of the St. Lawrence River, in the area of 1,000 islands, where the dressing got its name.

Many of these islands had very expensive and elaborate homes, particularly the ones you could see on the U.S. side of the St. Lawrence River.

We also took a day trip to Ottawa to visit my nephew Craig and his wife and two children. One was the same age as Naomi. Craig was in the Ontario Provincial Police, and he also had a service dog.

Craig was actually assigned to do undercover work, so was spending time among drug dealers, etc. He actually was quite dirty and unshaven – he had not bathed for two weeks.

Craig and his wife owned a pet cemetery and did funerals for pets. It was quite a successful business: they would do the service and arrange for the burial.

Craig had a hemorrhage, and problems in abdomen eight years after we were there, and he died at 52 years of age.

We also went into Smith Falls and visited with Terry McKintyre and his mother. Terry had worked for me; his aunt Marion Hamilton was also visiting.

Cher

In 1979, I married Chery Magyar, who worked for a bus company out of Lethbridge. Her parents farmed at Enchant; I had very little to do with them. We were married in a private ceremony before a notary public. We had a daughter, Naomi, born in 1981. She went to school in Taber and became very active in jumping, riding and other horse events, and was also very good in gymnastics.

Cher's mother gave Cher money to buy 160 acres of grassland and 20 cows. I continued to farm and run cattle, and Cher had her own horses – a lot of her interest lay with horses and riding.

When Naomi was six years old, we bought her an appaloosa mare for her gymkhana work. Cher and I separated in 1988 and 1989, and because of the difficult divorce I had with Marj, I was determined that would not happen again.

Naomi was attached to the farm, and it was obvious that it was the best place to bring her up. I transferred Cher's land around and put the home quarter, with the house and buildings in Cher's name.

This eliminated any cash settlement or maintenance and was the best arrangement that my legal council could direct me to do.

In 1980, I was advised by my accountant to form a limited company, so I put most of my land and holdings into Tim Brewin Ranching Ltd.

I allotted shares to Bev, Dan, Sandra and Dixie. This worked well, and all new acquisitions were done through the company.

In the late 1980s, interest rates went from 8% to 18% in two years. This put a tremendous strain on my farming operations, as well as Dan's.

Dan met Georgie Cassidy and lived for a while in Taber and Lethbridge. Georgie was a very nice girl. They moved to Calgary and bought a house and started their life together.

Dan and I rented land at Vauxhall that was irrigated by a large pivot; we grew soft wheat and malt barley. I took equipment from Purple Springs to Vauxhall.

In 1988, Dan enrolled in classes in Calgary. This left me and the trainee to do most of the work on the home farm, plus the Vauxhall land.

One of the people I had met on 4-H provincial council was Pat Bak from Grand Prairie. She was offered, and accepted, a job with the exhibition board in Lethbridge, and later with Canberra Foods in Lethbridge. I sometimes hired her to come and help me with harvest at the Vauxhall location.

Dan came home some weekends, whenever possible, but my work load was overwhelming.

I entered into a debenture loan and repayment plan with the bank. Dan, too, was having trouble meeting his obligations on his land debt. The bank offered us both a plan – putting everything into one operation, which was not a fair solution for Dan. He decided to let go of his land. It was very obvious he was very troubled over the bank's offer. He was afraid he was letting me down. He and Georgie came down from Calgary to see me and told me they did not think the farm was in their best interest.

Dan had also made his way through university in Saskatoon, and he wanted to go in a different direction, even though this went against what we had worked and dreamt for so many years. We both realized this was the best decision.

So, I told Dan that I, too, wanted to leave the farm and do something else. We arranged for an auction sale and sold off most of our equipment, cattle and other assets. I made arrangements with the bank to release my debenture loan, and to clear off any debt I had with the bank.

We had also won two lawsuits, one against our fertilizer supplier for loss of crop and damages, on the fertilizer application for two years in a row. The other was against S.M.I.R.D. Irrigation for flooding and damages they had done on my land.

The total of these lawsuits was over $25,000. I discussed all this with Pat, and we both decided moving to B.C. would be enough of a change, and we could start a life together out there.

We bought a conversion van with the $25,000. Pat also had a car, and a $21,000 cash settlement from her husband in the sale of their property. I paid monthly support for Naomi until she was 19.

Pat's husband was physically abusive to her, so she left the farm she had worked hard for. Pat and I were both on the provincial council. Her and two council members from Medicine Hat often traveled together to the 4-H centre in Wetaskiwin.

Dan was very involved when he was on the farm. He worked hard in the summer, but I did all the work in the winter. We had built up a cattle herd of over 300 head, and in 1982 and 1983 Dan went to university in Saskatoon. Rod and his son, Kerry had bought a large truck and semi-trailer and were often on the road with it.

I would hire Kerry to help me whenever he could. He was very capable and loved the farm work. I continued to get trainees each summer, but I spent a lot of time on the tractor, particularly in the spring.

In 1987, we rented the 640 acres at Vauxhall. It was 30 miles from home, so it was quite a distance to move machinery back and forth, but it was good land.

The owner of the land had vertigo and needed someone he could trust. We did very well on that land in the two years we farmed it.

I also traded some of the irrigation lands to other farmers, so I could grow sunflowers on clean land. Sunflowers are very easy to grow and showed a reasonable profit. I did not have a combine for them – in fact, only one person in southern Alberta did, and he had three of them. He would do custom combining on the sunflowers.

His combine had 32' headers, and he could harvest 160 acres in one day. They really yielded, and you had to make sure you had the trucks for him. I usually had at least six farm trucks that held 400 bushels, and four or five semi-trucks that each hauled 4,000 bushels available when he came.

You had to wait until after the first killing frost to harvest sunflowers, and sometimes we harvested them with snow on the ground. They were all delivered to the sunflower plant south of Burdett, which was 18 miles from my farm. This was where they made Spitz. The sunflower seeds were well sorted: the larger seeds were used for Spitz, and the smaller ones for bird seed. Spitz paid three times as much as bird seed.

When I delivered them, I often brought home screenings from the plant for my cows. To feed them to the cows, I would just open the truck end gate, lift the hoist and spread them out in a row.

Combine to Bev and Keith's

Keith Jones's family farmed at Balzac and were well-known for the purebred cattle they had. Bev continued her university in Edmonton. After Keith graduated, he lost his dad, I think it was 1984.

Keith, his brother and his mother took over the farm operations. Bev and Keith were married December 1984, and they lived on the farm.

I believe in was in 1985 that it was a very wet harvest for them, and they had trouble getting their crop off. Dan and I had been able to get ours done, so I decided to send my combine up to help Bev and Keith.

My brother Rod went up to operate it for me. I had a very large combine, and it was difficult to transport. I made the arrangement with my local New Holland dealership to transport it for me. It barely fit on his truck. Each large tire hung over the side by six inches. Rod helped them finish their harvest – he did appreciate the chance to operate a combine again.

He felt really needed, because he had left the farm himself. He appreciated the chance to get to know Bev again, and her husband Keith.

When my nephew Brent was in his late teens, he had several friends in the district that hung out together, and occasionally liked to party.

The four of them – Brent, Keith Hooge, Blake Fletcher and Tim Fletcher would sometimes end up at my place late at night. I would see a light coming up my driveway about 1am, and soon they were at my door wanting to party.

Occasionally, they would call me on the two-way radio first, but more often they would just come in. This would end up being an all-night-long event.

In the morning, I would make them breakfast before they went home. There was not point saying "no", because that just made it more of a challenge for them. It really was a lot of fun.

We did try to get even a few times after they got married, but I don't think their wives appreciated the noise and the work as much as I had.

Those get-togethers were very special to me.

Cher, Naomi and kids

Cher did not make it easy for the kids to visit. It was fine when Sandra and Dixie came to the farm, and all five kids were present. But sometimes when I took Naomi up to Bev and Keith's, to stay with her and the other kids, Cher would come up with stories why she did not want those visits.

I had many small thefts on the farm, of tools, fuel, etc. Most I did not solve, but two of them I do want to mention.

I noticed that my neighbour would have to quite often use his half-ton to boost his swather.

I farmed right beside him and seen this several times. One morning my battery was missing from my swather, and when my neighbour came to work, he started his swather without having to use his truck.

I went over to him and told him he had two choices: either bring me a new battery or bring mine back. He bought me a cheap one, but as mine was at least four yours old, I felt it was OK.

Sometimes tools would be missing from my equipment. Usually, we took them out at night; I often carried quite a lot of tools in my swather.

One day when I went home for dinner, they all went missing. One of Jack's hired men was using a truck that you could easily tell the tire treads on.

I could tell that truck had been in my field. I went over to him and asked him about my tools. He played dumb until I reached in the back of his truck and took out one of my pipe wrenches. He went on about how he had no tools. It was not up to me to supply him with tools. He got a good talking-to, but he had a habit of stealing.

Dan had bought his land in 1982. The Alberta government had come up with a scheme they hoped would get young people into farming, under what was called the Alberta Development Corporation. It was poorly thought through, however – poorly planned and implemented. In the end, it literally ruined and broke many young farmers. It was a 20-year loan of $200,000.

The lending agents were poorly-trained, and some, in fact, were dishonest. Every parcel of land was suddenly worth $200,000, whether it was profitable or not. The agents played with the numbers until it looked profitable. For instance, they would put down barley that was only worth $1.50 a bushel, and claim it was worth $4.00.

My farm at Purple Springs, approximately 1988

Most of the young farmers also had to get their dads to back them with a guarantee, often using land as security. Almost every farm son took out this government loan.

By 1990, 80% of them quit-claimed. Many of the agents bought some of this foreclosed land, once it was quit-claimed. The dads of the young farmers were not allowed to buy it back, and most of it was sold .50 on the dollar to large farmers, strictly on speculation.

Once, one of the agents at Taber bought 640 acres very cheap, but after several protests he had to re-sell it.

I had always been very careful not to include the home 160 acres of my property as security to the bank, therefore it always had a clear title. Dan's decision to go back to university has proven to be the best plan for him and Georgie, and he has done well. He and Georgie have three kids and a lifestyle they can be proud of.

Leaving the farm

Now my plans had to be switched to my future – where to move and what to do. I knew I wanted to continue ranching and working with cattle. I placed ads in some farm and livestock publications, to be a ranch manager. I also had a good contact with Bob Mitchell, agriculture advisor to the Bank of Montreal in B.C., and some opportunities became available. Some of these were:

1. The manager and administrator of a buffalo ranch at Ft. Smith in the N.W. Territories. I made many phone calls and inquiries, and seriously considered that opportunity, but it would have meant two years of part-time training and going to university in Yellow Knife. In the end, I would have mostly been in an administrative position, 25 miles from the ranch and the buffalo herd;
2. I also received an offer to manage the cattle herd at the Tatla Lake B.C. Ranch. I was contacted by Andrew Smith, an accountant in Williams Lake; arrangements were made for me to fly out for further discussions on a Monday morning in late 1989. On the Sunday night before, I got a phone call that I should perhaps delay my trip; the owner of the ranch and the bank were going back and forth with lawsuits; the owner eventually ended up getting charged with fraud, theft of cattle and equipment, etc. He had immigrated from Germany several years earlier and his wife had lots of money, and eventually the ranch was returned to her;
3. I received an offer from a lawyer, Jack Cram, in Vancouver, who had bought a 300-head ranch at Hedley, B.C. and was in need of a manager. I took Pat with me and we flew out and he gave us a proposal. He was missing 22 head of yearlings, and had the R.C.M.P. investigating them, thinking they had been stolen. When looking over his winter feeding area, I noticed he was watering his cattle in the river; I suggested that the cattle had gone through the ice and drowned. He would not even consider this, but next spring the carcasses floated down river to Keremeos, and actually blocked the river under a bridge. He was a very different person, and was eventually disbarred from law practice; we did not consider his offer for very long;
4. But we did visit with Don Adgerton at Princeton, who owned the Nico Wind Purebred Polled Hereford Ranch. His main business was a metal distribution business in Abbotsford, B.C., and he was quite well off. He only had 105 head of cattle that he showed all over western Canada, and I would be responsible for doing this. He and his wife also had three houses they rented out for short-term holiday stays, and they wanted Pat to run that business for him. I was not impressed with the quality of his cattle; but he did make me a good offer, and we drew up a program where we could improve his herd. I had a difficult time committing to his offer, though, even though he came to Lethbridge two or three times to see me;

Over the next three years, both he and Jack Cram tried to encourage me to manage their operations. Plans continued in the sale of mine and Dan's equipment, and settlement with the bank, which we held in March 1991.

In the meantime, I was contacted by Bob Gibson from Penticton. He had bought the Bobtail Ranch years earlier and was having a difficult time keeping good management and staff. The ranch ran 850 cows. The range was quite large, and it varied in elevation between 1,500 feet at the ranch headquarters, to 7,200 feet at Hedley Meadows.

The first manager Bob had after he bought the ranch, was Dave Ralston, who had to put together an excellent cow herd, and was a dedicated and knowledgeable manager. The problem was, both him and Bob had interest in the same girl.

Pat and I went up to Calgary and met with Bob and his girlfriend at their apartment. We spent the afternoon together, and had supper with them, where he made me a good offer to manage his ranch.

He said he made up his mind 15 minutes after we met, and he offered me the position.

The Bobtail Ranch had been in existence for over 90 years. It was originally a cattle and sheep operation, owned by a pioneer named Gardner. He sold in the 1950s to Joe and Farley Brent, who eventually lost it to the bank.

It was located 21km west of Penticton on Ridley Creek. It bordered the Penticton Indian Band on the east, the Green Mountain Road and the highway to Keremeos on the south, which also was the access to the Nickel Plate gold mine and Apex ski hill.

The Brent brothers had developed the ranch, and also used it as a recreation operation – a dude ranch. But it also had an excellent purebred cattle herd. They had put in dams, developed irrigation, stocked a large lake with fish, raised and released pheasant, built two very large homes, tennis courts and a swimming pool. There is a mountain named after them – Brent Mountain.

Bob Gibson offered me the full-time management position, where I would be fully in charge of the ranch, the accounts, irrigation and staff. He had the world-famous rodeo cowboy Kenny McLean as his cow boss.

There were four young people on his irrigation crew, Alfie George on the farm, along with a drug addict on the farm crew. Steve Roberts was a cowboy working under Kenny. Bob's offer included a small wage for Pat to do the books. I would be in charge of arranging for all cattle sales, buying bulls, etc.

He had an agreement with Kenny McLean to allow Kenny to own a stud, four brood mares, and have his own small business breeding horses.

Bob felt that Kenny had really taken advantage of this position, and one of the things Bob insisted on was that I was to fire Kenny within a year. The ranch also had a logging operation that I would also be in charge of – buying and selling the logs, as well as getting permits on both private and Crown land.

The ranch had a lot of land under irrigation, but also rented hay land from individuals from the Penticton Indian Band.

Tim and Pat 1993

A good relationship with the owners would be crucial. The north boundary of the ranch was up the McKaulty Road. Two large logging companies operated in that area.

There were four creeks that supplied water to the ranch, and there were four diversions and several dams.

This was one of the best ranches in B.C., but Bob Gibson also carried a lot of debt, and the ranch was very under-funded. He had over-extended himself when he bought the ranch. His girlfriend, Bridget Daniels lived on the ranch and received a wage.

Bob also had a sailboat which was very expensive.

At the time, Fred Lindsay was the manager running the ranch, and I was to take over on May 1.

My own farm sale was set for April 15, so the time frame did not allow me to go to Penticton to see the Bobtail Ranch. I told Bob I had to take another month, and for the next three weeks he phoned me every other day. He finally convinced me to take this position, without ever seeing the Bobtail Ranch.

This started out OK – a good move for me and Pat. I was able to settle everything on my own farm and arranged it that Naomi had a good home and Cher was looked after.

Two years later, the Alberta Wheat Pool sent me a cheque for the reserves and dividends I had accumulated over the years, amounting to $26,500. Cher was able to get hold of that cheque and deposited it in her bank.

In the end I decided not to press charges, as the one it would have affected the most was Naomi. However, I really needed this money, as I had to completely furnish the large house at the Bobtail Ranch. Pat did make sure I always had the money to make the support payments for Naomi.

After my farm sale, we loaded up the 24' horse trailer, the truck and the conversion van with some of my belongings and furniture, as well as some of Pat's furniture. We went to Bev and Keith's and left for B.C. around 5pm.

Dixie came along with us to help move onto the Bobtail Ranch. I had no reason to keep the horse trailer in B.C., as the ranch had its own stock truck and trailer.

So I agreed to bring the truck back to the farm for Cher and Naomi. There was a problem with the brakes on the truck, however. We got as far as Golden, and had to replace the front brake, drum, rotors, etc.

This delayed us for three days. I had taken the truck into my dealer in Taber before I left, and he was supposed to make sure the brakes were in good shape to make the mountain trip.

I went back to him when I took the truck back, but they would only pay about 20% of the bill.

We arrived at the Bobtail Ranch in the evening, and the manager's house was supposed to be empty, and ready for us to move into.

But Fred Lindsay was still busy building a new house in Kamloops and was behind schedule. We were put up in a two-bedroom bunkhouse the first night. It was over-run with mice, so I told Mr. Gibson we would not stay there again. He had built a log guest home the summer before, and we moved into that.

Bob had written up an agreement for me to sign as a full-time manager. I was to be fully in charge of the entire operation, hiring and firing a lot of men, and with full signing authority.

We did make a few changes; but it was agreed on Bob and I could work together.

It was agreed that Fred would stay on for two weeks to show me the operation. In fact, Fred only worked with me for one day.

It was Alfred George that I relied on. Steve Roberts proved to be an excellent cowboy – very reliable and capable.

When I got to Penticton, I met with Bob Mitchell, agriculture specialist for the Bank of Montreal, and Reg Enns, bank manager for the BMO in Penticton.

I already knew both these gentlemen. I knew Reg from Vauxhall, Alberta. They were very good at explaining the past history, and what I could expect at the Bobtail Ranch.

So much fraud and ranch failure had happened in B.C., particularly in the Cariboo and at Tatla Lake.

To get a full understanding, one should read *The Gang Ranch* and *The Gang Ranch Real Story*.

Also, *The Tatla Lake Ranch History*, and about Wayne Gardner, a logger and real estate agent on several ranches.

Cattle had been hidden under camouflage nets, so the bank could not see them. Many cattle were stolen. One bank manager compromised himself with logging fraud. Bob Gibson learned well from all that went on with the ranch foreclosures and debt.

Bob promised me a pension and long-term employment, but this was never honoured.

I have been asked many times if it was hard to leave the farm I had worked so hard for. Perhaps it was, but it was also a bit of a relief as well. I was under so much stress, and I knew I had to make changes.

I felt I had let my kids down some, but I also knew I had tried extremely hard, and had been successful for the most part. I had accomplished a lot in my area and had made many changes.

The biggest concern I had was with Dan. He, too, felt he had let me down, which was not true in any way. I had been able to see the kids all get a good start in life and was truly proud of them.

The night before I left the farm, I went up on the hill west of my place where I could see the area and my farm very well.

I actually felt a great sense of pride, of accomplishment and relief, as I knew I was leaving, and that I had done it. I thought, "It looks great," and I knew I could move on with support and with pride.

The Bobtail Ranch and ranching in general

The Bobtail was in financial difficulties and in danger of being foreclosed on. I accepted the challenge at the Bobtail and moved there in April the next year.

The ranch was owned by Bob Gibson; it had range and hosted 850 cross-bred cows. The cattle and range were well-looked after by Kenny MeLean, and the head cowboy Steve Roberts.

The condition of my hiring was I was to be fully in charge of all accounts and take over irrigation. Also, I was to lay off Kenny McLean within one year. Pat Bak and I moved there together; she was to do the payroll and books.

There were some good employees on staff, including Steve Roberts and Alfie George in charge of the farming and haying. The ranch rented hay fields from three different Indian families on the Penticton Reserve who I learned to trust and respect. One of the first challenges was the road block the Indians put on the main access road to the ranch.

Also, illegal logging was being done both by the Indians on ranch property, but also by the ranch on Crown land. I was in constant meetings with Forestry on that issue, and also on our grazing tenure.

The Indians used our range to run their horses both summer and winter. The ranch had the water rights to Farely Lake, which supplied domestic water to about 30 residences in Green Mt. Road. We also controlled the water levels and use of water on Brent Lake. But those residents soon decided they would support me when they respected the fact I was fair and decent to all water users.

Reserve residents Tammy and Joe Pierre had a big concern with kids on motor bikes chasing their horses. I gave them permission and unlocked the gate, so they could use the back access to our Crown range. Soon after, Joey stopped to tell me that they had solved that problem. They roped a couple of teenagers while chasing their horses.

They broke up their bikes and made them walk the six miles back to town. They told me where the kids' bikes were. I went and looked. Their bikes were all broke up and thrown over a 100-foot straight-down bank. Problem solved.

Some young members of the reserve were very involved in drugs but thanks to Abe Kruger, he kept them from the ranch.

In the fall of 1993 Bob said he could not meet expenses, not even payroll. He showed me promissory notes owed to him for spring 1994. Pat and I knew that three employees needed their monthly pay to make payments of their own on trucks, etc.

Pat had a $25,000 G.I.C. that was due to mature. We decided to lend that money to Gibson on the condition that he give us a post-dated cheque to repay it in October after he sold the calves, and also a promissory note for $25,000 plus 6% interest.

Even though we were in control of the bank account, ranch expenses and income, we were worried he would try to stiff us. When we sold calves at the O.K. Falls auction market he was there. The total calf sale income was $350,000. I had given Pat a $26,000 cheque on the ranch account.

Pat went to the office, got the calf cheque, took it to the bank and deposited it. She presented the $26,000 cheque for payment on the loan.

Bob was very pissed off when he went to the auction market to pick up the calf cheque and found out Pat had picked it up two hours earlier. He definitely intended to renege on his obligation to us.

Turn out on Crown range was April 15. In 1994, we turned out on that date. On April 24th Bob came to me and said he had a premonition and he wanted all the cattle rounded up and sold. This was an impossible task in spring.

With fresh grass and many of the cows 25 miles up on range, what had happened was that the bank had foreclosed on Gibson and the Bobtail Ranch. The B.M.O. asked me to be in charge of selling off the cattle, bulls and horses. I made arrangements with Bruce Wilcox and Wendell Monical to pay in April, 85% of the cattle using my cattle records, to determine numbers.

They were to pay the remaining 15% in November after roundup with more definite numbers. They were to provide the roundup crew. My condition was that they hire Steve Roberts to assist in the roundup, as he knew the range and the cattle. By then Steve was running his own operation with his brother at Lac La Hache. He had married my daughter Dixie. This proved to work out well as they had a successful 97% roundup. We had a reputation herd at the Bobtail and the cattle sold very well.

During my time at the Bobtail a lot of crime surfaced by neighbours, etc. Bob's girlfriend had a nine-year-old daughter, Mandy. An older lady who immigrated from Czechoslovakia was hired to babysit quite often. The babysitter had a 17-year-old son. A riding area and stable was owned by a single lady in Penticton, who went missing. Her body was found the following spring. This young man from Czechoslovakia was charged and convicted of her murder.

I had hired him for six days to change irrigation pipe as it turned out just days after he killed this lady. I had fired him and called Pat on the radio and told her to make up his cheque.

The ranch office was in our house basement. When he went to pick up his cheque, Pat would not give it to him until he gave her a social insurance number. They had quite an argument, but Pat also was a strong lady with a temper. Pat phoned his grandmother to come pick him up. When he went by the barn he stole a pair of Steve's cowboy boots.

It took three years to convict him and deport him.

Alfie and Helen George had a grandson disappear. He was searched for by police, neighbours and friends for over eight weeks. His body was finally located in the dump at Merritt. He had been killed by a friend because this friend had stolen a bike and was afraid Alfie and Helen's grandson would tell the police.

Helen attended every day of the six-week court trial. Due to an error in the court recordings some testimony was missing but because Helen had recorded everything, they were able to refer to her notes and her accurate documentation was used and played a part in the conviction of the guy who had committed the murder.

These two murders were very upsetting because they were so close to home. I have often wondered about the young man alone in the office with Pat.

We had a lot of rattlesnakes at the Bobtail Ranch; one of the irrigation changing pipe boys seen one he thought was dead. He picked it up and threw it at another worker. The snake hit the kid, fell to the ground and slithered away.

So much crime was going on at the Bobtail or around the ranch. The Penticton band members were known to be involved on drugs and the drug trade. We were working at the ranch when Penticton had the riots during Peach Fest. Cars loaded down with bricks and turned away by the police on a regular basis. Stores were ransacked and windows broken until the whole town was locked down and Peach Fest was cancelled for a few years.

When we left the Bobtail, we went on a nine-day cruise to Alaska and then I took on the job as manager for Les Madsen on his BX Ranch in Clinton. He promised all sorts of benefits such as shares in cattle, a pension, etc. For only two and a half months I did all the haying, riding and cattle care. He had purebred Red Angus and raised bulls, calving in January and February. He rented pasture from Mrs. Ogilvie (yes, the heir to Ogilvie Breakfast Foods.)

Anyway, the young bulls were riding the cows and other bull calves, and about 20 ended up with prolapsed rectums I had to sew up.

I was asked by the B.M.O., and also Andrew Smith, an accountant in Williams Lake, if I would take on the job as manager of the Fraser River Ranch. This ranch was really in disarray and I knew it would be a real challenge. It employed five people and some were taking advantage of the ranch.

Pat

Pat and I got along very well together. She helped out wherever she could: moving irrigation pipe, calving, haying and feeding cows. We were together most of the time. She also loved to garden, and soon had a beautiful flower bed. We worked together on the cattle records. Bob had everything on a computer, but you couldn't take that to the barn with you.

We entered every cow on a recipe card – all that cow's history.

Pat was well-accepted by my family, and well-liked. Gerald visited with us for a month in September and October, helping with the roundup and the ranch calf sale.

He and Pat became good friends. They both had to have their oatmeal porridge, were quite intellectual and loved to indulge in lengthy conversations.

My nephew Jim brought my brother Alfred to the ranch for a week that summer, too.

He and Pat also got along great. Alfred was 78 years old – he was in great shape and still had thick, black hair.

Pat made a point of telling him how well he looked, and that his brothers were all bald, but he still had a full head of hair.

Pat fixed up a special bedroom for Naomi. Dixie brought her to the ranch in July, and for three weeks at Christmas. Bev, Keith and the boys came out, and they also brought Naomi.

They had a bad accident at Field, B.C. and had to take my van home to Calgary.

In September, Pat and I traveled to Grand Prairie and met all her family. I got along quite well with her mom and dad.

Pat was very close to her dad. He was glad she was with someone who treated her well. Her parents often talked about their homesteading days – raising the family in Dixonville.

So, one day I asked if we could go see the homestead. Her mother and dad were very excited about showing the old farm. It was at the time Pat's parents were living in Brewyn. They had a remarkable garden and gave away many vegetables and a lot of produce to the neighbours.

Her mother won many ribbons and prizes at the Fall Fairs for many years. I met Pat's bother, Joe and his wife Pauline. Joe was a heavy-duty mechanic and had badly injured his back. Pauline was a nurse.

I met many of Pat's relatives. Most were farmers, so we did have a lot in common. I met Pat's son Les and wife Laurie, and her daughter Theresa.

Theresa had a one-year-old girl named Kristine. She visited us often over the years. She loved the swimming pool on the ranch.

Pat and her granddaughter were very close. It was thought that Theresa's husband was a drug addict, but Pat brought Theresa to the ranch for several months to get her away from that lifestyle.

I got along very well with Theresa as a father figure – her own dad just did not seem to care.

On our way home from Grand Prairie, we went to southern Alberta and Pat got to meet most of my family. She was well-accepted and developed a good friendship with my brothers and sisters-in-law over the years.

Pat was also a great grandmother to all my grandkids; I always cherished the time I could spend with Pat.

We both played a lot of tricks on one another. Her sister, Margaret and husband Lawrence visited in June for two weeks. Margaret's nickname was 'Bunny' and that's still the name I know her by.

Margaret was the Canadian ladies horseshoe champion for two or three years in a row. At the ranch, Kenny McLean was determined he could beat her at horseshoes, so many evenings were spent by the pool and the horseshoe pits.

We had close contact with many of our friends from Alberta. Joan Niblock and husband Larry came to stay with us for three weeks during roundup. He loved to ride and went with me on roundup many times.

He did not want to go home. When we said goodbye he told me he thought I had the perfect life, riding and working with cows in the mountains.

His final comment was, "And you actually get paid to do it."

Ted Youck and his wife and daughter visited for 10 days. Their daughter was the same age as Dixie. Dixie traveled back and forth from Alberta several times that summer. She lived with us for the most part. I think Steve had a lot to do with that.

Dan and Georgie brought two other couples to the ranch the following winter, and they used our place as a base to go skiing at Aspen.

Pat was a great organizer. When I got my first paycheque, she sat me down and said, "We're going to start saving for retirement right now," so $200 out of every cheque from that day on went into our retirement savings plan.

When I took the truck and trailer back to Alberta, Pat stayed at the ranch. This was during spring run-off when it washed out a lot of the Green Mountain Road – this was the main road to the ranch.

She got to know Bridget quite well. Bridget had a six-year-old daughter that loved to spend time with Pat around the swimming pool.

Bridget had her own horses and spent most of the time with them.

She actually proved to be a problem for me with the books and ranch expenses.

If I was short on funds, Bob was supposed to send money from Calgary, but that didn't often happen in time. He had the attitude that I was always to pay bills two months late, and I was not to pay interest on any account.

This was difficult, and I talked to a few of the suppliers to make these arrangements and apologize, explaining that this was the way I was supposed to run the business.

They were well aware of this, and told me, "Don't worry about this – it's all added on at the top of the account."

So, their interest was paid that way.

Our salaries were actually paid out of the Calgary office. Bob had a great dental plan and several other benefits, which was a big help to us.

Pat was a hard worker. She hated to waste time socializing with the other ranch wives, who often came to visit her. Pat finally sat down with them and told them, "I like you all, but I just plain don't like the coffee and visit."

Most of the maintenance and are for the pool also landed on Pat's shoulders, but everyone on the ranch benefitted from the pool.

Bridget did help out with that a lot, but the rest of the wives just took advantage of that benefit.

Steve Roberts was excellent with the cattle herd and at breaking and training horses. The young people doing the irrigation worked out very well that first year.

Pat, I and Alfie put up most of the hay, but the ranch still had to buy about 40% of the winter feed requirements.

That winter we hired a fellow named Tom to help us feed.

Alfie did not work for the ranch in the winter, so the feeding was left to me, Tom, Steve and Pat. It was mostly small, square bales that we fed to the 800+ cows, 100 yearlings and about 40 bulls and 40 horses.

We were short about 30 cows in the first roundup that fall, and Pat and I spent a lot of time looking for them. Just before Christmas, we went looking for a Christmas tree, and came across a large number of tracks in the snow. We followed these tracks for three miles in the truck, and came across 15 moose, and realized it was moose we had been tracking.

Steve later explained to me how to tell moose tracks from cow tracks.

Pat had diabetes, and always carried what she called a 'pen.' If she felt an attack coming on, she would inject glucose in her mouth. Several times I came into the house and found her passed out on the floor.

I would assist her to take the glucose. A couple of times she was right out of it, and I would have to use another source of sugar. On three different occasions, I found that forcing orange pop into her mouth would help bring her around, but when she did come around she would be really mad, spitting out that orange pop.

Helicopters and small planes at the Bobtail Ranch

When riding the upper range on the Bobtail Ranch, we would sometimes come across old sheep camps. When Gerald came out, we compared stories and looked up some of the history of the ranch. We found out that it was the original Gardener Ranch, which was the same operation that one of our hired men at the farm in Purple Springs told us about.

He had worked on it in the late 1930s. Bob Gibson made arrangements to buy the ranch in the early 1980s. He worked for a large oil company, and he hoped they would buy it from him, and he could turn a quick profit.

They did not go along with this scheme, and would not put money into the ranch, so Bob tried to take it on himself.

But he was always short of operating capital. He had been lucky that Dave Ralston had managed it for him and kept it afloat. Bob had many big ideas in life, such as playing the bagpipes. This also consumed a lot of his time and effort. He also took training and got his helicopter license.

In part, because Forestry and Lands were mapping out much of southern B.C., on our upper meadow at Hedley, there was a helicopter landing pad, complete with extra drums of fuel.

Bob, however, never became much of a helicopter pilot, and when I came to the ranch, his copter was being repaired in Abbotsford. He had crashed it and badly damaged the rotors.

It was very costly to repair, and it took more than two-and-a-half years to fix it. He tried to get me to fly with him, but I was warned not to.

I do not know what became of his helicopter - perhaps it was sold to pay for the repairs on it.

I did hire a helicopter on several occasions to look for cows and deliver salt to our upper meadows. The first time I went up in a helicopter looking for cows, we flew up and over Brent Mountain. I was just looking straight down, when all of a sudden there was no ground underneath us – just blue sky as we had flown over the edge of the mountain.

That was pretty alarming.

I did manage to show a profit at the Bobtail Ranch for two years, but after the bills were paid, the extra money did not go to pay down the debt. The bank manager phoned me about what I was going to do about this. All I could do was pass on to Bob that the two of them had to work out how they were going to proceed.

There had been a few airplane accidents on the range at the Bobtail Ranch over the years. There was a large draw and open area coming up out of June Creek at the base of Brent Mountain.

This was a very steep landscape, but it did not look like it. This draw often had a downdraft to it whenever there was a west wind. Many small planes flew into this without realizing the danger. They would realize too late that there was a problem, and that they could not climb out of it.

There were several stories of accidents in that area. Three years before I came to the ranch, there was a small plane with two aboard that went missing. It took six weeks to find the crash site, at the base of Brent Mountain.

The last fall I was at the Bobtail a plane with three men went missing and they found it crashed in the same area three days later.

They used my house as a base to drive up as close as they could to the crash site. I was able to help them some, as I had herded cows in that area, and knew a lot of the trails and roads, so could provide them with quick access.

Along the McNaulty Road, about four miles past where our trails into Hedley Meadows turned off, Lance and I were following the tracks of two bulls. As bulls sometimes did, they just kept going deeper and deeper into the trees.

We followed them, and all of a sudden came upon an old airplane wreck. It was from a crash, approximately 10 years earlier, when government surveyors were mapping the area.

Four men had been killed in that crash. They recovered the bodies, but the plane was too smashed up to try to salvage it.

We often hired a small plane to help us find cattle in the fall, usually using a pilot named Fred Wray. He operated a pilot training business out of Penticton.

He became a friend and would often come out to the ranch and ride with us on his little paint horse.

Fred was over 70 and had asthma quite bad. We always worried about him when riding with him, and really worried when we flew in his plane, but he was a very capable pilot.

One time he did really worry me. We were searching for cows in the Isontok Lake area, and all of a sudden he told me he had to turn back down the mountain toward Summerland.

He had flown into a steep area with a downdraft without realizing it.

We flew straight down the McNaulty Road and followed the highway to the airport at Penticton. The low fuel light was on for several minutes before we finally landed.

I actually was very glad I had Fred as my pilot that day.

Hedley Meadows

It was a four-mile trail from where we parked our truck at Mile 26 on the McNaulty Road, to our camp at Hedley Meadows. We had to use pack horses to take our supplies, salt, etc., into camp.

It is a special talent to properly use pack saddles, one I never did get good at. The camp trailer at Hedley Meadow slept four. The cattle did very well on those meadows in the summer. You could trail the cattle two different ways to get there: one up the McNaulty Road, or one going up from the Brown field over the top of Snow Mountain, and up to the trails at Hedley.

We usually made it a four-day trek and stayed there whenever we went up to Hedley Meadows.

In 1993, I unloaded 60 blocks of salt at different locations, using the helicopter to deliver them to the salt sites.

We covered them with tarps and this made our salt ventures much easier. The helicopter could only carry myself, the pilot and six blocks of salt.

One of the irrigators on the Bobtail Ranch was a fellow named Mark Peterson. Mark was 6'7" tall and weighed 300 lbs. He worked hard, but he also was diagnosed with depression.

Because of that, he could not live on the ranch, and had to live in a home in Penticton. The other employees used to tease Mark a lot, but Pat made a point of taking Mark under her wing, and he became a good friend for many years.

John Parsons was the local agricultural representative, and he got me involved with the local livestock association, which took in districts south from Summerland to the U.S. border, from Rock Creek west to Princeton. His office was located in Okanagan Falls.

He visited the ranch every other week that first summer, and advised me what fertilizer to use, and crops to grow, and so on. He also got me acquainted with the Conservation and Forestry personnel, as well as range agrologists.

I started going to the cattlemen's association meeting in June of 1991. Some of the local ranches were willing to help.

Allen Weins from Summerland, Alex Trebasket from Karemeos and Trevor Jolley also gave me good advice.

The veterinarian the ranch was using was Dr. McKenzie - his office was in OK Falls. Dr. Janice Waldie was the vet that would come out to the ranch on call from the vet clinic in OK Falls. She did our preg testing, and semen testing on our bulls.

Pat and I became very good friends with Janice. She, in fact, invited us to her wedding in Belize in 1996, but we were unable to go.

Willie Messersmidt had range on the south of our range; he worked on the Apex ski hill in the winter and left most of the ranch work to his wife. Willie seemed to be accident prone and relied on the Bobtail Ranch for help.

The Minton, or Aspen, guest ranch was at the southeast corner of the Bobtail range. A lot of problems surfaced with that dude ranch, as they tried to use our ranch as part of the guest ranch tours. They eventually got in trouble for lack of insurance on the dude ranch business.

Jamie McKay was an equipment operator for the Gormelly Brothers sawmill at Westbank. He was a grader operator for that logging company, so he knew the range. He also liked to ride, and Bob took advantage of this, and got him to repair fences on range without paying him.

I got along really well with the natives on the reserve, such as Basil Paul, Tommy and Joey Pierre, the Krugers and the Lasards. The Penticton Indian Band put up a road block on the Green Mountain Road that summer, to stop people from going to the ski hill. This also blocked the road to our ranch. I pulled out all the maps and figured out that the road to the reserve on Shingle Creek, that the band used, was partly on Bobtail Ranch property.

So, I went to one of the band council meetings, and pointed out that we could also block the road to the reserve. I won that one, and by the time I went home the block had been removed.

Bobtail Ranch had an excellent cattle herd of approximately 850 cows and 150 yearlings. Dave Rolston had started a cross-breeding program of Black Angus cross Hereford cows, by having the Hereford herd of the Brent family to begin with.

Bob had also taken advice from the Simpson Ranch in Alberta and introduced Charlois bulls as a terminal cross.

The calves usually sold for two or three cents per pound premium. Also, their Black Angus cross heifers were in demand. We ran approximately 15 Black Angus bulls, 10 Herefords and 20 Charlois. Our Charlois were bought at Henry Mann's annual sale in OK Falls.

Henry was a big fan of E.P.D,s (expected progeny differences) and you could rely on good, sound bulls. They were not all full-blooded Charlois, as he sometimes would introduce other breeds, such as part Simmental, to achieve higher rates of gain.

I further developed the cow herd during the four years I was manager, by buying high-performance bulls.

The first year, Kenny McLean liked to go to the bull sales, and did the bidding on the bulls. But he was easily influenced by neighbour ranchers and would sometimes over-bid our budget on some marginal bulls.

He was determined to buy Angus bulls from Wayne and Jill Hughes at Lumby.

We took two trips to their farm at Lumby and bought three two-year-old bulls. I selected two of them, and he selected one.

We took them home, and he tried to move them to the bull pen on horseback. They had never been handled by a horse before. The one he had bought went berserk. It got 'on the fight' and charged Kenny and his horse.

It sent them both flying, injuring Kenny and the horse. It was obvious that the bull would hurt someone, so I returned it to the Hughes.

The ranch owned seven horses, and Bridget owned two that she used to take part in English riding. Kenny and Paula owned approximately 15 horses, and Bob himself owned two.

Steve was the one that did all the horse shoeing, and he broke most of the ranch horses. He would always go to the barn about 6am and feed the horses, so that the saddle horses were fed and ready to go to work at 7am.

Kenny and Paula took a trip to Texas for two months one fall. Shortly after they left, one of their own mares got quite sick. I took it to the vet in Penticton, who suggested I take it to a horse vet in Kelowna.

The horse was plugged up—it had impaction. The vet, Sheila, kept it at her clinic for two months, and finally the horse improved.

Kenny had left instructions with Steve that he was to go check the brood mares which were still up on range. Steve found a young mare, dead. She had caught her head in a log. When we reported this to Bob, he went berserk. It turned out that this horse was one he had bought from Chunky Woodward. It was out of the famous Peppy Sam stud, and he had paid quite a bit of money for it.

At first Bob tried to blame Steve and I, but I finally let him know that we never even knew he owned this horse, and why would he allow it to run with the brood mares?

He finally put the blame where it belonged – on Kenny and Paula.

When Kenny cam home from Texas, he was pulling a horse trailer with four young horses. I think her dad had given them to Paula. The horses were penned in the horse trailer, two in the front part and two in the back, with just a short petition between them.

Kenny had not paid a lot of attention to these horses, and when he stopped at the Canadian border, he found that the horses in the back had eaten most of the tails off the two front horses. I do not think he was feeding them properly, and the horses simply got hungry.

All four were in very poor shape and took some time to recover.

That fall, we had a very successful sale in October. Most of our calves were sold to local feed lots, and the heifer calves were sold to a rancher at Rock Creek.

We started calving in March. Pat and I checked the cows at night, and Kenny and his crew looked after them in the daytime.

I remember one time, coming home from town and seeing a cow calving as we came up the road. I told Kenny about her, but he just ignored it and didn't go look. At quitting time, I made him bring her in to check her. She had a set of dead twins inside.

Kenny almost got sick and thought I should be the one to deal with her. I simply said, "Kenny, you just found out the difference between 'cow boss' and 'manager,'" and made him clean up his own mess.

The next spring, Steve told me he was leaving the ranch - he and his brother Bruce had taken on operations for Iris Wright at Lac La Hache.

When Steve told Bob, Bob gave him a lecture about how wrong he was, and how he'd never make a success of ranching on his own.

It's ironic that today the Bobtail Ranch is still in bank foreclosure, and Steve is running a very successful ranching operation.

Steve and Dixie were married and have three sons and a daughter. They have done very well and are highly respected. Steve was a pick-up man at many rodeos. I honestly believe that Steve is the most capable cowboy I have ever seen, both with cows and horses. He is also very excellent with his cattle dogs.

Just before Steve left, I hired Rick Petrie. He was great on the farm and could also ride and work with the cattle.

Rick and his wife, Bonnie, had two boys the same ages as Bev and Keith's youngest sons. Rick and Bonnie also became great family friends to all my family, and Pat and I to theirs.

When we came to the Bobtail Ranch, one of the irrigators who was also hired to help feed cows in the winter, was Mark Peterson.

Pat and I made sure that Mark knew he was an important part of the crew. He would often visit with us. His parents lived in OK Falls, and we got good support from them.

The third year at the Bobtail, Mark went missing, and no one knew where he was. Everyone looked for him, and the police put out a bulletin to try to find him.

After two-and-a-half weeks, Mark showed up at our door. He asked me not to contact his parents, or anyone, but asked to stay at our place for the night. He explained that what had happened was that he had a girlfriend.

She had been previously living with another guy, and asked Mark to help her move her belongings. When Mark showed up at the door, this other guy met him with a rifle.

It scared Mark, and he went in his car in the bush for the two-and-a-half weeks. He was afraid to go into town and asked if he could stay with us for a few days, and we said yes, with the agreement that we could phone his folks.

He agreed, and they said they'd leave him alone for a few days. After four days, they came to see him, and spent the afternoon with him.

Mark eventually went back to their home, and a week later came to us and wanted our opinion. He wanted to come live and work at the ranch. He had taken himself off all his medication, to find out if he could function on his own.

He did not feel the treatment he had been receiving had been getting him any better, and said, "I will either get better or go the other way."

We supported him in this decision, as did his parents. It was the smartest thing Mark could have done. Within six months, he had another girlfriend that he was living with. He did good work on the ranch, and truly learned to function on his own.

Mark had a small Hyundai car, and would drive around town with his head out the sun roof. We would be in town, and all of a sudden would hear him calling our names. We'd look around and see his little red car with Mark's head sticking out the roof. Mark became a lifelong friend.

Alfie's grandson lived in Merritt, and he turned up missing. Everyone looked for him, and they found his body in the dump. One of the people who searched for him was a so-called friend who turned out to be the guy who killed him.

It was over a bicycle that the friend had stolen. He was afraid that Alfie's son would go to the police. This was very hard on Alfie and his wife, Helen. Helen attended the trial every day in court, and she wrote down everything that was said. In the end, the defense differed with the trial lawyer on some of the testimony.

The court asked Helen for her notes, and it helped convict the killer, who was sentenced to life in jail.

After the first month at Bobtail, Bob asked Pat to do all the accounts. He was a real big spender, and he paid Pat $300 to do this. We hired a man from Penticton to pick rocks and help out at the ranch. I gave him a paycheque for $210, but he somehow changed it to $2,100.

He changed the amount, took it to the bank, and somehow the teller at the bank cashed it.

When the cancelled cheque came back to Pat, she noticed it right away. We went to the bank and they agreed it was the bank's error and reimbursed the ranch's account.

They told us the teller would be laid off, but first they put in a buzzer in all the teller stations that was connected to the police station. The very next day, the same idiot came in with another altered cheque and went to the same teller. She pushed the buzzer, and the police were there within minutes and arrested the idiot.

Bridget occasionally hired a lady to clean her house, and sometimes babysit Bridget's daughter, Mandy. This lady had an 18-year-old son, who Bridget talked me into hiring to help with the irrigation for a week.

There was a woman who owned a riding stable in Penticton who went missing, and this boy was seen with her wallet.

He claimed he had found it. Because they could not prove anything else, he was not charged. The next spring the woman's body was found in the bush. The coyotes had been at it, but they could still identify it.

They were able to prove this boy had been seen in the area. He was arrested and eventually convicted and sent back to his home country, which was Czechoslovakia.

He truly was a bad dude. When Pat paid him off after he worked for me, he came to the office, which was downstairs in our house. They got into a heated argument, but because he did not have a SIN number, she would not pay him. He also demanded more money from Pat.

Pat backed down from no one, and the boy finally left. He stopped at the horse barn to phone his mother to come pick him up.

Steve kept a pair of cowboy boots at the barn, and this little idiot stole them.

When investigating the murder, the police came to my office and asked to see all my records. This guy had $41,000 in his bank account. It turned out he was dealing drugs. He told the police that he earned the money working on the Bobtail Ranch.

I got quite a chuckle out of that and told the police that I must have been paying very well, since he had only worked for me for one week.

Soon after he left the ranch, the kid phoned us and said he was in the hospital in Kelowna. He had his SIN and wanted Pat to meet him in the park in Kelowna. She felt it would wrap up her payroll and was going to meet him.

I stopped her, but I always worried about the argument he had with her in the office, and about what would have happened if she had met him in the park in Kelowna.

He had killed one lady – would he have done something to Pat, too?

During his trial, he was on TV after he was sentenced, with him coming out of court and laughing and fingering the police.

It was very interesting, the four-and-a-half years managing the Bobtail Ranch.

It was truly a good operation, but needed a lot of upgrades: new equipment, and so on. Bridget at times could be very helpful, and other times very difficult.

She would put on dinners and get-togethers for all the ranch employees on special occasions. She also, however, interfered with the ranch employees, the horses and more.

Some of the men would go out of the way to deliberately aggravate her, particularly when it came to feeding the horses.

At times, it felt like I was more of a babysitter trying to walk a tightrope, between her and managing the ranch.

One day, Bob headed off to Calgary. Bridget had driven him to the airport, and she told me he was very annoyed with Kenny and Paula and said I was to lay him off. Apparently, he had a meeting with them the night before he left and was not happy with the outcome of that meeting.

I was supposed to pay Kenny off, using the agreement that Bob claimed he had with them and their horses. I had never seen any agreement, so I told Bridget that I needed a copy of it. She faxed me over an agreement that I'm sure had been written up in a big hurry, and never had any real teeth to it.

Kenny and Bob's understanding had been put in place long before I came to the ranch. So, I told Bob that he had to be present when I talked to Kenny, who obviously had a different understanding as to what he was limited to do – feed for his horses, pasture, etc.

Kenny was not happy. And he told me he was giving me six weeks' notice and was quitting.

Kenny could be a very nice person. He certainly was very respected as a bronc rider – he was world champion on the rodeo circuit

He truly was highly regarded in the world of rodeo. If only he had been able to control his drinking – that really held him down when he was getting older.

I had several talks with Kenny. He was a great instructor to cowboys in bronc riding, and in fact, all rodeo events. He received many awards and trophies.

He also loved kids. I always suggested to him that he should work with young people, as he would have been very good at it. However, his drinking always was a problem, that he could not, or would not, try to overcome.

Kenny and Paul left, and moved over to the exhibition facilities at Princeton in the spring of 1992.

Part way through turnout, Steve told me he was also moving on. Rick moved back to Saskatchewan, and this left me without a cowboy crew.

There was a neighbour named Myrt, who had previously worked at the ranch for Dave Ralston.

Her husband, Ken, who was a conservation officer who came and helped me out. I also hired other friends and part-time help. I put 'help wanted' ads in the paper, and got a reply from Ken O'Reilly from Tatla Lake, along with great references. He sounded ideal.

I asked him to come in for an interview, which he did. He brought along letters he claimed were from his boss at Tatla Lake, giving him glowing reviews.

I agreed I would hire him as soon as he could provide me with a criminal report for the R.C.M.P. A week later he showed up with all his belongings and a girlfriend, but no criminal check. He used every excuse to avoid going to the R.C.M.P. and getting the criminal check.

I finally took him to the R.C.M.P. in Penticton, and they arranged for a report to be sent to me. When it came, there were a lot of minor offenses, such as petty theft and fraud.

I had a long talk with him and hired him on a one-month trial. During this time, he got in very good standing with Bridget and Bob, but for sure he was a real dud as a cowboy.

He did, however, put me in contact with another cowboy from Tatla Lake named Sean Barrett. Sean was a good man, and certainly very capable, but he, too had a bit of a drinking problem. He seemed to be able to control it, however.

I also hired Lance Trebasket from Keremeos, who was a good cowboy. Lance's dad and I had become good friends the first year we came to Penticton.

His dad and uncle have a ranch at Keremeos. They were both very active on the Native council in and around the Okanagan.

I was in the bar with Alex and his brother when a few neighbours came in one evening. Alex had been bragging that he had all his cows in so he could relax. One of these neighbours came up to him, sat down, and told Alex that he had seen six of Alex's cows coming down the road and opened the gate for them so they could come on home.

Alex was truly embarrassed and sat there for the rest of the night saying, "Never tell anyone you have all your cows in. Make sure you always say you're out a couple, so you don't look foolish when someone else finds some of them."

This Ken O'Reilly proved to be far less of a cowboy than I needed. He wore green garbage bags whenever it rained, as he did not even own a raincoat. One day I told him he had go to cow camp up at Hedley Meadows and stay there for four days and check the cows and the range.

He left with two horses, and when I asked him why he was taking two, he said one was to use as a pack horse. He could not even put on a pack saddle, so I made him take extra saddle bags.

His girlfriend was away, and yet he packed meat and supplies for two.

One of the regular bar girls in Summerland phoned the morning he left, and asked Pat to give Ken a message that she wouldn't be able to go to Hedley Meadows with him.

He was gone for four days, and when he come back he had lots of wild stories about grizzly bears and cows stuck in creeks, and so on.

The next Monday morning I took Sean, Ken and Rick up to Hedley Meadows to check everything out. Sean told me that Riley had taken another lady from Penticton up with him the week before.

The first night at Hedley, I poked through the fire pit and trash, and found a partly-burned fancy red nightie. The next morning, I told Ken and Sean to get breakfast while Rick and I saddled the horses.

We took the fancy nightie and hung it on Ken's saddle horse. He was quite annoyed when he seen the burnt garment. It was the brunt of a lot of jokes. He was teased for three days straight.

When we got back to the ranch, I told him he was being laid off. This was early October.

He played the landlord and tenets act and was able to stay in the house at the ranch until December 15. Bridget was very angry because I had evicted him just before Christmas.

That October we held a ranch calf sale right on the ranch. We put on a huge pancake breakfast. There was close to 300 people at the sale, so it was very successful.

We had also had a great round-up with 97% of the cows gathered before the sale.

Pat and I went to Alberta in November, and before I left I drained all the irrigation pipes, and left instructions how everything was to be fed. We had 120 yearling heifers that were in their own pen along Ridley Creek.

I had installed new automatic waterers that summer, so water was not a problem.

It has been an open fall, and there was still a lot of green growth on the hay fields. The day we left, Bridget decided the yearlings should be put on the hayfields at the Paul Field, which was one-and-a-half miles from the corrals.

So, she had Lance and Sean reconnect all of the 8" mainline pipe, all one-and-a-half miles of it. This was to get water to the Paul Field so the yearlings could drink. The next day it turned really cold: 20 below.

I got a phone call in Alberta from Sean, saying that most of the yearlings had wondered off and were on the reserve, and the pipes were all frozen. We headed right back home.

Sean and Lance had unlatched a lot of the pipe, but more than 40 8" 40-foot-long pipes were frozen and split. Some of it we could weld, but the next spring I had to replace a quarter of a mile of expensive pipe.

Also, Sean and Lance were only able to locate about half of the yearlings.

The next day Lance and I went riding on the reserve and found all but 27 of those yearlings. They were on the east side of Ridley Creek. We could not find the other 27. They day before Christmas, these 27 head wandered up the road. I believe Tommy and Joey Pierre had found them just above Penticton and had brought them home for me.

The Natives loved to sneak on the ranch property to fish in Brent Lake, usually by cutting the fence. So, Bob locked all the gates to try to stop the Indians' access to Crown land above the ranch. He also bought a huge gun safe and had it delivered.

All these things annoyed the Indian band. Abe Kruger often visited with me and supported me with any problems I had with the Natives.

He was a very large man, and most of the Natives were afraid of him. He also loved to play jokes and tricks on all my employees. Anyway, I gave Abe a key to all the locked gates and let him know I wanted to work with him and the Native band council.

When they blocked the road to the ranch from Penticton, we could get access to the ranch by way of Summerland.

We got to know some of the conservation officers in Penticton and Summerland. We sometimes encountered bears, cougars, etc. when riding. I asked one of these officers what I should do when riding, for my own safety.

He told me to carry a gun at all times, even though it may not always pass inspection.

The third year we were at the Bobtail, Pat informed me she was going to be gone for the day. She left at 5am and said she might be back late at night but would not say where she was going.

What she had done was, she read all the regulations and became fully familiar with all the rules and regulations of bringing a pistol to Canada from the U.S.

She went down to Wenatchee, bought a 22-caliber pistol and took it to customs at Osoyoos, where she was told she could not bring it into Canada.

She produced the regulations, which said that she could in fact do so if the R.C.M.P. signed for it and accompanied her to Canada customs. They could have it cleared there, and then deliver it to the local R.C.M.P. in Penticton.

None of the customs people in the R.C.M.P. were aware of this wording in the law. They phoned Ottawa and found out that Pat was, in fact, correct in her interpretation of the rules.

Eventually, they all signed off on it, gave her the gun and gave her two hours to report to the R.C.M.P. in Penticton.

She met this deadline with less than 10 minutes to spare. The R.C.M.P. brought the gun to the ranch, and personally delivered it to her. The next day, the sergeant in charge of the Penticton R.C.M.P. came to the ranch to sign off on the gun so we could keep it in our house.

He said Pat had interpreted the rules correctly, and everything was legal. She gave me that gun for my birthday. I asked her why she went to all that trouble. It was because she had went to the Rod and Gun Club in Penticton and asked for their help in purchasing a pistol.

The president of the Rod and Gun Club was very arrogant. He said he would help her lawfully own a gun but said that you can buy one in the U.S. and said, "The Rod and Gun Club would help you if you were real nice to me, and if I help you enter into Canada."

She told him to go to hell.

Taking over management at the Bobtail Ranch was a huge challenge. The ranch was in need of a lot of upgrades. Pat and I took over the ranch during spring calving.

There was a problem with scours and pneumonia in the young calves. The cattle watering facility needed repairs and upgrades. The fencing and corral repairs had been neglected.

The irrigation had not been stored, or proper attention paid to it. There was no one in place to handle any of the repairs, and maintenance of machinery and equipment was virtually non-existent.

The cattle herd was under the care of Ken McLain and Steve Roberts, but a lot of work was needed on the trails and on a turnout program.

Fred Lindsay had been the manager, but only spent two days with me. I had been told he would stay on for at least a month, but he already had a job in Kamloops with B.C. Livestock. He had no further interest in the Bobtail Ranch, or in helping out Bob Gibson get his operation in order.

Pat and I spent many hours going over records, deciding the best way to move the ranch forward. Bob seemed to have little interest and virtually no money to put into the ranch, and basically just did not seem to care.

Pat's and my first projects were calving, turnout and the irrigation. The ranch employed four young people to do the irrigation, two men on the farm crew, a cow boss and a full-time cowboy.

Bob Gibson had bought the ranch six years earlier from the bank. It had been owned by Joe and Farley Brent, who Brent Mountain is named after. They ran a purebred Hereford of 800 head. The cow herd was a very good one, with mainly purebred Hereford cows.

Most of the irrigation was done by 3" hand-lines irrigation pipe and 1.5 miles of 5' wheel line. There were five main pumping systems, which consisted of eight dams with 6" electric pumps.

Irrigation lines were only moved once a day and covering the hay fields was very slow and inefficient.

The hay fields were seeded to a mixture of alfalfa and Timothy grass. They were in poor shape and not very productive, and the machinery was also in poor shape.

Most of the baling was done by 5' Heston round belt baler, and a 4' Bear Cat round baler. The hay was cut with a New Holland 10' disco mower, and the hay was raked with a Fern Lande 6' rake and a small 35 horse power Massey tractor.

There was a heated work shop, but very few tools. I had brought along all my tools from my farm, and Pat and I spent the first two weeks putting together a plan on how to move the ranch forward.

We were very fortunate to have Alfie George to help us and give us direction with the irrigation and hay.

Kenny and Steve Roberts were very capable with the cattle herd and turnout. The Crown range went from an elevation of 1,500 feet at ranch headquarters, to 7,200 feet at Hedley Meadows.

Bob was very little help in giving us direction on how to operate the ranch. His girlfriend was Bridget Daniels – she lived on the ranch and was paid a good salary. He lived in Calgary and visited the ranch about once a month for a few days but was not active in the ranch operations.

It was obvious that most of the hayfield needed to be worked up and re-seeded. Alfie was put to work doing this, and we also had to overhaul all the equipment and get it ready for haying.

One of the big problems was that the machinery dealers in Penticton were poorly equipped to supply repairs for the machinery.

I soon made arrangements to order all my repairs from the New Holland and Case dealers I knew in Taber and have all the parts flown to Penticton. Otherwise it was often 8-19 days' wait to get the parts through the dealers in Penticton.

Alfie came to work at 6am every day, but left at 4pm, so was not always available for swathing or baling. One of the men was very poor with the equipment, and with helping Alfie. We laid him off the first week, and I hired local help.

It was also important that I get to know the range and the cattle movement. We moved the cattle onto range by four different turnout trails and roads. One was up over Brent Mountain, one was over Snow Mountain and to the Hedley Meadows. It was two weeks before I went up the main range. A lot of work was needed to cut out and maintain new trails to facilitate the use of the land and range.

We rented hay lands from four different land owners on the Penticton Indian Reserve – different areas we used to turnout to utilize the different bulls.

We kept the Hereford bulls separate from the Angus and the Charolais bulls. We did have some problems with cougars and black bears.

One of the problems was that the dead calves and cows were usually dumped in one area. That encouraged the bears and eagles to feed on the carcasses from these dead animals. It was also obvious that the corrals and winter feed areas needed better water troughs and corral upgrades.

I purchased five new concrete automatic waterers and installed them on concrete pads. We also upgraded the corrals and sorting areas and were able to put up approximately 65% of the feed we needed for that first winter. We purchased the other 35%, mostly from local ranchers in Summerland and Keremeos.

The majority of this was small square bales that were stored in a large barn and hay shed.

It was very fortunate that my brother Gerald came and worked for me the first two months that first fall.

Jamie Mckay did a lot of the fencing for me the first few years. We also had very poor vehicles to do the irrigation, and the stock trucks were in terrible shape.

I soon became good friends with a mechanic in Summerland – he kept my vehicles in reasonable shape.

The four main lakes and dams we used for irrigation were Brent Lake, June Lake, June Creek and Deschamp Creek. All of these dams had been poorly maintained, and we had to remove lot of logs and debris from them.

When cattle were moved to Hedley Meadow, there was a trailer and cow camp we used there, and there were also trails over Snow Mountain, as well as a Forestry lookout tower on Brent Mountain that had a good heater and cook stove. Most of the rest of the range we would access on a one-day ride from the ranch.

Steve was a very capable cowboy, but Kenny was often gone to rodeos from Thursday to Sunday.

Truly, there were some challenges at the Bobtail Ranch, but it was also obvious that it had been a good operation with a lot of potential. One big challenge was finding and keeping good employees. Another was enough money to pay the bills.

With good planning, we were able to get through the first summer and plan ahead for a second year. For the next four years we had good calving results and good calf prices.

However, it was discouraging to see that so much money was wasted; and very little went back into the ranch for improvement or upgrades.

Bob spent very little time at the ranch, and we seldom seen him. Pat and I were fully in charge, and we planned and made many improvements.

We got along very well with the neighborhood ranchers, and with the cattle associations, and with Forestry and the range agrologist.

I was able to increase the amount of range, to where we were running 950 head by adding the Messerschmitt grazing permits, and the Stemwinder Range. The ranch was bordered on the south by the Green Mountain Road and the highway to Keremeos, as well as the Aspen Ski Resort and the Nickle Plate Gold Mine.

The north boundary was the McNaulty Road, and the east boundary was the Penticton Indian reserve and the road to Summerland.

We did not share range with anyone else. Jack Howard had 50 cows on range to the north.

Isnoltly Lake and Clark Lake pastures were used for early turnout, as was Roddy Flats, Augur Lake and June Creek pastures. The cattle were turned out on May 15. It was an easy ranch to move cattle on.

The main problem was that a lot of logging trucks also used the roads on Crown range, and often gates were left open.

We did have some theft of calves, but Conservation and constant riding did keep that under control.

We had a very large swimming pool, tennis courts, fishing and lots of recreation.

Weeds were a big problem; common weeds were Hounds Tongue, Canada Thistle, Wild Mustard and Burdock.

Pat put together an excellent system of recording: keeping records on every cow and calf. Bob had used his computer, and had his own system, but it was not efficient or user-friendly.

He expected us to take all the computer sheets to the corral when we worked cows and enter the records at the chute. This was time-consuming and subject to a lot of errors.

Pat set up every cow on a recipe card, all numbered and in sequence. This worked very well – every animal had their history on an individual card.

The next big problem we had to solve was drinking facilities for the cows. The water lines were only buried three feet deep, so were subject to frost. That first summer we dug up almost all the water lines in the corrals and cattle yards, and buried them all six feet deep.

I also installed new concrete heated water troughs. The older metal water troughs were not property grounded, and many animals drinking from one got an electric shock. It was an easy fix to properly put in round rods, and ground every trough, but it was time consuming.

The water intake to provide the drinking water also had to be redesigned. It was too shallow and subject to freezing. I put in one continuous-flow water trough to the heifer pen, with a ¾" water line that flowed through the trough and simply drained back into the creek below the trough.

This worked very well. Before, they had chopped a hole in the creek for the heifers to drink from. This was very slippery for the heifers. With this improvement, the winter feeding worked much better.

We still fed a lot of small square bales. I did not mind that too much because it gave you a chance to see every animal as you fed.

We usually finished feeding by noon each day. I had a crew of four to help with the feeding, and it was all done by tractor and wagon, using small square bales.

There were two ladies that lived along the McNaulty Road. They boarded problem kids. It was good income for them. They usually boarded 8-10 boys at a time and home-schooled them. These ladies had about 10 cows, but no bulls. They would buy apple pulp and put it in the corrals to entice our bulls in to breed their cows.

This proved to be a sore point between us. I eventually had to get Forestry and Conservation in to put a stop to this.

Many problems surfaced at the Bobtail because of things like crime and theft.

Most of this was an easy fix but needed more support from the ranch owner. Bob would not pay much attention to the ranch. Because of this, the operation was at times quite stressful. The sad part was that the Bobtail Ranch was truly a great operation. I still think of it as one of the best ranches in B.C., but it did lack support from the owner and his family.

Bob hired various bookkeepers and accountants, but they interfered more with the men, and did not really support the ranch. His main accountant was a vegetarian who did not support the ranch or any beef operation. The last year at the Bobtail Ranch, Bob hired his sister Gail, and brother-in-law Allen to help out.

This was a positive step, but he always had some scheme that he wanted them to help put into place.

Unfortunately, the bank slowly withdrew its support from the Bobtail Ranch. This proved to be the downfall of the ranch. In the fall of 1993 Bob could no longer meet his obligations and payments at the bank. He could not meet payroll.

Pat and I lent him $25,000 for three months, but the next April the bank foreclosed on the Bobtail Ranch.

Our turnout was April 15. We had all the cattle out on range by May1, and on May 6, Bob came to me and asked me to get the cattle back in because he wanted to sell them. He claimed he had a premonition. He had, in fact, been foreclosed on by the bank.

It was an impossible task to round up all the cattle in May. I made arrangements with Bruce Wilcox and Wendell Monical to pay us 85% of the value of the cow herd, based on my records and cattle numbers. The cows would then be delivered by November 1.

The last 15% would be paid based on actual cattle numbers that we got in. This worked very well, and we were ale to round up 95% of the total numbers of cattle.

In April and May, when word got out that I was leaving the Bobtail Ranch, I got three different job offers within a week. One was managing the Bar X Ranch at Clinton, to begin July 15. Another was managing a ranch in Princeton, and the third was to manage a ranch at Redstone.

The Bar X position at Clinton seemed to be the most attractive for us, so we accepted that position and left Steve Roberts to round up the Bobtail cattle.

Bar X Ranch

This position offered me a good salary, and the opportunity to run 25 cows of my own, with full management of the operations.

That ranch was owned by Les Madsen from Kelowna, who manufactured chain link fencing. He would bring his welders from Penticton shops, to Clinton for three days every week to do work on the ranch. He paid them very little – usually a steak supper and a bottle of beer on a Sunday afternoon.

The Bar X Ranch only had 150 cows, but I was fully in charge of the cow herd, the haying and cattle movement. Pat and I had decided in January and February of 1994 that we wanted to be married on the Bobtail Ranch, so we made arrangements for our wedding on June 4. We planned a honeymoon to Skagway, Alaska on a cruise ship for nine days.

Dixie stayed at the Bobtail and looked after it while we were gone. When we got back to the ranch we hired a moving truck and moved all our stuff to the Bar X Ranch in Clinton.

We had 80 people at our wedding. We put up a large tent and hired caterers. Most of my family came out – Frank and Colleen, Gerald and Marg, my sister Eleanor, my five children and all my grandkids.

Dan was my best man, and Pat's sister Bunny was her maid of honour. Bunny's husband Lawrence and Pat's parents also came and stayed for three days. It was a good time for everyone to get to know each other. Most of our guests were neighbours, or people who had worked for us.

I was very proud of the work and improvements I did at the Bobtail Ranch, and Pat was very proud of all she did, including the beautiful gardens and flower beds.

I only stayed at the Bar X Ranch for two-and-a-half months. Les did not live up to his promises. From there, we were unsure what we were going to do. We actually looked at buying a bed and breakfast operation in Peachland, which had a large number of walnut trees on it. We thought it would be a real challenge for us.

However, in September we were offered a position at the Fraser River Ranch near Williams Lake. It was a full management position, and we accepted it.

The ranch was owned by Reinhart Bradner. This ranch also held many challenges, but Pat and I ran that operation, plus the Buckskin Ranch and the Springfield Ranch, for 30 years.

Rodeo years

As a member of the Taber rodeo committee and a director of the Taber exhibition board, I spent a lot of time with the other directors and board members.

I also got to know many of the cowboys and rodeo contestants. I usually worked at the timed events end of the rodeo arena. I made contact with a lot of the professional cowboys, and we often socialized together after the rodeos. I got to know most of the bull fighters and the rodeo clowns.

One I became very good friends with was Kelly Lacosta. He worked as a bull fighter in rodeos all over the U.S. and Canada. He and his wife also had a western store in Medicine Hat that I often shopped in.

After Kelly got hurt, he spent most of his winters doing leatherwork. He spent his summers in Medicine Hat or traveling the rodeo circuit. He sold memberships in his store to purchase western wear, allowing you a 20% discount on anything bought in his store. He was well-known for things like his bull whips and head stalls.

Pat and I visited him in Scottsdale, Arizona when we traveled there in 1993. He had us bring him six 15' long bull whips. Pat brought back a lot of leather, and she made me some chaps, some leather curtains for the bathroom, and more.

On that trip, we rented a little red Mustang convertible for a week, traveling around Phoenix and area.

Daines Western Store set up an outlet in Kelowna in the Cherryland Mall, and when we lived in the Okanagan we often shopped at the store.

The manager was a lady named Leanne, who always treated us well and gave us good prices. Along with one of her friends, she often came out to ride and help move cattle. She later moved to Lamlies Western Store in Calgary

A Rancher's Story

In 1992 Pat and I decided we wanted a dog. Steve had a very good border collie named Annie, and Ken had a very good one named Molly.

I didn't ride often enough the first year at the Bobtail, and I didn't feel it was fair to get a cattle dog.

So, Pat and I decided to get a golden retriever. We paid $150 for it; it was a great pet, but it was a retriever, so it brought everything to our doorstep.

We named him Bear, and soon realized he was not a good dog for the ranch. He got to be quite large, and we put an ad in the paper, asking $100 for him.

Within three days, a father and two sons came to look at Bear and struck up an immediate friendship with him on our lawn. I told the boys they could have Bear for their own, as long as they took good care of him.

We often seen them around Kelowna together.

Bear could not have been placed in a better home. We soon decided to get our own cattle dog, and stopped at a sheep ranch south of Golden, B.C., where they had a nine-month old border collie for sale. We bought this dog; his name was Boy.

We soon named him Boyd, and we had him 13 years. He became an excellent cattle dog and was a great friend and pet. He went everywhere with us. Boyd became good friends with my grandsons, particularly Greg, and it took very little training to teach him how to work cattle.

It was just natural for him. I loved to ride and work cattle with Boyd. I used him at the Bobtail, and also took him with me to the Bar X in Clinton, where he was a constant companion.

One time I remember with Boyd was when Les Madsen, the ranch owner, came to the ranch on a Wednesday evening. He had a list of two purebred heifers, a cow and calf pair and a mature bull he wanted me to bring in so that he could take them to the Red Angus show and sale in Red Deer the following Friday.

He wanted those cattle collected in one day. At the Bar X Ranch, the range included Big Bar Lake, which was almost like a park.

In the middle of the area was a set of corrals that most of the ranchers and Forestry shared. On the Thursday morning, I loaded up the horse in the stock trailer at 5:30. I took Boyd and we traveled the 11km to the corrals at Big Bar Lake.

About 30 head of cattle were lying together about 100 yards from these corrals, and I could see from the truck that every one of the animals Les wanted was in that small herd.

I let Boyd out to keep the cows together, unloaded my horse, and within 15 minutes had them all in the corral. It took about another 15 to sort out the ones I wanted, and I had them loaded in the stock trailer by 9am.

Then what? I had given Les a big lecture about not giving me enough time to get these cattle, so I did not want to go back to the ranch. I fixed some fence, repaired some gates, and then took a back road to a small restaurant at 154 Mile.

I had lunch, and then checked some more fence, and got back to the ranch about 5:30pm. Les was so glad to see all the animals he wanted and said, "I knew you get them all."

I still impressed on him that he was never to do that to me again. I also told him I had to ride hard all day, and that he was just plain lucky to get his cows.

He sold these animals in Red Deer for over $60,000.

Big Bar Lake was known for fishing and recreation.

At the Bar X there were a lot of interesting neighbours that lived in the area. One of these was a lady named Marian Hariott, whose husband had passed away. He had been the last cow boss to trail cattle from Ashcroft up to the Gang Ranch.

One other lady who lived on Meadow Lake Road was a Mrs. Olgilvie. She had inherited a lot of he Olgilvie cereal estate and was quite well off.

She would often feed the coyotes and cougars from her back porch, much to my annoyance.

Les Madsen rented pasture from her, but the two of them hated one another. I had to make all the arrangements on her rental agreement.

We did not have a telephone at the Bar X Ranch. Telus would not provide the poles or line, as the houses were too far apart. The summer I was there, I got 20 home owners together and we convinced Telus to provide the necessary telephone service for everyone on Meadow Lake and Big Bar Road.

One unique feature of the Bar X Ranch was an abundance of alkali lakes. One large lake of about 1,500 acres was known as White Lake because of the white alkali. Early settlers would make large wooden boats, or small barges. In the winter, they got large blocks of this white ice and filled the wooden barges, which were about 40' long.

In the spring when the ice melted, the alkali in the bottom of the barges would be about 8" deep. It was sold and shipped to Vancouver, to be used for things like soap. This was a huge undertaking for over 100 years in that area.

The Kerrs originally owned the Bar X; they sold out to the Harpers, who later moved to a ranch east of Kamloops.

When I was at the Fraser River Ranch, I bought 250 head of bred cows from the Harper Ranch. The government took over that ranch and gave it to the Natives.

I also bought 50 head of cows from the Bobtail Ranch, and these became the foundation of the cattle herd at the Fraser River Ranch and were excellent cattle.

The summer at the Bar X Ranch, I did all the riding and all the haying. We built two bridges over a creek out of semi-trailer steel decks, which I expanded to be 12' wide.

I fell on one of these steel decks and injured my back. I damaged three vertebra that have bothered me ever since.

Les Madsen's main business was manufacturing Lynx brand galvanized gates and panels. He had a small plant in Kelowna and another in Edmonton; he did very well at this business, selling gates and panels all over western Canada.

He bragged to anyone who would listen that he was worth $14 million dollars.

Les was very difficult to work for. He would come to the ranch every Thursday evening. He was supposed to bring up the paycheques, and the cheques to pay the account, but he never did this. His wife, Diane, always had to bring them up sometime during the weekend.

The cow herd at the ranch was mainly Red Angus, but he also had a lot of Guernsey-cross cows. These were very difficult to handle.

Les decided to do a lot of fencing, as well as building a large barn 200 by 80', and a hay shed 100 by 60'.

He hired a crew from Lytton to do the carpentry work on these buildings. He ordered the rafters, tin, poles, etc. I designed these buildings for him, and he hired a large crane to put up the rafters at $200 an hour.

One Monday morning, the crane truck came at 6am. I was going riding and could not be home all day, but when I rode past the building site on my way to Big Bar, a small wind had come up and they had not secured the rafters.

I rode over to Les and the contractor and told them to make sure the secured those rafters. Les's only remark was that at $200 an hour, he wasn't going to waste money doing that.

He wanted the rafters put up as quickly as possible. I rode over to Big Bar Lake, and about 10am Pat heard an ambulance come into the yard.

At first she thought it was me, but what had happened was that they had not secured the rafters, and they all blew down like dominoes.

The contractor on site broke his back, and when I came home about 5:30pm, Pat told me what had happened. Les was waiting at my house and tried to convince me that it was all the contractor's fault, as Les knew he could be in trouble with Workman's Compensation.

I made it clear to Les that I would not support him on that claim, and the next morning I let Les know I was quitting and gave him two weeks' notice.

This did leave him in a bit of a jam, as he only had two other men working on the ranch.

One only worked part time, doing things like fencing; his name was Jerry Spoonmire. The other was a very good man, who was from Switzerland. He lived at 70 Mile and drove the 50 miles to the ranch every day.

I suggested to the Swiss boy that he apply for the position I had at the ranch. Les was only paying him $1,100 a month. I told him to insist on a salary of $2,500, which he did. He worked at the Bar X for at least three years after that.

We had a lot of strange experiences at the Bar X in the short time we were there. We lived in an almost-new small log house, with one bedroom on the main floor, a loft, storage room, small living room and small kitchen. There was a deck that ran all the way around the house.

About 300' away was a chicken house that had about 200 young roosters just learning to crow at daylight.

He also had 20 geese that loved to chase Boyd, but Boyd did get even.

Les got a small dog that he wanted me to train for cattle work, but it was a useless mutt, so he kept it penned up. Whenever it got out it would chase the geese.

The last week we were at the Bar X we took my horse Lester up to Steve and Dixie's, and when we got home and pulled back in the yard, there were six dead geese. Les's dog and Boyd had had a field day.

The Bar X Ranch was in an area where there was a lot of mosquitoes. I had to keep barrels with a smudge burning in them all the time for the horses. Also on range there was a real breeding area for horse flies. We always had to wear heavy shirts because of them.

One day when checking the cows at White Lake, we found a newborn pair of orphaned twin calves. We took them home and bottle-fed them. Les promised Pat she could have one if she kept both alive. He bought a crazy Guernsey milk cow that I had to rope in order to milk, but the calves thrived and grew fast.

One Sunday Les had a neighbour and his wife in for a barbeque. In front of Pat, he gave those calves to the neighbour lady. Bad move on his part, because Pat really tore a strip off him.

Another Sunday a neighbour and his wife stopped in for a visit. She wore a jacket with flowers on it, and about 10 hummingbirds swarmed and attacked it. She had to sit in the truck to get away from them.

Four years after we left the Bar X, Les sold it and bought a farm at Cache Creek with some range and irrigation. He had that operation for two years. He sold out his chain link operation and moved to Edmonton.

He did hold a few bull sales for his Red Angus bulls in Williams Lake for three or four years, but he did not keep good track records, or his bloodlines, so his sales were not well-attended.

He attempted to buy the Buckskin Ranch – the ranch that Fraser River Ranch bought in 2000 – but he was not successful.

After giving our two-week notice to Les, I was able to finish up the haying and get most of his cows in for September 1.

We had no plans of what we would do, but had looked seriously at a 40-acre parcel of land in Peachland. It also had a six-unit Bed and Breakfast, a half-acre of walnut trees, as well as cherry and apple trees. It would have provided a decent income.

In the meantime, we decided to take a trip to see Pat's family in Berwyn, Alberta. The accountant at Oliver Smith Accounting in Williams Lake was looking for a manager for one of his clients – a man named Reinhart Brandner, who owned the Fraser River Ranch across the Rudy Johnson bridge.

The accountant's name was Andrew Smith.

As we went north out of Williams Lake, we could see the Fraser River Ranch from the highway. Pat made the comment that perhaps we should go look at this ranch, as perhaps ranching was still in our blood.

We drove over to the ranch; it was very run down and in rough shape. It was badly over-grazed, the cattle were very poor and you could tell that the ranch was poorly managed.

We went in to see Andrew Smith, and he filled us in about the ranch and yes, it was badly in need of a manager.

Andrew had heard of me and asked if I would consider the position; we agreed that a lot would have to change first. He asked me if we would stop in when we came back from Peace River country and said he would have the owner there for me to talk to.

We stopped in to see Reinhart five days later. One condition I had was that I would have to be completely in charge; Andrew and Reinhart agreed to most of our terms and conditions.

FRR, Buckskin and Springfield Ranches

Our first impression was that Reinhart was a real gentleman. He was sincere, appeared honest and did not sugar-coat anything. He really wanted his ranch to be turned around.

The ranch had four employees, plus a cow boss, Jack Ward, and his girlfriend Bernice Grinder. The foreman was Ken Lafoy. Ken had the best interest of the ranch at heart. He was a good farmer but admitted that he did not like cows. He was a lot of help to me when I became manager.

The first condition we gave Reinhart was that we had to have complete control over improving the cattle herd and the range, and that we would only be responsible for the number of cattle we actually rounded up by October 15. This was not the numbers shown on the ranch books, which said there was supposed to be 650 head of cows and calves.

Our October count was actually just under 450 head – 200 short.

We also needed a ranch truck, which we agreed to buy and rent to the ranch. The men were to be completely under my control and instruction.

The house available to us was a four-bedroom older house in bad need of a good cleaning.

The previous manager was a man named Mark Carr. He was to stay on under my instruction and do logging and land clearing for a period of one year. It was agreed that I would be the one who worked with Forestry on the range turnout and the logging.

I was introduced to all the men, and let Reinhart know some of the changes I would have to make, and he accepted that.

I also made clear that my starting salary would be no less than $2,500 a month. Pat would be paid $200 a month to do the books, and we would need to be in charge of all the accounting, etc.

Andrew Smith would continue on as the accountant for the ranch, and we were to take the books to him once a week. The ranch was to rent a ¾ ton truck from me, with the payments set at $350 a month.

Reinhart and Andrew did not agree to this salary but did agree to think about it overnight, as did Pat and I.

I was to phone Reinhart at 7am the next morning, but I lost his phone number. We stayed overnight in Williams Lake, and had to drive out to the ranch the next morning to get his phone number from Ken Lafoy.

So it was 9am before I was able to get in touch with Reinhart. He had become very anxious, and readily accepted all my terms. We agreed that the house was to be cleaned up, and that we would take over September 4, 1994.

Ken Lafoy did nothing to clean up the house or yard, so our first bill to the ranch was for $600 for Pat to clean it up. Jack Ward and Bernice tried to put together herd records, but they were very poorly done.

The next day we sat down with Reinhart and went over the books and the ranch assets. It was obvious that a lot of what the ranch was supposed to own was not there. So Reinhart asked that we do a complete inventory, complete with our values.

We did this and found a lot of fraud and schemes going on. One of the previous managers had done a lot of logging and sold the wood under his own name. Most of the ranch employees used the ranch fuel and got repairs on their personal vehicles. Bruce Bowe was really honest and reliable.

I remember one item that was supposed to be in the barn was a Leatherman knife. The books showed that the ranch owned eight of them. When I showed this to Reinhart, his comment was, "What is this Leatherman knife?"

When I explained it to him, he said, "I always wanted one of those."

I said, "You actually do: you own eight of them."

What had happened was that every worker had one and had also given some away as birthday presents.

I met with all the crew as a group, and laid out the new working conditions, the house, and so on. Most were very upset and threatened to quit. I made it clear that they only had a job under my direction. I laid out their salaries. None of them quit, but within six months I had laid off every one of the except for Bruce Bowe.

When we sold the calves that first year, the average weight was a terrible 289lbs, so I knew that was to be our first challenge. Reinhart agreed to spend money and buy 110 cows and bulls that I selected. That's when I bought those first cows from the Bobtail Ranch.

Bruce Wilcox and Wendell Monical sold off most of the Bobtail herd, and this gave me an excellent cow base to start from at the Fraser River Ranch.

Within four years, our average calf increased in weight to 410lbs.

I met with Fred Knisivich, the range agrologist, and Ross Fredell and we went over the ranch and the plans ahead. At first, they were very sceptical as I was the fourth manager in less than three years, but when Pat and I left their office, Fred commented to Pat that he was glad to finally have an experienced manager at the Fraser River Ranch.

He also told me to get rid of Jack Ward as he was not an honest person.

Fraser River Ranch was not an old ranch. It had been owned by the Kelly families, and some of it had been owned by Dr. Greenway. It consisted of several different parcels spread out over 80,000 acres of mainly Crown land.

In order for me to talk more about the Fraser River Ranch, I need to go back and address some things about the ranch, the area in general and Reinhart's involvement.

I was truly fortunate to have Pat at my side. She was a true rancher's wife – worked extremely hard and was highly respected by the neighbours and the ranching community.

She did a lot for the ranching industry, for the other ranchers and for Reinhart and his ranch for almost 30 years.

Tim Brewin and Keith Altwasser at FRR

The Bymans built all kinds of houses

FRR silage crew: Andre, my grandson Jack, Everett Byman and Mike

At FRR overlooking the valley from the Rimrock

Train trestle from FRR house

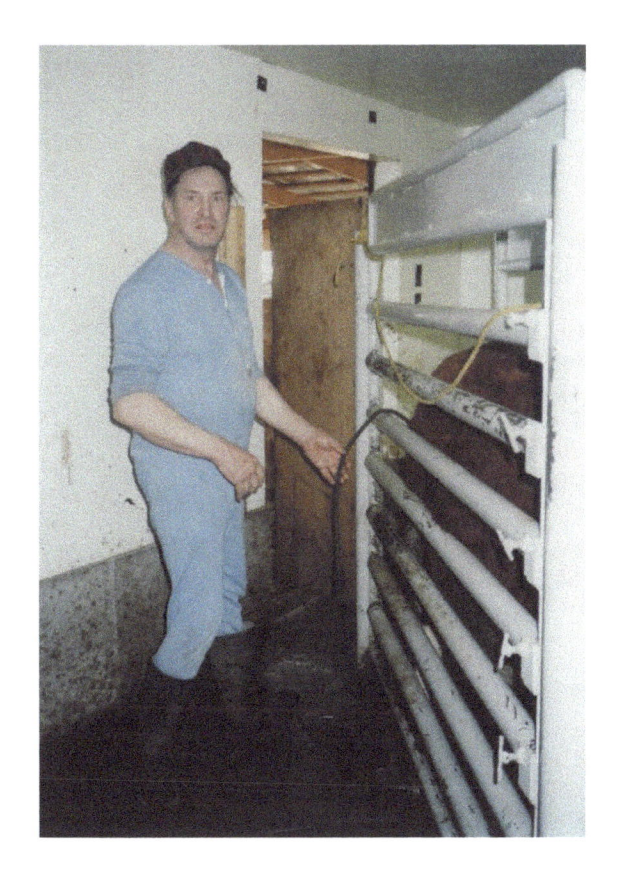

Tim cleaning up after a difficult calving at FRR

Denny and Everett with shuffleboard trophy at FRR

Bruce gets silver bit for 18 years service at FRR

Tim judging at Camrose in 2002

Kevin Kaufman and Pat, shuffleboard champs

The shuffleboard trophy that lasted over 20 years

Gordon Woods and Tim with trophy

Pat, Bruce, Gordon Woods at New Years Party 2002 at FRR

Christmas 2007 at FRR

Brand inspector Len Ablitt at FRR

Tim and Boyd at FRR

Sheldon Purdy and Reinhart at FRR

The ranch extended west from the Rudy Johnson bridge for 37km north/south along the West Fraser River for 20km. It included the ranch headquarters, Soap Lake, Freese Lake, Emerald Lake and Pre-emption Meadows.

It also included the Aspen Valley Ranch and meadows, what we called New Place, Salmon Meadows, the Mile-a-Minute range and Lowry lands.

Reinhart and his brother Axel had bought the operation in 1980; they added onto it and wanted to do a lot of development.

Reinhart was prepared to put his own money into the ranch to move it forward and expand it.

Most of his money was deposited in the ranch bank accounts from his mother in Austria. Reinhart bought his brother out in 1984, so was the sole owner.

Pat, Reinhart and I spent many long hours the first six months to determine how best to move the ranch forward.

It was obvious that the cattle herd needed to be improved and more land developed for pasture; more winter feed was needed, and we needed to enable cattle movement and increase productivity.

Mac Graham owned and developed the Aspen Valley Ranch. He installed a Pelton wheel for electricity on Mackin Creek, putting in one-and-a-half mile of power line to the Aspen Ranch buildings. He had a swimming pool, and also developed a lot of flood irrigation on the meadows.

Mac had lost that part of the ranch to the bank, who in turn sold it to the Natives; they pretty much let it go and then it was turned back to the bank.

And that's who Reinhart bought it from.

Reinhart had also bought several more parcels of land surrounded by Crown range that the ranch controlled.

This helped a lot for me when I was doing the expansion. Other ranchers, such as Rudy Johnson, Erik Reay, John and Alex Moon, Jim Couiltard and Neil MacDonald ran cattle together as a group, and called it the Mackin Creek Ranchers Association.

Reinhart, however, did not want to work in a co-op environment. He split off everything north of the 100 Mile Road as his part of the range. When Reinhart bought the ranch, it was at the time Pierre Trudeau had imposed no foreign ownership of property in Canada. This meant that Reinhart had to set up Andrew Smith as his director and trustee to hold the ranch for him.

Reinhart himself bought property in Florida and moved to west Palm Beach. He would visit the ranch five times a year for about a week at a time, but he would walk his ranch, so got to know it very well.

One thing he recognized and was very adamant about was that he knew he needed to develop more irrigation.

The second week I was there, he took me across the river along the Williams Lake cut-off road and showed me a plan he had to divert water on the west side of the river down Collins Creek to irrigate farm land to increase his irrigation.

He asked me to explore that idea and present him with a feasibility study for all pipelines, dams, pumping stations and a pivot system.

The first winter, I spent many hours on this. I came up with a plan, a design and a cost of $320,000 for the entire project.

Plus, $150,000 would be needed for the pivot irrigations system, dam and pumps.

When I presented this to Reinhart, he told me that he had set aside $500,000 for this project and asked me to proceed.

Woody's Welding also helped Harold with the welding on this project.

Before this, a lot of the hay was produced at Pre-Emption meadows, Aspen Meadows and on 480 acres of crop land seeded to rye or barley that was put up for silage.

Most of the hay was put up as round bales. As I expanded the cattle herd, we also had to expand the feed supply. We purchased hay, but also improved the farming methods. The first balance sheet I was given showed that the ranch was valued just under one million dollars, and Reinhart made it clear that he was prepared to invest in any capital projects.

He and I agreed on that, and that the expected income for the calves and cow sales had to pay for all the operation and expenses for the ranch itself. Pat and I were able to operate the ranch at a profit until 2001. At that time Reinhart's brother Joerg bought the Buckskin Ranch and expected the Fraser River to pay for all the labour and operating costs of that operation.

Joerg did put in a lot of money and machinery and did buy some cows.

Very little ranching had been done on the west side of the Fraser River before World War II. The Gang Ranch and Mel Moon were some of the exceptions.

Smaller operations such as the O'Keefes, Couiltarts, Coopers and McKays also had small ranches before the war.

In the 1950s. a large group of Americans from Florida bought huge tracks of land for cattle ranching. Some of these investors were Mack Graham, Gordon Bell and Herb Chestley. They called their operation Northern Ranches. They spent huge sums of money on land purchases, but their operation never showed a profit.

Herb Chesley did stay involved, and developed his own operations, which involved the Pre-Emption Meadows and other small parcels, and his home place on Tingley Creek. The majority of the ranchers, however, were Americans who were escaping fighting in the war.

Two years before we arrived, a German farmer brought his wife up to settle on a parcel of land called Mile-a-Minute. He set her up in a cabin and went back to Germany. She ran out of supplies and tried to walk back to town. The snow plow operator found her frozen body on the side of the road.

Rudy Johnson was a successful rancher and logger. He also built the famous Rudy Johnson Bridge across the Fraser River in 1967. He and his wife had three sons that worked the ranch with him. It seems like there had been a lot of friction between land owners and ranchers – there were a lot of stories of fights and shootings, and so on.

Pat and I made if clear from day one that our only interest was to operate the ranch for Reinhart. Some of the locals, such as Garth Lloyd, tried to get us involved in the local in-fighting, but we could easily see through these local games.

The area west of the Fraser River and into the Chilcotin was really not developed much until the 1950s, when ranching and logging took hold. When we came to the Fraser River Ranch, it was a real challenge, as everything was really just getting developed.

Also, a lot of trapping was being done, mainly for muskrats, martens and fishers. It was a big challenge for Pat and I, as Reinhart was really anxious to see his ranch expand. This meant a lot of land clearing and logging. The logging was a new venture for us, but was, in fact a profitable one for the ranch.

Forestry told me that close to a million dollars worth of logs were taken off the ranch and sold by previous managers. One story was that Reinhart and Andrew Smith called in the R.C.M.P. to investigate one logger selling the logs to a small mill by Mcleese Lake. They were able to determine that this was logs from Reinhart's land, but charges were very difficult to prove.

Reinhart hired his nephew to monitor all the loads that went out. This nephew was from Austria. He did this for over a week, and the ranch paid him for it. In the end, there was only one charge – Reinhart was using a foreign worker to work on the ranch without a work visa.

So, this was one of the first challenges Pat and I had.

The ranch workers used ranch fuel in their own vehicles at will. One of the wives went to town every day, charged whatever she wanted to the ranch. It seemed they had no conscience.

Pat and I did inventory after one week, and then got the whole crew together to lay out new rules.

One man said, "You're cutting our wages," and I said, "No, I'm stopping your theft."

They were used to starting work at 8am, taking a full hour for lunch and two half-hour coffee breaks. It was very annoying to watch a man turn his tractor off at exactly 12 noon and sit in it watching his watch until 1pm.

I set working hours from 7am, and that meant to be at work at 7am, not coming in the shop to drink coffee and do up your boots just to waste time.

The interim ranch manager was Ken Lafoy. Dave Still was a farm employee, and a truck driver, and Jack and Bernice Ward, who lived at Aspen Valley Ranch, were in charge of the cattle.

Bruce Bowe was the best man – he was good with haying and equipment and was also a very good cowboy.

Two young people were hired to move irrigation pipe, which took them about four hours a day. Mark Carr was doing the logging, and he, too had full use of ranch fuel, as well as a ranch truck to use as his own.

They had bred 200 yearlings to large-boned Hereford bulls, and the next spring we had to do 38 Caesareans.

Reinhart did not know much of what was going on but was willing to allow Pat and I to make the changes that were needed.

Within two years, we were able to turn the ranch around and move it forward. We built up the herd from 459 head to 850; we bought good bulls and improved the farming and irrigation.

This worked very well until 2001, when Joreg, Reinhart's brother, decided to get involved, and purchased the Buckskin Ranch. I was hired as director and manager of that operation, too. Rudy Johnson had sold the Buckskin to Henry Houf in 1990.

Barry Bare was Henry's manager, and his main worker was Bill Johnson, a Native from Alkali Ranch. He was a very good man and a great cowboy, but he spoke very quietly.

One day Henry Houf pulled up to one of the farm gates to open it and go through. He got out and walked in front of the truck next to the wire gate. The truck rolled forward and pinned him to the gate. He was injured and could not do much for over a year.

When he bought the Buckskin Ranch from Rudy Johnson, he increased the size of the house so that it had nine bedrooms, three bathrooms, a large kitchen, and so on.

He also had a large room in the basement that he used as a classroom. His plan was to teach religious classes, and also have guests that he planned to treat for stress problems.

I don't think that he ever really got that going.

Henry sold the ranch to the Moons in 1996, and we bought it from the Moons in 2000. It had a lot of good hay land. The irrigation was supplied by gravity from the Buckskin Meadows and dams.

It had one small pivot, and one large one, plus 150 acres that was irrigated by hand lines.

In the next three years, I installed another six pivot irrigation systems. We could then irrigate 1,500 acres on the Buckskin Ranch alone. We also installed four more pivots at the Fraser River Ranch, and then had enough feed. We increased the cattle herd to 1,400 head.

We bought the Springfield Ranch, on the east side of the Fraser River, in 2004. I was hired to be the director and manager of that ranch, too.

We installed four pivots on the Springfield Ranch, and increased the cattle numbers to 1,800 on all three operations.

I introduced a lot of new crops, such as Triticale – a grain crop that is a cross between Durum wheat and rye. It's very high yielding and has great protein. I also introduced high-yielding oats and barley.

In 2006, Reinhart and Dieter Kellinghousen decided they wanted irrigation water from the Fraser River, two-and-a-half miles up river from the Brewin dam.

I worked out a plan and design for them but could not see how it was practical.

Vern Winger from Highlands Irrigation convinced them to install that system at a cost of $360,000.

It had to use diesel fuel for pumping, and when we got it all installed and ran it for 10 days, it was enough to prove that it was just not practical.

We shut the whole system down, and within a few days, the pumps, motors, winches, etc., were all stolen.

When we took over the management of the FFR, a lot of the hay was purchased. Some was produced off the Aspen Valley and Pre-emption Meadows.

Most of it was round bales. Some of it was left at Aspen to feed the cows in the late fall and the next spring. About 5,000 round bales were stored at Aspen in the hay sheds.

Another 3,000 were hauled to the main ranch. This was all done in the late fall; the ranch had its own semi truck that hauled 40 round bales at a time

Dave Still was the truck driver. He was able to haul two loads to the ranch every day.

This was very poor-quality hay. It was only about 9% protein, and the cows did not do well on it. I continued this practice for five years, then fenced in the Pre-emption Meadows and used it solely for grazing.

Pre-emption was 1,100 acres of meadows; later, we also fenced Aspen Valley Meadows and used it strictly for grazing.

But the hay from those acres had usually given the ranch enough feed for most winters, when it was added to the hay and sileage put up at the main ranch.

We would round the cows up into the Aspen Valley Meadows, wean the calves at that location in mid-October, sell off the calves and drive the cows to the main ranch in mid-November.

This was a 25-km cattle drive. We had a large open sileage pit at the ranch. The cows were fed mostly on open ground feed bunks along the corrals. After I took the herd numbers to 1,000 head, the feeding took most of the day in the winter time.

I laid Jack and Bernice Ward off the end of the first calving season. Then I hired Wes and Marian Metzer to look after the cows for one year. They were very capable, but were 65 years old, and the job was just too much for them.

I then hired a young family from Ashcroft for the next summer.

The third summer, Bruce Bowie and I looked after the cows and the roundup. Then I hired Mike McGuiness and his girlfriend, Lee Sanderson. They lived at Aspen Valley, as it was the center of the range.

Mike was a very capable cowboy but lacked ambition. Reinhart complained constantly about the labour cost for the cowboys. On one trip to the ranch, he went out to Aspen Valley about 9:30am. He found Mike still in bed, and the cows all in the hay meadows. Mike and Lee had also spread a lot of negative rumours about the ranch. That night Reinhart told me to lay Mike off. I did this, and hired Joe Engelhart, who was an excellent cowboy.

Earlier, I mentioned Reinhart had purchased several small parcels of land at various locations on the range. Soon after I arrived, he had bought two 40-acre lots at Dry Creek. He also had in place an agreement to buy 320 acres from Marvin Magnussen, four miles north of he main building at FRR, along the West Fraser Road.

It was a three-year agreement, and the Magnussens would live there for those three years. It was to be fully paid for by the end of that time.

Reinhart had me visit with the Magnussens to make the final payment two weeks after I took over management of the ranch.

Pat and I took the payment up on September 30. This was a very interesting visit. The Magnussens offered us a coffee, and we accepted. They asked if we took cream and sugar, and we said we did. On the table was a bird cage, covered up. Marvin said, "The cream's around here somewhere."

He uncovered the cage, and we saw a couple of feathers floating in the cream.

I hurriedly made up an excuse that I had to go pick up one of my men, so Pat and I quickly left. We barely made it outside when Pat had to vomit.

The Magnussen house was a very nice one. It was two stories high, with a large basement. On two sides was a great porch which adjoined the kitchen on the second level.

They had never disposed of any of their garbage or tin cans, but simply threw them over the side of the porch. It was a very smelly pile! I brought in a large excavator to dig a big hole, rake the garbage in and bury it.

We rented this house out to a lady who worked for Forestry. She was there for three years and loved to go for a walk in the evening. She told me that whenever she did, there were bear tracks over top of her footprints on her way back home.

I advised her not to walk there anymore, as the bear was likely stalking her. We set up snares, using a beaver tail for bait. Two days later we caught a large black bear in the snare, which we shot.

When I told Conservation officers about it, they asked me what paw was in the snare. I told them it was the right front paw. They told me this was quite common. Just like humans, a high percentage of bears are right-handed.

The Magnussen property was very valuable to the FRR. It had hay fields on it, and also gave us an alternative route for roundup, going into and back and forth from the Aspen Valley Ranch. It also gave us access to our hayfields along the Fraser River.

The government also put up some of the agricultural lease lands for sale. Three of these parcels were at Emerald Lake. The conditions were that you had to improve the meadows on this land. These three parcels were a total of 540 acres, and 110 of those acres were very productive wet meadows.

These lands also contained a large amount of good timber. I put Mark Carr to work brush-cutting thee meadows and hired a large single-bottom plow to turn the soil over so it could be farmed. I then seeded these 110 acres to tame grass. This was excellent pasture in the middle of our range.

We logged the remaining acreage and received enough money to pay for the logging and the land. It also had a small cabin on it.

When I was disking up these meadows, I usually left home around 6am. I never took Boyd with me, but Pat could always tell when I was coming home in the evening. Boyd would go lie in the driveway 15 minutes before I pulled in the yard.

In 1997, we had increased to the point where we needed a full-time employee for nighttime calving. I advertised this position. Jim Heaton, a 19-year-old boy from Quesnel applied for the position, as did a 19-year-old girl from Spokin Lake.

After we interviewed them, I decided to hire Jim. This annoyed Pat. She convinced me to hire the girl, Carol Campbell. Carol turned out to be an excellent choice and did the night calving for three years. The second year, I also had her operate the tractor in front of the sileage chopper.

Again, a wise choice. Carol did this for four years. One day she was driving the tractor in front of the sileage chopper, right along the road. Carol was quite a small girl, and one of the neighbours actually ran in the ditch when he seen this young girl on that large machine.

Reinhart's brother Joreg owned a large gravel and paving operation in Austria – he sold much of this in 2002 and used this money to buy into the Buckskin Ranch. He also sent some of his excess equipment from his gravel operation in Austria to the ranch.

Included was a large excavator, a 1060 Volvo loader that held over two yards of dirt – a very large machine. He also sent over a very good backhoe. I was told that he could not get a good price for this equipment in Europe, so this is why he sent it to the ranch. The book value that he put on this equipment was $200,000.

I had it appraised in Williams Lake. The value here was less than $100,000. This equipment was, in fact, very useful and a great asset to the ranch. Paul Ruddenklau from New Zealand came to the ranch in 2003; he was very good at operating the excavator, digging ditches and burying PVC pipe.

Paul was also very good with the cattle, with calving, haying and with the farming. His girlfriend, Tracy, came with him and they stayed from February to October.

A year later they returned to the ranch, where they got engaged and eventually married. Pat and I went to their wedding in Ashburton, New Zealand in 2005.

In 2004, I hired Jim Heaton to help with calving and work on the ranch. Jim was also very handy, and a capable operator of the excavator. He was also very good with irrigation.

He became almost like a son to Pat and I. Two of Jim's friends, Brian McDonald and Rooster McDonald, also came to the ranch to help with irrigation.

I hired Jim's cousin, Kevin Kaufman, in 1999 when he was 14 years old, to pack sileage for me. He worked for me for nine years.

In 2007, I decided it was time I should retire. I asked Jim if he would take over as manager of the Fraser River Ranch. When Jim, Bruce, Brian and Rooster went to the Lakeside pub to celebrate Jim's new position, Jim was killed by a whacked-out mental person, who stabbed him in the kidneys.

In 2008, I hired Mike Altwasser as an interim manager at the ranch. At that time, the ranch consisted of the original FRR, Springfield Ranch and Buckskin Ranch, and I was running 1,800 head of cows. I was the president, director and manager of all these operations.

FRR operated Springfield and Buckskin in trust for Joreg. Before this, in 2003, I had built the herd up to 1,500 cows. We were unable to produce enough feed, so the decision was made to sell off 300 head of cow/calf pairs.

We sold these in April, through B.C. Livestock in Williams Lake, and got excellent prices. Months later, B.C.E. (Mad Cow Disease) was detected in beef in Alberta, and almost overnight, cattle prices dropped almost 50%.

So, our decision to sell off some of the herd was a very lucky move.

In 2006, we built up a large calving and hay storage barn. It was 200' by 60', complete with 54 inside pens, all 12' by 12' with their own watering system.

There was an I.C.U. room, a kitchen and a good drainage system. The I.C.U. itself was 36' by 60', complete with concrete floors. I designed this barn myself, first making it out of cardboard. It really was an asset to the ranch, and we were able to improve our live cattle percentage.

Today we build a barn

The first load of lumber

Starting the barn

After one week

Week three; Bob Kelly was the contractor

Barn finished

New calving barn at FRR, 40' by 220'; contained 64 12' by 12' pens

Fraser River Ranch map

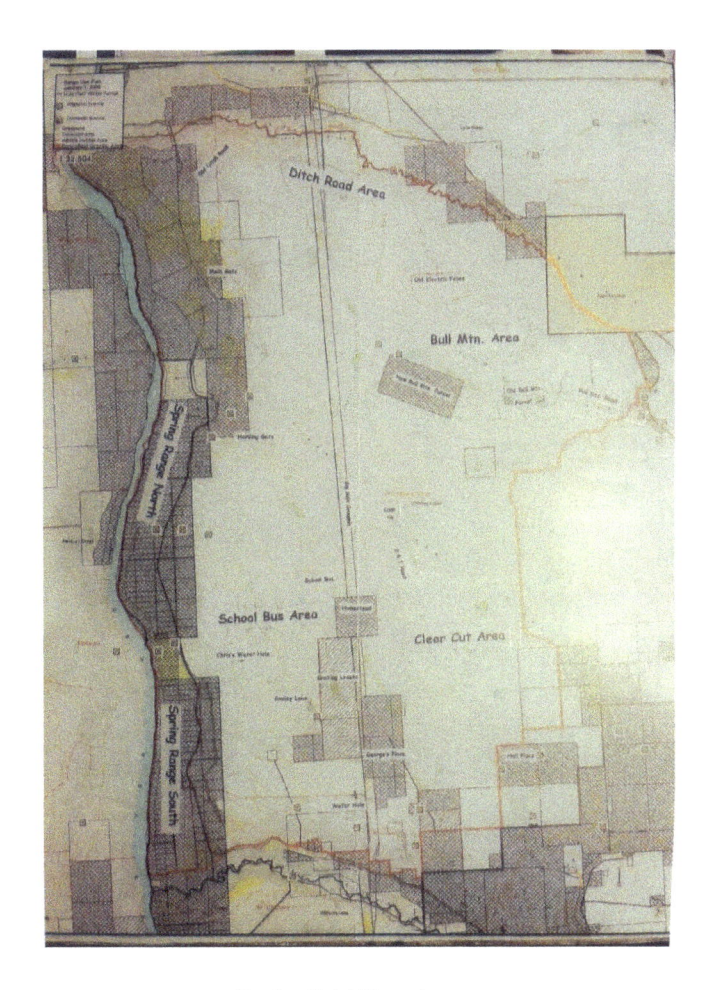

Springfield Ranch map

Filling the new barn with hay in 2007

View from FRR kitchen in 2006

Putting up silage at Buckskin

A Rancher's Story

Rudy Johnson Bridge connects Buckskin, Springfield and FRR ranches

Tim and cougar hunter with cougar killed in calving pen March 2001

— 183

Weaning at Aspen October 15, 2003

Weaning at Aspen 2002

Sorting crew in 2004 at Aspen; Jim Heaton (kneeling at right front row)

Branding crew 2006 FRR main corrals

Branding crew 2007 FRR; Jack, Camille and Carol (in front)

FRR sorting crew October 2004

Paul on the excavator

Some years following that, we had a live calving percentage of 96-98%.

The barn paid for itself within three years.

Pat helped me design the I.C.U. and the kitchen area, and we also incorporated a large office, with record-keeping desks and shelves.

A neighbour friend of mine, Everett Byan, worked for me for several years. He was a very good carpenter, and a great ranch employee.

Bob Kelly from Williams Lake was the main contractor I used to build the large barn. Eric Mirus had his own small excavator, and he did a lot of the drainage and installation of water troughs and water lines.

From 1998 onward, we sold the majority of our calves by electronic tape, through B.C. Livestock.

I sold them in large lots, usually 100 head, with buyers from all over Canada enrolled on this electronic tape method. That meant that many of our cows were sold to feed lots in Alberta, and as far away as Quebec.

Our calves did very well as feeders, and we developed a well-known reputation for supplying high-quality feeder cattle.

Reinhart was committed to expanding and improving his ranch. One thing he was sure would help realize that goal and move forward, was to install more irrigation.

His first idea was to utilize the run-off and snow melt in Collins Creek.

We spent most of his first visit after I was hired, looking at the feasibility of doing this. He asked for my input on hat it would involve, and I informed him that the following steps would need to be done:

1. Meet with the Minister of the Environment and the Water Branch to explore the possibility of getting a water license out of Collins Creek
2. Determine what area we would be able to irrigate
3. Map out a plan to divert and use the water
4. Measure the flow in the creek

5. Determine how and where we would build a diversion and a dam to store the water
6. Determine the actual building of a pipeline and other water diversions
7. Build a structure on the creek to facilitate redirecting and diverting the water
8. Do an archeological study of the area that would be affected

I visited with Bill Kloop, with the provincial water branch, to discuss all these areas of concern, and he informed me that some work had been done measuring and understanding the flow and amount of water in Collins Creek.

I was put in touch with the Federal Department of Fisheries to determine any concerns they may have, and whether or not Collins Creek was a fish spawning area.

I found out it was not; however, my inquiry did raise a red flag for them to study it.

I was lucky that Reinhart was already working with the Ministry of Agriculture on clearing the meadow and doing drainage work at Emerald Lake.

I asked these surveyors to look at the possibility of using Collins Creek as a source of irrigation, and where I could put in an area to store water, complete with a dam.

I got in touch with Vern Winger from Highlands Irrigation, who was very anxious to help out. He could see benefits to his business, selling pipe and irrigation equipment.

We went up in a helicopter, together with two bureaucrats from Victoria, and the water branch. We determined that the main source of water for the creek was 8km from the farmland, on the ranch along West Fraser Road.

Smaller creeks and run-off water also flowed into Collins Creek. For most of the way, we'd be able to use the creek itself, for the water to flow in.

Approximately two and three-quarters miles from our farmland, however, the creek took a turn away from our farmland, so we needed to put in a pipeline to divert the water to the dam.

Two dam sites were selected – one and a half miles north of the ranch headquarters.

Reinhart was logging and developing two parcels of land in that area. Both of these he controlled by agricultural permits. This meant he could develop them, utilize the sale of the wood, and that would cover most of the cost, and pay for the purchase of these parcels.

This meant that Reinhart would not need to put in a lot of his own funds to purchase these lands.

I arranged for the surveyors to locate the most suitable site for the dam, and to determine how much water would be required to irrigate 200 acres of farm land.

This was all moving quite fast, and I spent many late nights that first October exploring feasibility and the undertaking of Reinhart's dream.

When Reinhart visited the ranch again, in late October, I had a basic plan put together for him. He immediately asked me to continue exploring what all would be involved.

This would include measuring the flow of water in Collins Creek for the first two years, arranging for the archeology study, determining the method and route to divert the water to the dam site, as well as finding out the size and construction needed to complete the dams, and the area we would irrigate.

In early November, I borrowed a hand-held altimeter from Highlands Irrigation. I walked and mapped out a possible ditch, or pipeline, to divert the water. I put in ribbons every 100 feet with a slope or drop of half-an-inch every 100 feet.

I tied this pink ribbon to a tree, as this was all Forestry land. I did this on the area where I thought we could install the diversion in Collins Creek. This helped me to determine that the project was feasible – to build a pipeline along this route after the right of way was cleared.

Next, I got in touch with Duncan Baines. He had a ranch at Big Creek, and the Alexis Creek area, and was also an engineer who had done a lot of work on dams and water use in South Africa.

Duncan came to the ranch and met with Pat and me. We went over my plans, and Duncan was very helpful to me with this project, through to its completion.

He made it clear that he would be too expensive if I hired him full time to design this project. He suggested that he would come to Williams Lake every two weeks, so if I agreed to pay him one day out of 14, he would stop at the ranch to offer suggestions and oversee the project.

I was truly fortunate to get Duncan to work with me. He was impressed with what I had done and suggested that I continue moving ahead. He also met with Bill Kloop at the Water Branch and offered his input and suggestions.

I also put in a structure to measure the flow of water in Collins Creek. All I did was put in a 2' long board, 2' high, and I diverted all the water over the top of it.

I then simply measured the amount of water going over this structure every third day. This structure was put in four miles north of the ranch buildings, where Collins Creek crossed the West Fraser Road, just before it flowed into the Fraser River.

Reinhart was very excited about the progress that was being made. He phoned me once every night.

An archeology study was done May of the following year. The route I had ribboned out had an almost ideal slope for a pipeline.

The only area of concern was that one quarter-mile high point would require a 25' cut.

I met with George Giesbrecht, who had a large excavator, and got his suggestions on how to handle that obstacle.

He suggested that we use our D8 Cat to trim off 15', and then he would be able to trench in the pipe. I ran into a lot of obstacles with Fisheries and Lands. They were reluctant to encourage my project, but with Duncan's help, it seemed we were always one step ahead of them and prepared in advance for their bureaucracy.

Within one year, we were far enough ahead with the planning to begin the project. It would involve two-and-three-quarter miles of steep pipeline, two large 35-acre water storage areas with dirt dams that were 15' high.

This included a cut of 100' wide for the pipeline, dynamite, a quarter-mile of rock 4' deep, logging and leveling the actual route and right-of-way.

I then applied for all the required licenses.

I was only granted a 100' right-of-way for the road, the pipe line and the construction. We contested this, as the natural gas pipeline received a 600' right-of-way for 12-20" pipeline. We were not successful getting a wider right-of-way.

Duncan Banes determined that the equipment we had on the ranch would be all we'd need to build the dam for water storage.

This was the first license I was granted. I immediately put one of my men, Dave Still, to work pushing dirt down off the side hill, and building the dam using our D8 Cat. Duncan determined that this soil, when packed, should make an ideal earth dam.

It contained the proper amount of clay, sand and gravel. We also used our 930 loader and land packer to build this dam. It took 15 months to complete.

A site was selected for a second dam; however, this was never built, as there was not enough water in Collins Creek to fill two dams.

The D8 Cat was a very valuable machine. We used it to build the dam, level land, put in roads and make clear right-of-ways for fencing.

I hired different people to operate it. Jack Butler was one of the best operators and really knew how to move dirt and operate that Cat.

Dave Still was also one of the employees who operated it. Dave was supposed to do the maintenance and repairs on the Cat. Pat's brother, Joe, did a lot of work on Caterpillars for many years. When he visited the ranch in 1996, he asked Dave if he'd been cleaning the transmission and hydraulic filters.

Dave had not, so Joe immediately checked the D8 over, and had Dave shut it down and assisted him in completely the maintenance on the Cat.

The filters and the oil were extremely dirty. It was a good thing that Joe came along and knew Cat equipment, otherwise we would have had costly repairs.

I always made it very clear to all my employees that they were responsible for doing all the maintenance and service on any machine they were operating.

They were instructed to read the operator's manuals service requirements.

By the spring of 1996, I had all the plans for the pipeline, and all the licenses in place. Reinhart had asked me to find the required amount off 12" steel pipe to complete the project, and to arrange for the logging of the pipeline right-of-way.

We were put in touch with a used pipe dealer in Delta who had what we needed. On a trip back to Florida, Reinhart went to see him and made arrangements to purchase all the 12" pipe we needed.

Much of it was Yellow Jacket pipe from natural gas pipelines. It was all in excellent condition and had been removed from the Vancouver airport during renovations. Most of it was in 30' lengths.

I arranged with a trucking firm to deliver this pipeline to the ranch over the next months.

Harold Lindburgh, who often did the repair work on the ranch, and was also a very good welder, was from Alexis Creek.

He would often stay over in the bunkhouse and have supper with us. He saw what I was doing and asked if we would consider him as a contractor on the pipeline project.

He would also hire another welder from Likely named Woody Tettestone. It was very fortunate that I hired both of them.

I arranged with the Lorings from Riske Creek to log the pipeline right-of-ways.

However, we were called in to a hearing, as the Lorings went over the right-of-way boundaries. The forestry technician tried to lay a large fine on the ranch. I had thoroughly examined the area, and the logging that had been done.

And yes, it was a mess. The forestry technician claimed that several thousand dollars worth of timber had been destroyed. However, I'd spent three days walking and taking pictures of the damaged area. Much of it had been logged three years earlier. I measured it all out for the hearing.

For the hearing, I took four people with me: Harold, my Cat operator, one of my neighbours, and a friend who was also working on the project.

The Lorings were also supposed to attend, as they had made the mess, but they never showed up.

Attending from Forestry was a district manager, the assistant manager, a secretary and their legal counsel.

I also had gotten aerial photos of the area before and after the logging was done, and from the photos, we were able to measure the area in question.

The area technician, a fellow named Jeff, presented his case in detail first, claiming that we had done several thousand dollars in damage on Crown land.

I then produced aerial maps and photos, my measurements and my opinions. The district manager really reprimanded Jeff. He asked me, "How many men do you have here today, and how much is this costing you?"

He agreed with my estimates, and that only 1.9 cubic metres of Crown timber was affected, and made it clear to Jeff that he was never again to bring such a ridiculous claim before him.

He told me to take my men and get back to work. He also said I was not to use the Lorings for logging anymore. He suggested that I hire Lorne Hinche instead.

Lorne had his own skidder, loader and logging crew. I did hire Lorne, and he did an excellent job. I used him for several years as a logger on the ranch.

I do think perhaps a small fine was given to the Lorings.

Lorne proved to be very honest and reliable, and became a real asset logging for me, arranging for the sale of timber, and measuring out areas to log.

Lorne is a very large man, about 6'6" and about 300 lbs. He and his wife became very good friends.

The pipe started to arrive in June. Harold and George Giesbrecht, using his excavator, had cleared and leveled about a quarter mile of right-of-way for the pipeline.

Harold and I designed a large steel diversion structure, 16' by 16', complete with ¾ inch expanded metal on top to serve to screen the debris out of the water.

George and Harold installed that structure and made a turnaround area beside this diversion. And then the insulation for the 12" pipe was underway.

The construction of the dam and the completion of the storage area continued into the early summer. The plans called for a 15' high earth dam that was 350' long, but I built it 17' high with an overflow on the east end.

We were able to use the soil and dirt and material, mostly taken from the east end of the dam, from a small hill, and to push it and pack it properly to construct the dam.

Duncan Baines kept his word and visited the site at least once a week. Harold and I designed and installed 3' expansion joints, 24 air vents and 10 2" drains. We also had to install several elbows and joints. We had to dynamite an area, about a third mile long, as it was solid rock. We blasted it three feet deep and cleared away the sharp rock with a D8 Cat and replaced that material with dirt and sand.

I used Peter Abrahamsen to do the dynamiting.

On the 100' right-of-way we also built a 20' wide road. The pipeline also had to traverse a valley. We arranged the pipe so that it could push water over this valley. I had to install an 8" valve in the pipe at the bottom of the valley to facilitate draining, so that it wouldn't freeze in the winter.

Garth Wakefield worked for the provincial government, and one of his duties was to inspect the dams. On one occasion, he visited our dam while construction was being done.

He started in about how we needed to build the dam and needed equipment that we did not have. Duncan listened to him for about five minutes, then he asked, "Are you an engineer?"

Garth admitted that he was not, and Duncan simply said, "Well, I am, and at the end of the day I'm the one who has to sign off on this project."

He informed Garth that he had no clue, really, what he was talking about, so get the f*** off the site. We never seen Garth after that.

The water storage area flooded approximately 40 acres, 15' deep.

We did not dig or disturb the soil in the storage area itself, so the area remained pretty much sealed and had very little seepage from it.

We completed the pipeline October 1st, so had 45 days when we could use the creek water and divert it into the dam that fall.

Harold and Woody did an excellent job welding, as over 300 joints were welded, plus 20 air vents, eight air vents, and three expansion joints. There was not even one leak evident when we turned the water into the pipe over the entire two-and-a-half miles.

This Collin Creek project proved very beneficial to the ranch. We installed a large pivot and two wheel-lines. It irrigated over 200 acres of grain and hay each year and provided an additional 1,500 tons of winter feed.

I was supposed to leave a 3" pipe opening in the diversion to facilitate a non-existing fish hatchery. I left this hole, but often plugged it with a rock, so if DFO came along, I could say, "Well, I guess that rock just got stuck in there."

It was just a waste of irrigation water.

In 2001, Guy Scharf from Fisheries and Oceans and Sabua from the provincial fish habitat visited the pipeline and the diversion.

Bill Kloop from the water branch asked me to attend his office, as he had a concern because those two had turned off the water in my pipe, as they thought not enough overflow had been provided for future fish habitat.

They actually took photos of themselves turning off the water flow. They had done this without my knowledge. It could have caused a blowout, as the water pressure built up in the 12" line.

Bill Kloop said I could take them to court for tampering with a private pipeline. I chose not to do this, with the agreement that they would never tamper with the pipeline and the water flow again.

Very few problems have surfaced with the pipeline for the past 25 years. I named the dam and storage area the Brewin Dam, and that name is registered on several maps.

The Mackin Creek pipeline

Because the Collin Creek project was so successful, Reinhart asked me to design and build a pipeline to take irrigation water out of Mackin Creek and divert it to the ranch. In 1999, King Campbell with Ducks Unlimited approached me about this project.

He was aware of funding that might be available from several different sources. One of these was with the provincial and national water supply. Another was with the Northern Development Fund that was set up when some of the railway from Tumbler Ridge was sold to private investors.

Another source was a grant from Ducks Unlimited. King spent many hours designing a proposal that I could present to secure this funding, as it was a very large project. We hired Jeremy Cook as an engineer to design and forward this project for me.

I also hired my neighbour, Everett Byman, to work with Jeremy to map out a pipeline right-of-way. The pipeline was to travel eight miles.

After two years, Jeremy's cost estimate for this project was $2.5 million. We should have been able to get funding for $1.5 million, which meant that Reinhart and two other neighbours would have to invest $1 million.

Many obstacles surfaced before we could proceed with this project. One was getting the approval from Fisheries, as it was a fish-inhabited creek.

We had to get approval from all the neighbours, measure and prove that there was enough water in Mackin Creek and get the approval from three Native bands that it might impact.

I was told I would never get the Natives' approval.

Dieter Kelinghausan, who had worked with the Natives a lot in the past at Alexis Creek, agreed to get their approval for me.

He got it within a month. When I went to the Department of the Environment with the Natives' letter of approval, they could not believe we had gotten it.

Dieter had simply paid the chiefs of each band $1,000.

I worked with Jeremy for two years on the project. It finally was all approved, and the funding was in place by 2001.

However, in March of that year, the Northern Development funding and the provincial/federal water supply fund changed their criteria, and funding became no longer available.

This meant we had to withdraw our application. I still have the design and feasibility of this project; perhaps someday it will go ahead.

Pivots at FRR

During my time managing FRR, Buckskin and Springfield, I erected seven pivot irrigation systems, bringing over an additional 2,040 acres under controlled irrigation. This meant we were able to grow more hay and grain sileage. They were all auto-reverse and auto-shutoff systems. First, I would do a feasibility study to determine if I could put in another pivot. I would work with Vern Winger with Highland Irrigation to determine costs and productivity, and then I would work out the availability of water and electricity.

We would then clear and level the area where we wanted to the new pivot system installed. Next, we would apply for all the licenses, do the studies and impact studies and address Native concerns.

I would then log the area and put our D8 Cat to work leveling it. Highland Irrigation supplied the pivots, and they would arrange for two men for three days to help me erect the system. I used the ranch loaders and equipment, and usually men from the ranch to erect each system. Normally, all the pipe components, etc., would arrive on two semi-trailer trucks.

We would lay everything out in order, and it would take us about four days to have the system up and running. This all did take a lot of time planning and organizing but was perhaps the most beneficial improvement I made at the ranch.

Pump sites and irrigation systems

We utilized eight different pump sites to supply irrigation water to our various systems. Each had its own problems.

I had to install screens in all the pipelines and pivot hookups, because a lot of trash, sand and debris was in the water.

The screens had to be cleaned often – some every other day and some every five or more days. Electricity was used as a source of power for all these pumps. The pump in the Fraser River was used to irrigate 110 acres. This site was referred to as the New Place.

This river water was very dirty – full of sand and silt. This wore out the impellors on the pumps, and they had to be repaired every fourth year. It also wore out the sprinkler nozzles themselves.

Two 20hp electric pumps were used at this site. I installed them in a pump house that I could push up and down the river bank as the water in the river lowered or became high.

One night about midnight, Pat and I were coming home from town, and decided to go down and check these pumps. The river had risen about six feet. Luckily there was a tractor on site. We spent over three hours pulling the pump house to higher ground. The next morning the river had risen so much, we had to pull the pump up even higher.

If we had not done this the entire pump house and pump would have been lost.

At the second site for two 30hp electric motors, the pump and section line were winched in and out of the water at Brewin Dam on a track I had made out of 4" by 6" steel channel iron, that I had got from a mine using the mine car wheels.

480v electric cable also had to be pulled out along the tracks. This electric cable was copper, and it was stolen twice in six years.

These pumps supplied the water to the pivot on the road field and a quarter of a mile of hand line, and an additional half-mile of wheel lines.

Because this water had a chance to settle in the dam, it was quite clean.

The third site is the Lake House dam where I used two 10hp pumps to supply water to three one-and-a-half mile-long wheel-moved irrigation systems on the north field, and the house hay field.

This system required screens that needed to by pulled and cleaned every four days.

The second pump site in the lake field required two 20hp electric motors. This supplied water to three pivots. It used three large screens that needed to be cleaned every three days.

The next site, #4, was in the well and pump site at Hawkes Creek, that supplied water to the four pivots on Springfield. I used two 30hp pumps at that site.

This water also had a lot of silica and sand in it, that wore out the pump impellors every three years. It was a big job to remove and repairs those pumps and impellors.

All of the irrigation systems at Buckskin used gravity, and water from the Buckskin marshes. The water flowed down Buckskin Creek into a large 30' by 30' cistern that was 16' deep.

This cistern provided the pressure and volume of water to run pivots on the Buckskin Ranch.

Each of these had their own screens that needed to be cleaned, and the cistern itself had to be drained and cleaned every 10 days.

Other than that, the cistern was an excellent, almost trouble-free source of irrigation water that only used gravity – no power.

Every October, I had to dismantle, drain and clean out all these lines, and the pivot and drains themselves – this would always take me about seven days.

It would take three weeks every spring to get them all going again. I also diverted water from Salmon Meadow, and runoff snowmelt above the ranch headquarters.

I designed and built a large water storage area, just east of the ranch yard for irrigation. This provided enough water to irrigate another 300 acres. We installed four more pivot irrigation systems, and logged and cleared more than 300 acres that we could farm.

Joreg bought the Buckskin in 2001. We installed six pivot irrigation systems that all used the gravity water from Buckskin Lake.

In 2006 Joreg purchased the Springfield Ranch, and I was put in control as president, director and manager of both these operations.

We installed four more pivots at the Springfield Ranch on the east side of the Fraser River, using water from Hawkes Creek, and Willow and Whiskey Creeks.

We were able to graze and provide feed for over 1,800 head of cattle.

Reinhart and Joreg had me do all the negotiations when they purchased the Springfield Ranch from Mike and Brenda Okeefe, the owners. Mike and Brenda were very honourable people, and the negotiations went very well – we purchased all of the land, equipment and cattle.

Cliff Dorion had managed Springfield for 25 years. He was a capable and effective manager. I asked Cliff if he would stay on the manage Springfield Ranch, but he said he'd had enough after 25 years, and preferred to do something else. Cliff did help me with the irrigation and pumps on Hawkes Creek. He also worked for me, often running my backhoe and installing pivots and pipelines.

He was a good friend of Eric Mirus, who had a small track excavator and did a lot of the ditching and fencing work at all three ranches.

Eric had a lot of experience, and was very knowledgeable, installing pipeline, doing draining and irrigation.

We developed a very good reputation for having good cattle. Usually our calves would receive at least a 5-cent premium over other calves, and most went to feed lots in Alberta.

I was paid by Fraser River Ranch, but more and more I was working for Joreg on his ranches – either Springfield or Buckskin.

A lot of the labour for winter feeding was also paid by Fraser River Ranch.

More and more, all of these costs started to put FRR in a difficult position, with the revenue and with the standing at the bank.

In 2004, I rolled an ATV and damaged to rotary cuff on my right shoulder and re-injured my right ankle. I had an operation to repair the rotary cuff, but due to infection, etc, I had and still have very limited use of my right arm.

I could not rope or lift my arm above my head.

I tried, unsuccessfully, to get compensation from Workers Comp in 2005. Pat and I decided that perhaps it was time for me to retire and hire someone to take over the daily management of the ranches. We drew up an agreement with Reinhart to stay on as president and director of his ranches.

We also asked him for a long-term retirement agreement. He readily agreed to a package, if we continued long-term employment to oversee his ranches.

Pat put on a retirement party for me in 2005 at the ranch. Over 200 people attended, including all my immediate family.

We told Reinhart that we would stay on until the ranch was sold, which was eventually done in 2011.

When I took over as manager at FRR, Crown range was approximately 50,000 acres. It took in Crown land along the Coulitart Road, up the Aspen Valley Ranch. It extended another 11km onto Emerald Lake and included the range from Salmon Arm to Mile-a-Minute, and the privately owned 1,100-acre Pre-emption.

The Kinlock Meadow fences separated FRR from the Moon Ranch.

The map showed an old trail going from Windy Point and Emerald Lake, over to Pre-emption. However, these trails were all overgrown and this Crown range was not allotted to any ranches.

These trails also showed access to Frog Lake - a very large, wet area. The first fall Pat and I were at the ranch, we went up in a helicopter to look the ranch over, and were quite impressed with the Crown range between Windy Point and Pre-emption.

We took along aerial maps, which showed approximately 40,000 acres of an area called the Burn. A large forest fire had burned it off in 1960.

It had been allowed to burn over eight months. We noticed that all this area had overgrown with a lot of aspen trees, but also contained a lot of green grass.

It also had lots of water, as well as another 20,000 acres around Frog Lake, extending north to four private lots along Twan Creek. It also appeared from the helicopter to have good grazing.

I had asked many of the old timers about this area, and researched map throughout the winter. We also attempted several times to find the old trails.

In June of the next year, Fred Kinisivich with Forestry offered to take me up in a helicopter to see if we could locate the trails. Pre-emption would give us a non-stop range to connect to our Aspen Valley Ranch.

As we flew over the area, I kept asking Fred to fly further over so we could look at the entire area.

After about two hours of this, Fred made the comment, "You sneaky devil: you're not so much interested in looking for the trails, as you are in the vast area of range between the two properties."

I admitted that, yes, that was what I wanted to see.

When we got back to Fred's office, he pulled out all the maps that Forestry had of that area, and also any letters of interest anyone may have in that range.

No one else had even applied for it. I told Fred that I would be putting in an application for over 40,000 acres of that range, extending south 10 miles, and along the 100 Road.

At our next cattlemen meeting, district range manager Ross Fredel read out my application. All the other ranchers laughed, and said it was nothing but bog, bugs and mosquitoes. No one else had any interest in it.

FRR was granted 45,000 acres of range, which included Frog Lake, and all the range between Pre-emption and Aspen Valley, south to the 100 Road, and including Emerald Lake. This range proved to be very valuable – a huge asset to FRR.

Two years later, Pat and I decided to walk into Frog Lake from F Road, a distance of six miles. Pat insisted we both carry rifles, as it was also known that many bears were in that area.

It was a difficult 10-hour walk over dead fall, up and down hills, across bogs, and so on, but we did get to Frog Lake. It was the first time in a long time anyone had seen it from the ground.

Oddly, two years later, logging tenure was granted in that area, and the whole area was opened up and made accessible.

Grants became available for fencing of range. I arranged to have 12km of fencing put in on the west side of our range, including Pre-emption, 10km along the 100 Road, and 8km along the Coultart Road, and into Camp Creek.

This meant that all our range and private land was contained within a fenced area.

This was about the time I had hired Mike and Lee McGuiness. They moved into, and lived at Aspen Valley Ranch year-round, although they only worked in the summer for the ranch. I laid them off in the winter and they collected U.I.

In 1999 a fire destroyed the house in Aspen, and Mike and Lee moved into town.

Luckily, we had an $80,000 insurance on that house. Reinhart agreed to put in another $10,000, and Pat and I designed and arranged for a new house to be built.

In 2010 Reinhart bought the 320 acres adjoining the ranch headquarters, from Garth Lloyd. It had a good house on it, which we rented out to hunters for two weeks at a time. When Reinhart and Joreg came out in November, we took them over and showed them the Lloyd house.

That night the house burned down. We had no idea what started it, but we did have $200,000 insurance coverage. After a lot of investigation, that policy was finally paid out.

Another devastating fire was in 2003, when lightning started several forest fires on Crown land between Alexis Creek and Meldrum Creek, our ranch and north to the Alexandria reserve.

We had a large portion of our Crown Land burned out and were evacuated from the ranch. My grandson, Jack, was working for me, and we were put up in the Super 8 Motel for two weeks. Pat's back was really bothering her, so she went and lived with Joyce Ward in late July and early August.

As we were evacuated, we were not allowed to go back to the ranch. Our neighbour Everett Byman did not leave, and he was able to watch our place and keep the irrigation going.

Finally, I met with the R.C.M.P. sergeant in charge of the evacuation order. I convinced him that I knew the area well – where all the water, creeks and trails were, and that I could assist Forestry in fighting the fire.

Jack and I, two R.C.M.P. cruisers, four Forestry trucks and regional manager went out to the ranch. I showed them that I could be a lot of help

The next day, I was able to go back and forth to the ranch at will, and two days later I was able to take all my equipment and crew across the river to do my haying and sileage. I did know another route to the ranch via Springfield Ranch, bypassing the road block.

So, using my ATV, I was never completely isolated from the ranch, and was also able to buy groceries and supplies and take them to the six or eight people who had not complied with the evacuation order, and were confined to the west side of the river.

That fire burned out a large area from Alexis Creek to Alexandria. We did lose about four cows, but most moved around to wet meadows and were OK.

Forestry would not allow us to go check on our livestock on private property. A lot of damage was done to our fences, trails and meadows by the large Cats that were used to contain the fire, but we received almost no compensation for these damages.

After the fire, large numbers of mushroom pickers arrived, and camps were set up. Most of the people were very good, but some of them got lost quite often.

Picking mushrooms is so dirty, and I felt sorry for those people covered with soot. It was claimed that some of those mushroom pickers made very good money.

Their mushrooms were sold to buyers camped right in the burned-out areas. They boxed up the mushrooms, took them to the airport and they were flown to Vancouver the same day.

It was the pine mushrooms most in demand after a fire.

When I hired Mike McGuiness to look after the cattle, an agreement was made that he would also keep most of the horses at Aspen Valley.

During the winter, he and Lee had three horses of their own, and the ranch had six. The ranch was so supply all the feed.

That first winter some of the horses went through the ice on a small lake, and two of them did not recover. All of the horses were in poor shape, so I had them bring them in to the main ranch and we looked after them.

We had a lot of problems with bears and wolves. At Aspen there were a lot of drain ditches. The bears would chase the calves or cows into the ditches, where they would get bogged down, and the bears would kill them.

It was a chore every morning to examine the ditches; sometimes three or four cows would be bogged down and had to be pulled out. This was a task that Mike took on, and he did save many cows.

We lost up to 10 or 12 cows and calves each year from this. One morning I sent Pat up to help Mike check the ditches. Right in front of her on her bike, a large bear jumped on the back of a cow and took her down.

It's unusual for male bears to work together on a kill, but four five of them were doing this on our meadows.

Al Lay from Conservation told me that sometimes they would do this. We did shoot or trap several bears.

Another large problem we had was with the wolves. They would kill up to 30 calves each year on our ranch.

A survey was done on the 10 ranches in our area, and over 300 calves were missing each fall.

Wolves were responsible for most of these losses, although I still think two-legged 'wolves' were also at play.

I worked with Conservation on various committees and programs, to attempt to control the wolves. The problem was that we received very little support or help from the Ministry of Environment, or the provincial government. Wolves also had a huge negative impact on the Caribou and moose populations.

So many do-gooders do not want wolves to be controlled. I hate wolves. They are vicious, inhumane killers. They kill just to kill. I personally witnessed mature moose that a pack of wolves had ham-strung. They moose kept on the move as much as they could but suffered for several days until they were very weak and could not fight back – then it was an easy kill for the wolves.

The ranchers were left pretty much on their own to control the wolves, something we usually did in the winter.

We were not allowed to use poison, so shooting or trapping was our only method of control. Because most ranchers are not experienced with wolf control, there was very little success in reducing wolf numbers.

We also had a few problems with cougars killing cattle. We took out a few cougars. Often, they would attack the cattle close to the corrals or feeding areas. Sometimes it was scary to go out at night to check cows at calving time. You would hear cougars within a quarter mile of the calving area. They were hard to hunt. I did utilize two different cougar hunters who used dogs to track down cougars.

Pat and the bear at the wood store

There is a very neat store about 20 miles north of Mcleese Lake that specialized in selling things made of wood, and Pat and I visited there often.

One of the trips, when we came out of the store, Pat had to go to the outdoor bathroom.

She no sooner got in, when a bear walked down the road and went over to the outhouse, with Pat inside. I hollered at Pat not to come out, but of course she opened the door to see what I wanted.

The bear was right outside, but lucky for her, when she opened the door, the bear took off. We got a big laugh over it, and to this day refer to it as 'Pat's toilet.'

Department of Fisheries and Oceans DFO

They decided to put in fish ladders on Mackin Creek so the salmon could go upstream to spawn. They spent almost $500,000, installing poorly advised and designed programs. The ladders and culverts were put in too high, and when the flow of the creek slowed own, the fish could not access them.

This was supposed to be a three-year program, and in the end, it was abandoned. Highways and Fisheries took out the ladders and culverts and restored the road over Mackin Creek.

We went up and watched this operation. It cost Highways and also Fisheries at least $150,000 to restore the flow of water in Mackin Creek.

I increased the cattle herd, as well as the hay field and cropping area.

So, when we purchased Buckskin Ranch in 2001, our irrigated acreage increased, wo we had 800 acres of alfalfa and tame grass hayfield. We also had over 700 acres of irrigated grain field that we put up for sileage. This was labour-intensive.

Joreg purchased two large sileage trucks, and a self-propelled forage harvester.

It took a crew of six two months each summer to put up the sileage.

Buckskin had a very large nine-bedroom house.

One idea was to hire a foreman to look after the Buckskin operations.

Rudy Johnson had set up a very good feed yard, complete with scales, good useable corrals and sorting pens.

I did have to upgrade a lot of the water and troughs and put up more windbreaks. But there were actually very good facilities at Buckskin.

My plans were to operate both ranches together, selling off the majority of the calves each October, and only keeping about 250 of the best heifer calves for replacements.

I was not sure of the arrangement Reinhart had with his brother Joreg, as far as the ranch management, but Joreg did buy 300 cows. The arrangement seemed very one-sided, with Reinhart paying most of the costs.

We tried four different couples to operate Buckskin that first year.

None of them worked out, and by the spring Pat and I decided to leave all the crew in place at FRR and move over to Buckskin to run that operation ourselves.

This worked out well, as it was also close to the irrigation fields and the pivot, and I could be more involved with turnout and cattle movement

My neighbour Everett Byman took over the day-to-day operation at FRR, along with Bruce Bowie and Burt Gentles (another neighbour).

At Buckskin there was a very large lawn area and a garden that Pat really involved herself with. There were a lot of choke cherries, Saskatoons and crab apples, too.

This made for an ideal environment for the bears. I was also growing a lot of oats and barley, which bears love.

Pat loved to shoot nuisance bears. One day we found that a number of window casings had been damaged outside the basement kitchen, where a bear had been trying to get to into the basement.

One night I was at a meeting in Williams Lake, and got a frantic phone call from Pat. She was at our kitchen sink, and a bear looked in the window, nose to nose with her, four feet away. I rushed home to find Bruce and Pat surveying the yard with rifles and flashlights.

The next morning, we seen a black bear about a quarter mile from the house. We got close enough to each get a good shot at it, and it went right down. Of course, Pat said, "I hit it – you didn't," but it soon got up, limping badly, and charged down the hill straight at us.

We both got in another shot, and the bear veered off into some bushes along the creek. Paul Rudd came to the ranch to work for a year – he and Pat took out a few bears for me, as they both loved to hunt.

Another encounter was when I was winter feeding on the Buckskin Ranch. When I put out my first load of sileage a bear came out of the trees and went over and started scaring away the cows so he could eat sileage.

I went back up to the house, got Pat, and we came down with two rifles. The rifle Pat used was a 303 with a scope on it, which was mounted high up on the gun. The rifle I used was a 30-06. The bear moved off into a small grove of trees. We drove about 50 yards away from it and parked broadside to the bear.

We both got out of the driver's side and took up a position over the back end of the truck. Pat was about 3' from the cab and I was closer to the rear end of the box. We both sighted in, and Pat said, "Now!"

When we fired, the bear went right down. We drove over close to it and it was obviously dead. Pat took the rifles back home while I finished feeding. I drove over to the barn at FRR. Ivan Sampson came out of the I.C.U. just as I drove up. He walked past the passenger side of the truck and said, "Who shot your truck?"

Ivan was a very soft-spoken cowboy and he loved to play tricks. This time, however, he was not playing a trick. I walked around the passenger side and sure enough, there was a bullet hole about 1.5" from the top of the box where Paat has shot.

She had forgotten to take into account the height of the scope from the barrel of the gun. Her bullet has traveled through the truck box and probably also hit the bear. Pat did take a lot of ribbing about who shot the truck.

When I took over management of FRR we had a huge skidder that was in poor shape. It was costing us a lot in repairs to keep it operating, so we decided to sell it.

Sevena (Sens) Satre from Tatleoko Lake purchased it and fixed it up. He actually worked for Caterpillar so was a great mechanic. He traveled for Caterpillar but also had a ranch at Tatleoko Lake.

A few months after he bought our skidder he was out riding his fence line with a young man who worked for him. A black bear started stalking them, so Sens gave the young man the axe he was carrying. Neither one of them had a gun. They decided to split up and head home.

When the hired man got back to the ranch, he took a couple of other men with rifles with him and went back to look for Sens. They found where the bear had pulled Sens off his horse and killed him. They left the body there, with the hope that the bear would come back to it. He did, in fact, the next morning and they were able to shoot it.

There were as lot of black bears on the range at FRR. We would see one or two pretty much every time we were out riding on range. On day three of us were moving about 40 cows with young calves from Aspen to Emerald Lake. Shortly after we left Aspen, moving the cows along a narrow road, we seen a black bear up on the ridge watching us. As we moved along for the next couple of miles we noticed the black bear following us and getting closer all the time.

We all had rifles, so when he was in about 100 yards, we shot him.

Cougars

One day I went down to the irrigation pump at the new place. I noticed a lot of cougar tracks in the sand along the river. I began moving pipe around, and suddenly noticed a cougar in a poplar tree right above me hiding in the branches and leaves. He was standing up like he was going to jump. I had a 3" piece of irrigation pipe in my hand that was about 20' long. I threw it up at him, and he jumped out of the tree and ran off.

We also had a lot of cougars on the ranch and were always on the lookout for them. They killed calves, so we would bring out hunters with dogs to run them down. They would kill the cougars in our winter calving area.

Ivan Sampson

Ivan was a cowboy at FRR. Him and I became good friends. One day I pulled up in front of the I.C.U. and went inside. Ivan was busy cleaning up after extracting a calf from a cow and disinfecting the calf's navel. I congratulated him on saving the calf, and he quietly said, "Well, Tim, but the other one is dead."

He claimed that the cow had had twins. The live one was full black in colour, and he said the other one was quite small and it was grey. I helped him clean up, and I noticed a dead mouse in the gutter. I realized that Ivan was playing a trick on me, and the dead mouse was in fact supposed to be the 'other calf.'

I really enjoyed his little spoof, and many others he played on me.

In 2003 Pat and I traveled to New Zealand to Paul and Tracy's wedding – a great trip. We spend a month there visiting with Owen and Judith; it truly is a beautiful country.

We rented a motor home for two weeks and toured most of the south island. Owen also loaned us his car for 10 days, and we went through the Catlins and the city of Dunedine.

The day we left the ranch, Reinhart gave me $2,000, which was a great, unexpected surprise.

We developed many good friends who are like family to us today.

In 1999, I was elected as director on the Cariboo Cattlemen's Association. I was also put on the wildlife committee as a delegate with the Ministry of Environment.

This committee consisted of guides, outfitters, the local hunting association, as well as the Williams Lake and 100 Mile hunting associations. It also included the Ministry of Environment person who regulated the hunting.

We always had well-attended meetings, mainly because of the conflict between the different groups.

One issue that always came up was concerning the BC and Federal Wildlife Associations.

Wilf Phlieder from Quesnel was the president of this association. He was very active and had a lot of influence with the B.C. Government. His input did influence the allotments of hunting licences, and issues with the Ministry.

I always felt that the guides and outfitters had too much control, and many hotly-contested meetings were long and bitter.

The local hunters always demanded more control of hunting on private lands and use of ATVs to do so.

So, this put me right in the middle of many of the conversations.

The Ministry of Environment deer counters were inaccurate for two main reasons. First, they did them in the late spring, after many of the deer had already migrated back to higher ground. Second, many of their counts were done from a truck along the road, where they would only count the deer close to the road.

The ranchers started doing their own counts and reporting more accurate numbers. On FRR, we often counted as may as 1,500 mule deer in the early morning and the evening.

That number of deer did a tremendous amount of damage that the rancher had to compensate for.

Peter Fofenoff from the Department of Agriculture started working with me and Pat to address the problem. The Kootenays also had a lot of damage to their hay fields from elk.

They were very active and developed a program to do actual counts and costs of the damage the elk were doing.

We got them to come to a couple of meetings in Williams Lake to explain their process in getting compensation.

They had built 8' by 8' wire mesh enclosures, which were 8' high and made out of chicken wire that the elk couldn't get into.

They were able to accurately measure the amount of hay inside these enclosures, compared to outside the enclosures, where it was not eaten off by the elk.

This gave them an accurate record of the damage the elk were doing.

We designed a similar method to determine the amount of damage the mule deer were doing in our hayfields.

We did not require as large an enclosure, but realized we needed enclosures at many different locations. Peter Foffenoff worked with us, and we took a proposal to the Cattlemen's Association, where we asked for their support going to the Wildlife Federation, to get their support to go to the Provincial government.

We were seeking provincial government compensation for the damage the deer were doing. We got good support from Highways and the insurance companies, because of the large number of deer that were hit on the highways.

Our biggest problem was that as soon as we started putting a program in place, we would get some government employee that would come up with a similar program he wanted to head up and get paid for.

After two years, we finally got approval to go ahead with the programs on 16 different ranches. Enclosures were put up, and we hired a crop expert to work with Peter to do accurate crop loss documentation.

On that small number of hayfields, the results were mind-boggling. We proved that ¾ of a ton of hay per acre was being eaten by the mule deer. We then had the information we needed to approach the government for compensation.

Hay was $100 per ton, so if you had a 100-acre hayfield, that would be a $7,500 loss you would suffer.

Compensation was paid to these 16 ranches, and the next year we expanded the program and 108 ranches took part in measuring their losses. Over $4 million was paid out that second year.

This soon came down the pipeline, where Environment realized more had to be done for deer control, so more hunting licenses were issued. This programs still continues today, but I understand only about $250,000 was paid out last year.

The program expanded to include the Peace River, and northern B.C., and also to include moose and Canada goose damage.

Pat did much of the work, along with Peter Foffenoff, putting this program into place, but there was a rush of government employees lined up to take credit for it.

Locally, it was known what she had done, and the local ranchers always showed their appreciation for her.

The third year of the program FRR alone got a payment of $180,000 in compensation for the damage deer had done to our hayfields.

I served as a director for Cariboo Cattlemen for 10 years. Often, Pat and I worked closely with Conservation officers and local hunting concerns.

We became good friends with four or five of them. Al Lay is one we still count as a family friend. Al is now retired and lives in Penticton. He and his son, Jared, and his friend Rod Cook, come to the ranch to hunt every fall

There is a cabin on the ranch they stay in. We often play a little crib and drink a little Crown Royal.

Al was a conservation officer in charge of predator control for over 30 years.

He has many experiences to share. I'm not sure if all the stories he tells are true but getting together with him is a great time for three of four days.

A lot of these Conservation officers referred to Pat as 'Mom', and at her funeral in 2012, four of them dressed in their uniforms and served as an honour guard.

The three ranches

The three ranches bordered each other. FRR was 105,000 acres, Springfield was 30,000 and Buckskin was 12,000, for a total of 147,000 acres. 20,000 of that was deeded, and 125,000 was Crown range.

I hired separate crews at each ranch, but because they were close, I was able to utilize a lot of the staff on all three ranches.

In the summer I employed 21 people, and the heaviest work load was in the spring and early summer when we were calving, doing turnout and gearing up for irrigation and haying.

In the winter, I cut the crew to around 10, and everyone helped with all the tasks. I organized roundup and weaning, with myself and four cowboys I'd have with me. That went over two months in the fall during roundup.

As president and manager of all three ranches, Pat and I did spend a lot of time in the office, and also on legal issues and planning – mainly in the winter.

Boyd

It was a real pleasure to have Boyd with me; he was a good pet, a great cattle dog and a good friend. When we got to FRR, he got more work, and spent almost all his time with me. He was very smart and attentive and loved to work cattle. He needed very little direction. Boyd was also a tease and could be naughty at times.

He was almost like a human. He always had to sit by the passenger door with the window open. Pat would have to sit in the middle. He would nudge himself behind her, and when we came to a gate, move over so she could get out and open the gate.

One day, she got out to open a gate and stepped into a very fresh cow pie. Her feet went out from under her, and she landed flat on her back. Boyd looked down at her. I heard her say, "Dog, you'd better not laugh."

He looked over at me and there was no doubt he was laughing.

We kept over 200 bred heifers in the pen, just below our house, so we could watch them closely at calving time. We would move them into smaller pens, sort them, and keep them in a small pen about 100' by 100', so that they were easier to check at night.

This became an important duty for Boyd. We usually did this about 5pm, just before the rest of the work crew went home. Boyd was always there to help.

If we were a little late, Boyd would start rounding them up himself, into the smaller pen. It was a pleasure just to watch him work these cattle.

Boyd was a lover, too. Mike and Lee stopped at our place one afternoon. They had a female dog in heat at Aspen, 25km from our place. That afternoon, Boyd snuck off without us knowing it. Lee came home about 8pm to find that Boyd had traveled the 25km and had bred their female.

Another time, Jim and Nancy Curie had a female in heat. They lived six miles from us. We had kept Boyd in the porch that night, but at midnight Pat decided to let him out to pee. After about three minutes, she tried to get him back in, but he was gone. We jumped in the truck and took the road for four miles to try to cut him off.

He had taken a short cut across a pasture. I turned the truck around, so the headlights would shine up the road. I waited about 10 minutes and told Pat to watch and see if Boyd was coming.

I turned on the headlights, and sure enough, 300' up the road, there was Boyd coming at a fast pace, heading for Jim's. Poor dog – he was so devastated that he had been outsmarted.

Boyd went almost everywhere with us, from Peace River to Saskatchewan, and to Dan's in Winnipeg. He was never any trouble, always stayed in the vehicle. We let him out every three hours to pee. I still drive by all his favourite stops and refer to them as 'Boyd's pee stops.'

Boyd had three bad accidents. Once a pork bone got stuck in his stomach, and they had to cut it out, along with part of his stomach. This took a toll on him for about three weeks.

Another time, Rooster ran over him and broke his right hip. We had to take him to a specialist in Prince George to have it pinned and repaired. He was in a cast for three months.

Boyd loved popcorn and ice cream. At Dairy Queen Pat would often rotate the cone for him to lick. After being at the vet clinic, we often took him for an ice cream cone or some popcorn.

All the staff at the clinic loved Boyd, and he did get special treatment.

When he was 13 years old, Boyd developed bad arthritis. The vet advised that we put him down. This was very hard. Pat and I and the vet all cried. Pat made him a coffin, and we buried him in view of the house.

We have a large drawing of him, and Boyd will always be a part of me.

Injuries

In 1999, I was driving about 10 pair of cows to the corrals using my ATV, going through the trees. There were several cut-outs, or holes from old logging, and as I went along the top of one of these, about 6' deep, a cow charged me. She sent me and the bike flying into the hole.

I realized a sharp pain in my right shoulder, but she kept on charging, hitting both me and the bike. I fell off the bike, and she stood on my right ankle. This was the ankle I had injured 20 years earlier. I was finally able to get a stick and beat her off.

It hurt like hell all that night. The next morning, I went to the hospital, and they x-rayed my shoulder and ankle. I had a badly-torn rotator cuff in my shoulder and more damage to my right ankle.

I was referred to a specialist in Kamloops, and there I was put in an air cast for my ankle but was told I would have to eventually have to have surgery on my shoulder.

Later, this all caused arthritis.

I did continue to walk on my ankle, and it did improve some, but I was referred to a Dr. Pethabridge for my shoulder. He was a specialist who did a lot of work with the Canadian Olympic team.

I was scheduled for surgery the following January. My arm was put in a sling for two months. The following January, I was booked into a private clinic for three days to repair my rotator cuff. The operation went well – I was told it was a complete success.

I went home, and three days later I woke up to find that the incision site on my shoulder was, in fact, infected. I went to the hospital in Williams Lake – they wanted to lance and drain it.

In the meantime, Pat phoned the specialist in Kamloops, and he told her not to let them do that. She was to get me to Kamloops as soon as possible.

By the time we got to Kamloops, a large white swelling full of pus had formed, about the size of a ping pong ball.

They were remodeling the hospital in Kamloops, and I was put in a waiting room, where there was a lot of dust, and workers going back and forth. The infection in my shoulder burst while I was waiting.

I went immediately into surgery, where the doctor tried to clean it out, but he had to cut away some of the muscle and tendons. I was in the hospital in Kamloops for 17 days, most of the time on an I.V. to try to control the infection in my body.

When I was released, my arm was again put in a sling.

This was a work-related accident. We had paid into Workers Compensation for several years. At first, they offered a lump sum payment instead of a monthly amount. I fought with them for more than seven years, trying to be treated fairly.

They assigned their own doctors, who gave me the run-around from one advisor to another. I had to appear in Kamloops every month at the Work Safe B.C. office.

I was bounced from one advisor to another.

Every one of them came up with some phony procedure to avoid payment to me.

They sent me to Prince George to see a specialist, regarding exactly what my impairment was. I appeared before three different medical specialists. One report said I only had 19% use of my arm and right shoulder. I could not lift my arm above my head and could not use a hammer or a rope.

That run-around was the biggest farce I ever experienced. They eventually paid me $960 a month until I reached the age of 65, and after three years they decided to give me a lump sum of $4,100.

During this time, WorkSafe B.C. was under a lot of criticism. One of their staff was shot and killed in the Kamloops office. That office was locked down like a prison, and even the front reception was behind bullet-proof glass. You were escorted to and from the office.

This injury did result in the lack of my ability to do many of the jobs or tasks that had to be done on a daily basis. It resulted in us having to hire extra staff. Workman's Comp treated Pat much the same in the year 2000 after she got sick with Ecoli, and also when the bale fell on her.

We had put up a large stack, eight bales high, of square bales – each weighing 900 lbs. They were 3' by 4' and 8' long.

Gord Neal stopped in one day to say the stack was heating. I went down to have a look and removed four of the bales. Pat decided to walk over, and as she did one of the bales rolled over and hit her.

It actually knocked her out. I got her in the jeep and called Jack on the radio to have an ambulance sent over.

I took her home and got her in the half-ton. The ambulance said they would meet us on the way to town, which they did. She was transferred to the ambulance, which took her to the hospital.

She had three broken ribs, a broken sternum and a badly injured shoulder. She was in the hospital for six days and had very poor mobility for over three months.

The hay, in fact, had not been heating.

Because I was the manager and had to sign all the Workman's Comp forms, and Pat was my wife, Workman's Comp made it very difficult to allow our claim. Eventually, Pat did get a small monthly cheque of $600.

Concerning the Ecoli, the sewage drain on the heifer ICU barn plugged up. Pat worked on cleaning it out for two days. She must have ingested some of the manure and got very sick.

She was in the hospital, and unable to look after herself for two weeks. Dr. Reece was our doctor; he researched what she had, and it was determined that it was HR27 Ecoli – the same as had infected people in Walkerton, Ontario.

He was told what to do to treat it. One thing he was not to do was to give her any antibiotics. This was difficult for me to understand, but in the end, he treated her in the best way possible. Again, Workman's Comp was very unfair in the treatment for her claim.

These problems were all complicated by Pat's diabetes. In 2009 she also developed kidney stones. She was sent to the Kamloops Regional Hospital, where they were to treat her. They decided to smash them or break them up instead of operating and removing them that way, in hopes that she would simply pass them.

This was done, and it put Pat in a tremendous amount of pain. On one trip to the hospital for a scheduled operation, she was admitted at 9am for a 12pm procedure. I was told to wait at the hospital, and they would call me at 4pm. I hadn't heard anything, so went back to the hospital and found out her operation had been delayed because of another emergency.

She was then scheduled to go into the O.R. at 6pm. I was told to phone at 9pm, and when I did I was told she would be in recovery until 10pm.

At 11pm I still had not heard anything. I had to go through a night watchman to get into the hospital. He phoned to see where Pat was, but they could not find her.

The night watchman got very angry. He contacted several different nurses in different departments and made it very clear they had damn well better find her and get their act together so they could let us know what was going on.

At midnight, they finally found Pat in the recovery room. She was fine and got a kick out of the fact that she'd been 'lost.'

All these injuries and problems resulted in many health issues for Pat, and she was often very depressed.

In 2004, I was walking in the heifer barn to check on a cow that was calving. There was a steep 6' slope that was very icy, and my feet went out from under me. I fell backwards and broke my leg.

I was put on crutches and told to stay off it for four weeks. I suggested that we should hire some help, but Pat would not hear of that, and took over my place on the calving crew.

She was perfectly capable and did an excellent job.

Over the years our workers had a lot of claims with Workman's Comp that were paid out. Many of these were not legitimate. One of the truck drivers claimed he smashed his thumb greasing the truck.

He had actually done it by clubbing a fish. Another truck driver claimed he had hurt his neck driving the truck on the field. He actually injured it driving off the dock into Dugan Lake.

These claims were paid out on reports that were not accurate, based on lies about how the injuries happened. Some of the employees used the W.C. program to get extra paid time off.

I hired a lot of locals, many young people, to irrigate. Many of them were from the reserves.

I always needed at least six people to move the irrigation pipe. Chad Stump from the Alexandria Band was my main irrigator for four years. He usually had his own helpers. I also hired some of the neighbours to help out on the ranch, including Everett Byman, who helped me for many years.

He was an excellent carpenter and did a lot of the repair work and the fixing up. He also remodeled some of the houses and did a lot of the corral work.

Everett also worked in the field doing tractor work, did calving and helped with the cattle. He was a very reliable neighbour – he helped me install some of he pivots and pipelines.

Him and his wife Maureen owned their own place six miles north of the main ranch. When the Springfield was purchased, I relied on Everett to do a lot of the work and the organization at FRR, as I became very involved at Springfield.

Burt Gentles and his wife Patty lived at km 67 on the 100 road. He worked for me for two summers and was a good man. His three sons also worked for the ranch at different times.

Their cousin, Derek Gentles, worked for me at Springfield for three summers.

Gordon Woods and his wife did a lot of the fencing on the ranch for eight years – they built approximately 20 miles of new fence, both at FRR and Buckskin.

Don Chambers lived 15 miles to the north. He and his three sons also helped me on the ranch. The first was Doug, who worked for me for two summers. He was a great worker, but unfortunately, he got into a fight in Merritt, and shot and killed another young man. Then he hid out.

Doug was very well liked by many friends and neighbours, and they wrote reference letters to try to stop the R.C.M.P. from tracking him down and killing him.

However, Doug ended up taking his own life.

His brother Soupie worked for me for three summers, and another brother, Matt, worked for me for a summer.

The closest ranch to the south was the Moon Ranch, owned by John Alex and Frances Moon. Our cattle often mixed on range, the Moon cattle often came home across our range, and each fall we had up to 60 head of their cows mixed with ours.

Eric and Diane Reay had a ranch at Meldrum Creek. They were very good people, were well-liked and very active in the community.

Further south was the Cotton Ranch, owned by Grant Huffman and Dean Bonner. A few of their cattle also mixed with ours. Dean had his own small airplane and would often fly me over our ranch to help find cows in the late fall.

Jim Coulthart and his wife Vi lived up the hill six miles from us. They had their own range and herd of cattle. He had a long-horn bull that often got in with our cows.

Herb Chesley had a ranch 20 miles north of our place. His ranch bordered us to the north, and our cattle often mixed, too.

Herb was a very good neighbour. One day I came along the road one mile from the ranch, and he was having trouble. He had about eight cows and calves in a stock trailer, but the side door had come open, and his cows were out on the road.

He did not know what to do. Pat and I helped him keep them together and drove them to our corrals and he loaded them back up. He was sure glad that Pat and I showed up!

Jake Sherbauer lived 10 miles north of us. He and his wife Tracy were good people. Jake loved to ride and helped me out with things like roundup and branding.

Scott Fareless lived four miles north of the ranch - he was also a great neighbour. He loved to walk and would often tell us of any concern he seen with our cows on range.

Tom Salley was the one of our neighbours we could not tolerate – he was a troublemaker.

Another very good neighbour was Willie Meldrum, who lived south of the ranch. He did a lot of logging and had his own guide license.

I made many changes when I took over management of FRR. The way they did the branding was an unbelievable process. They would crowd all the calves into a corral, run in and try to grab one and wrestle it down. It was very hard on the calves, and on those doing the work.

I changed this to where we would rope the calves by the heels. Two people would hold then down for processing; we would usually do 200-300 in one day. The most we did on one day was 500.

My son-in-law Steve was always a big help at branding, sorting and shipping. His dad, Denny, would also come out and help rope. I usually did all the castrating myself, and we would get in a crew of about 20-15 people to help with all this.

Steve also did a lot of my horse shoeing, and when we bought the Springfield, I hired Steve to move the cattle on range.

Denny sometimes helped Steve – they were very valuable during roundup and sorting at Springfield. Steve was a very capable cowboy and helped out a lot on my ranches.

He also really knew cattle; he breaks and trains great horses and has good cattle dogs.

I honestly believe that Steve is perhaps the best cowboy in the area. He also does pick-up at many of the local rodeos, and is very involved with 4-H, minor hockey and coaching baseball.

Dr. Bruce Kay

The Williams Lake vet clinic was owned by Dr. Bruce Kay. He employed vets, but he did most of the work on the large animals himself.

He was the vet on our ranch for most of the time we were at FRR. He did our preg testing, and most of the vet procedures the ranch needed. He was an excellent vet. He also had a great front-end staff in his clinic: Cindy, Karen, Becky and Bruce's wife Louise were long-time employees. They were knowledgeable, efficient and very helpful.

The ranch bought almost all of our medicines and supplies from his clinic.

He would put on clinics or field days from time to time, and always had a large supper every fall for his customers, complete with great speakers and reps from medical supply companies.

We became very good personal friends with Bruce, but we also relied on his help and advice on almost all concerns.

When I built the large barn at the ranch, I designed the ICU based on the one in Bruce's clinic. One of the vets in Bruce's clinic was Eileen Alberton, who was the vet in charge of Boyd with his hip and stomach concerns.

Bruce kept us informed on herd health and advised us on things like scour treatments.

During the Mad Cow outbreak in 2003, Bruce kept us informed on what steps we should take.

This disease had a huge impact on the Canadian beef industry, as many countries banned Canadian beef imports. This resulted in prices being reduced by up to 60%.

Several ranches invested money to operate a slaughter house outside of Salmon Arm. It was a great facility and a great idea, but the Federal Health of Animals would not give us the support that we needed.

They refused us access to waste product disposal, such as intestines and blood: this all had to be transferred to a facility in Swan Lake, Alberta where it would be properly disposed of by incineration.

This refusal eventually broke our slaughter house facility. FRR had invested $10,000 in this venture, which was a loss to the ranch.

I had sold 60 head of slaughter cows to this facility. We had a real battle getting paid for these cows. I was eventually paid for them, but the lawyers in charge of the foreclosure of the facility and the bankruptcy did everything to try to make me give back the money.

I just ignored their demands, and after two years, they just gave up – they had no legal case.

Advice I got at my wedding reception to Marj in 1960

I got some good advice from three old-time ranchers. One of them was Jack Paul, a well-known cattleman and farmer who was injured when he was younger when a boar hog ran his tusk up Jack's leg, tearing muscle and tendons. He had a bad limp from that day on.

Another fellow was Allen Baker, the owner of the Bar U Ranch at Longview. The third was an older Norwegian man who had quite an accent. I went up to get a drink after the wedding reception. At the time I usually drank Scotch whiskey. Olaf the Norwegian seen this and invited me to the table where the three of them were sitting.

The first time I met Olaf and we shook hands, he went on and on about my firm handshake. To him, a person with a firm handshake was honest, hard working and sincere.

The three of them went on about hard work and opportunities in life. One thing they said was that you only have three chances to own and develop a superior cattle herd in your lifetime, as it took 29 years of hard work, and a great deal of patience, to develop a good herd.

So, if you ranched for 60 years, you'd be lucky to develop three good herds.

The second thing they said was that you'd be lucky if you owned three good horses in your life, and the third was that you'd be lucky if you owned three good dogs in your life.

I developed a great herd of cows on my own ranch at Purple Springs. I have owned three great horses: Billy, Jingles and Lester. They were all great cattle horses and were great to ride, with great stamina. They were also great with my kids.

I have also owned three great dogs: Sport, when I was young, Boyd, my almost-human cattle dog and great friend, and now our young dog Brandy – an excellent pet.

So, in the eyes of those three old-timers, I have fulfilled these three opportunities in my life.

Cattle drives

I used to drive my cattle from my farm at Purple Springs to the ranch Frank and I owned at Skiff. We would take about 150 at a time, an all-day drive of over 16 miles, going across country. Some of it was also on the gravel roads.

It was take six or eight of us, and often several of our kids and three or four horses. Some of the longest drives I organized and headed up were when we brought the cows home from Aspen Valley Ranch to the benches and hayfield at the headquarters of FRR.

We would trail 600 or so cows the 25km in mid-November.

This would involve one person leading with a bale on the tractor, with six or eight cowboys scattered along the road amongst the herd, keeping them moving and making sure none wandered into the bush.

We would start the drive at about 8am and arrive either at the main ranch headquarters just before dark, or if we came down through the Magnusson place, we would get them to the hayfield about 4pm.

Pat would go to the front and count the cows through the gate. This was often a cold, wet drive on horseback. I remember one time it was just starting to snow when we left Aspen, and it snowed hard all day. When we arrived at the hayfields, though, it was clear with no snow. When we went back up at 6pm to get our trucks, there was two feet of snow on the ground that we had trouble plowing through.

We also made several smaller cattle drives, to and from Emerald Lake, with 150 or so head. This was a 13km drive. We made several from Pre-emption to Windy Point and Aspen Valley of about 100 head. This was a 16km drive, too. We made several drives of 100 head up the 100 road to Buckskin Meadows.

In the spring, we usually made a drive of 150-200 head the six miles up to Salmon Meadow. This was done when the calves were young, so it was always a very slow drive.

Another difficult drive was when we moved the cows up on the range at the Springfield Ranch. This was five miles, and again with young calves and about 400 head. This trail went uphill, so the dogs and horses worked very hard all day.

It was always very difficult to keep the young calves together with their mothers.

Gathering the cows for branding was also pretty intense. Often, we would gather them on the hayfield for a few days beforehand, then bring in 250-300 head to the corrals early in the morning. I always took at least 20 people for each branding: three ropers, eight wrestlers, three doing vaccinations, two branding and two doing the de-horning.

Usually, Pat and someone else did the book work and the records. Pat was a great organizer at the brandings. Usually we had a branding party afterwards, where we served up the testicles for a great feast.

One challenge we always had was to gather the cows that were out late in the fall. It was often difficult to get all of the bulls in until late November and December.

This usually involved searching for them and bringing in two or three at a time. This was often done in rough, cold weather. I hated riding when there was a lot of snow on the trees, as it would fall off and you'd be wet all day.

I always rode with an Australian Outback long slicker, chaps and often long johns and a heavy winter coat. At lunch we usually made a fire to warm up. I had a horse named Pete, who learned to sneak up and take the sandwich from your hand.

I had several cows charge me during branding or in the barn. Some were very protective of their calves. One hit me in the kidneys and I had hard time walking for a few days.

Another time I put one in a small 12'x12' pen. She hit the panels, which in turn hit me, injuring my chest and shoulders. The same cow did the same the next day to Everett.

I had one cow I needed to move out of the calving pen with her newborn calf. She was really mean. I got on the tractor, which didn't have a cab. I dropped the rope on the calf, and pulled it up on the seat with me. The cow decided to follow her calf, so I had to bail off the tractor.

We always tagged and processed the newborn calves as quick as we could after they were born, so you have to be very careful, as this was the time when the cows were most protective.

One time when we were sorting up at Aspen, we had six bulls in a small pen and they started to fight. Pat grabbed a cane; I hollered at her and told her to get back, but one of them knocked another into a panel that moved about 4'. This panel hit Pat, and sent her flying, injuring her chest.

Another time I was working a cow in the cattle squeeze, cutting off a horn with a de-horning cable. She threw her head and caught me square in the face. Pat took me to the hospital where I needed 16 stitches and a clean up.

Feed requirements

I always planned for 33lbs of feed per cow for winter feeding, either sileage or hay. At FRR we usually had at least 850 cows, 300 yearlings, 60 bulls and 15 horses. This meant we needed at least 2,000 tons of feed at FRR, another 1,200 at Springfield and 800 at Buckskin.

This meant I either had to put up or arrange for at least 4,000 tons of feed each year.

We usually fed on top of the ground on the hayfields, or we'd be reseeding on the hayfields the next year. This way we utilized the manure as fertilizer.

The heifers were fed in the feed bunks. It took about three weeks each fall to clean the manure out of the corrals where we kept the cattle in the winter. We had a large feed wagon for feeding out the sileage. It held seven tons of sileage at one time, and we used ground bale busters to rake up and feed out the round bales.

I used a 930 Cat loader to fill the sileage wagon at the sileage pit.

We used a four-wheel drive tractor with chains on both front and rear wheels to pull the sileage wagon. The wagon was very heavy and would sometimes push the tractor around on icy roads.

One time I was going to the Buckskin pivot fields to put out a load of sileage. The road was very icy, and there were a few small curves in the road. I geared down, but as I went around one sharp curve the tractor started to slide.

I could not control it. I was pushed off the road and over a small slope for about 15 feet. The wagon started to jack-knife and the tractor started to roll. I was very lucky, as the tractor came up against a fir tree that held it upright. I had to hire a large winch truck to get the tractor and wagon out.

We did not feed in that field again when the road was icy.

There was a great view from the kitchen window at FRR. We looked across some of the corrals and the house lake, across the pastures and the working corrals.

Looking across the river you could see the large train trestle that spanned Hakes Creek.

This was a great view when the sun came up and it shined on the train trestle.

From the Lowery property, you could see up the river for about three miles. The river wound its way and was truly beautiful. If you rode up on the rim rock above the valley, you had a great view of several of the pastures and many of the farm fields.

At Pre-emption, there were many wet meadows, and you could go up on one of the hills and see for miles. In the wintertime, you would often see moose on the meadows at Pre-emption.

It was great to ride though Aspen Valley in the late fall and see all the fall colours: the ground would be just covered with colourful leaves.

At Buckskin, we had a 20ft waterfall that fell into our irrigation system. And at Buckskin you could look over the river bank and see several hoodoos with the river below. From the Rudy Johnson bridge you could see a small island with the remains of a small cabin on it.

Apparently, someone had moved onto the island and cut down enough trees to make a cabin and a shed. He used a rowboat to go to shore where he kept his bicycle, which he used to go to town or visit a neighbour.

Often Pat and I just went for a drive on the ranch, taking different routes and enjoying what was close by to see.

Even though Reinhart owned the ranch, he did not realize everything there was to see. He drove or walked a lot of it at his leisure. One time when he was out, he asked me to show him all the range. I picked him up at 7:30am, and took him to the west end of the ranch to Twan Creek, our cow camp, and so on.

We toured back roads until 5pm when he had to go back to his house to make some phone calls. He wanted to know how much of it he had seen, and I said, "You've seen perhaps 25% of it."

We spent two more days driving FRR, Buckskin and Springfield, and he decided to take aerial photos of it all. I always enjoyed going to Buckskin Meadows in the summer, as there were several loons on the lakes. There were also a lot of wild geese and many wild geraniums in one of the pastures.

When we weaned the calves at Aspen Valley, we gathered the cows in the different meadows for two weeks before doing the weaning. Usually the calves were pre-sold for delivery at a certain date.

We would bring the cows and calves into the corrals at daylight and start storing them in the various lots. There would often be lots of 100 head gathered in each pen.

These calves were weighed and sorted, and the truck would start to arrive about 2pm, when they were loaded and hauled to various buyers and feedlots. These lots were often in Alberta, and the calves would travel nonstop to their destination, often hauled for 12-14 hours.

If it was a longer haul than 15 hours, they were unloaded, fed and watered, and loaded back up to complete their journey.

I was very fussy about the trucks, and the delivery of our calves. I insisted the buyers received the calves in the best possible condition.

We sorted them according to weight, colour and condition.

Our tan calves were very much in demand.

I insisted that the trucks had to be clean and filled with fresh bedding; Pat wrote up a list of the conditions and procedures to load our calves. The buyers appreciated the extra effort and the quiet way we handled the calves that they purchased.

The day after the weaning, we would round up all the cows and put them through the squeeze for preg testing.

This usually took about two-an-a-half days of hard work. The open, or culled cows were kept separate all through the hayfields for approximately a month to put on extra weight. They were then sold at the auction market in Williams Lake.

We generally had a 10 to 12% culled rate, so the sale of our culled cows, and the proper care of them were an important part of our income.

We purchased a lot of our Charolais bulls from Keith and Cheryl Altwasser at Lumby, and got our Brisco Charolais at Golden, or from the Rawe Ranches at Camrose.

Our Hereford bulls were often bought from Ray Stienburgh at Cranbrook, or Deanfield Herefords, or Jim Turner at Kamloops.

We also purchased Hereford bulls from Marine or Fred Zimmer at Lumby, as well as other local breeders.

Our Black Angus bulls were often bought from Crosby Ranches at Dawson Creek, Todd Marchant or Heart Ranches at Claresholm.

We culled at least 15 bulls each year so had to replace them.

I always bought good quality bulls, which were usually replaced every six years, so our bull purchase costs were a big expense.

After Joreg bought the Springfield Ranch, FRR operated it in trust for him. I was president, director and manager of FRR, Springfield and Buckskin.

I hired different foreman who helped me operate theses ranches, but it was very hard to find reliable, responsible people.

The best employees I had I will list in order:

Pat, who did the accounting, also helped with the cattle, did the yard work and took responsibility for a lot of the ranch business. We hired Joyce Ward to do the books, payroll, and so on. She would prepare the cheques to pay the accounts, which I signed every two weeks. Pat and Joyce worked great together.

Everett Byman worked for the ranch for over 15 years He helped with farming and the harvest and was my main carpenter. He took a lot of the work load and responsibility off my shoulders+ and was also great with calving.

Bruce Bowe was an all-around good cowboy; he drove truck, did farming and helped a lot with the irrigation.

Jim Heaton was a good man: great at operating the excavator, good with the cattle, and was very responsible and reliable.

Kevin Kauffman did the irrigation and helped with the farming. He also packed sileage, and starting at age 14, helped me feed in the winter. Jack Roberts, my grandson, also packed sileage and did farm work for me for four summers – he was very reliable and responsible.

Tom and Jill worked for me for two years. Tom drove Cat and helped with the farm work. They were good people.

Cliff Dorion was managing Springfield when we bought it; he also worked for me part time and was a great help with the irrigation. Paul Ruddenklau from New Zealand and his girlfriend Tracy were good workers, and they became very good friends.

I used several trappers at the ranch; one was Sheldon Purdy, and there was also Ben and Ian Mobbs.

Roy and Chad Stump helped me for four summers, Karen Sinclair worked for me as a truck driver and Todd Lloyd helped me with the farming and the irrigating.

Angie Moon worked for me for two summers as a cowgirl, and also helped with the farming.

Katri and her boyfriend from Australia worked for me for two years and did a lot of the fencing and general farm work.

Avia from Norway worked for me for six months and become a very good friend; Pat and I actually adopted her as a granddaughter.

Shannon Smith helped out in the yard for two years and became a good friend of Pat's.

I also hired many others for short periods of time. In all the years I managed the ranch, I only had a conflict with three workers who I fired on the spot.

Lorne Hinche was my logger for over 10 years.

When Joreg bought Springfield, I hired the whole crew that was working there. Most lasted two years. I then hired Dwayne Halverson as my foreman for a year-and-a-half, and his brother, son and wife also worked for me part time.

They were questionable employees at best.

I have no doubt forgotten to mention at least 20 employees that worked for me at various times.

In the summer, I would have between eight and 16 workers, and approximately eight in the winter time.

Derek Gentles worked for all three ranches at different times. He was good with the cattle and the heavy equipment.

I had problems with one employee using drugs; we had a zero-tolerance drug policy.

Steve Roberts, Dixie and their kids often helped out on the ranch and with the cattle work. In 2009, I hired Mike Altwasser to mange the FRR ranch, and when I retired he took over as full-time manager.

I also hired Gord Neal and Wendy Dixon as cowboys at the Aspen Ranch for three years, and they were later hired as managers at the Springfield Ranch when I retired.

Harold Lindbirgh was often hired to do the mechanical work, and the instillation of the pivots and irrigation systems.

Woody Tetterstone was a very reliable welder for all three ranches for several years.

Eric Mirus owned his own small excavator, and I often hired him to install water lines, sewage lines, and repair various pipelines and irrigation ditches. He was, in fact, a very valuable part of the operation and was reliable and very knowledgeable.

Downtown Service did a lot of the repair work on the ranch vehicles.

The ranch payroll averaged about $160,000 every year, not including my salary.

Pat had a very good flower garden and developed great yards at both FRR and Buckskin. She loved her garden and growing flowers – this was something she really enjoyed.

At Springfield, there were two log houses, as well as a good garden that included raspberries and strawberries. Pat also looked after these yards.

She loved to pick Saskatoons, chokecherries and wild raspberries and did a lot of canning.

Mack Graham had built a large arena when he owned the Aspen Valley Ranch that was 400 feet long, complete with an announcer stand. I used this building for hay storage.

When we were successful in getting the range permit for Buckskin, we had to install two regulation cattle guards on the main road. We put these in ourselves. They worked very well and are still in use today.

We had to build new fence from Buckskin marshes to Bear Lake, 2km long. I hired Gordon Woods to build this. There were some bad vibes between Gordon and Forestry, but he built the fence to his own standards.

It was a very well-built four-wire fence. I had to log and clear the right-of-way.

We often would see Bighorn sheep at Buckskin, and also at what we called the slide area on the West Fraser Road.

They migrate between that area and Cotton Ranch at Riske Creek

Each spring we had a big problem with Canada geese. They would bring scours into our calves, as well as other problems, as they stopped at every feed lot as they migrated north.

Jack Butler and Pat Jasper loved to hunt these geese in the fall. It was not uncommon to see several flocks of 200-300 geese for four weeks in April and May.

We did have several bear encounters, one I will never forget. I was walking from one field to another along a steep bank at the River Place, picking wild raspberries as I went along. I looked into a small opening between the bushes and came face to face with a black bear about 10 feet away.

I backed away, and when I got about 50ft away, I looked up the bank. I guess he was afraid of me as I was of him: he was scampering straight up the 200ft bank.

Another time, I had to walk to my truck across a 6' high rye crop. Suddenly, I could smell dead animal. I broke out into a large 40' round opening that contained a lot of bones and a couple of deer carcasses. I was lucky the bear was not there!

The fuel tank at FRR started to leak with a steady drip, so we removed it. We had to dig down about 20' to get to the bottom of the diesel fuel leak.

The leak went straight down and contaminated the soil in an area about 2' around, and about 20' deep.

We often visited with Gordon and Vi Woods; they loved to play crib and Pat and Vi were good friends.

Reinhart was very committed to increasing irrigation acreage and doing water improvements.

We often went over many ideas and possibilities, and I spent many hours studying maps, water licences, etc.

The four main areas we decided to work on were increasing the water flow in Collins Creek, utilizing the snow melt above the ranch headquarters, increasing the flow in the house lake and utilizing the three or four small streams that slowed above the ranch buildings and in Garth Lloyd's.

Paul from New Zealand was very capable at operating my excavator. He was put to work ditching and cleaning up several bog areas that fed Collins Creek. This took a lot of skill to prevent the excavator from getting bogged down.

Several times, Paul would have to use the beam and the bucket on excavator to lift the track off the ground and put a tree or some trash under the track to free up the machine.

He also ditched about a half mile through Jim Coutart's farm, draining that area for Jim's benefit, but also delivering the runoff into Collins Creek.

We had to dynamite some shale rock for about a quarter mile to get the ditch deep enough. Pete Abrahamson did the dynamiting.

We hired him to drill through about 3' of solid rock and blast the ditch deeper. This was a very slow process, but this ditching did increase the flow in Collins Creek enough so that I could install and operate wheel lines and irrigation on another 80 acres.

Salmon Meadows held a lot of water that we used to fill our house lake every spring, using a series of pipe and ditching. Above Salmon Meadow was Long Lake – a large lake fed by Spring Lake.

We improved the ditch between Spring Lake and Long Lake, pumped the water from Long Lake to Salmon Meadow, and diverted enough water to our house lake to enable us to irrigate another 140 acres.

First, we had to log and clear 80 acres.

I hired Jack Butler, an excellent Cat operator with a keen eye to operate my D8 Cat and do this work for me.

We then increased the pumps and installed an additional three miles of 8" pipe from the house lake to provide the water for these new pivots.

I also had to have B.C. Hydro move six power poles so the pivots could complete the necessary circle.

Everett Byman and Burt Gentles did a lot of the work installing these new pivots.

After Joreg bought the Buckskin Ranch, Reinhart had me install five new pivots. Three of these required logging and leveling of approximately 150 acres of very rough land.

Jack Butler had to fill in one ravine, over a quarter mile long and 20' deep. It took him about two months.

We also hired Lake Excavating to bring in two large earth movers and scrapers to level another 80 acres.

There was one hill that required a 15' cut. Joe Monical helped me prepare this land for farming.

I designed and installed this pivot myself using FRR ranch labour. We also wanted to upgrade over two miles of hand line irrigation, both at Buckskin and at the River Place.

I priced out wheel line irrigation at Highland Irrigation in Williams Lake. They wanted approximately $11,000 for each quarter mile system. I looked around and found a small dealer in Westlock, B.C. that would bring in used wheel lines from Alberta for $5,000 each.

The dealer's name was Brock Eys. We purchased six of these systems from Brock. He would deliver one each week. We had to erect them ourselves; three of these were installed in the hayfield at Buckskin, and three were installed at the River Place on FRR land.

Joreg did purchase a lot of irrigation equipment, but FRR provided all the labour and everyday expenses. We also needed to put in 3km of 8" PVC pipe. Jim Heaton operated the excavator or most of the work. We put in three miles of new four-wire fencing, as well. The extra labour costs for all this work was approximately $500,000.

This increased the irrigation acreage on both ranches by over 1,200 acres.

This new irrigation land was then used to grow more hay and grain sileage and make both operations self-sufficient in feed requirements.

Joreg purchased a new John Deere forage harvester and two tandem trucks, etc, to enable us to harvest the sileage.

Jim Heaton had hay fever bad, so he could only operate the forage harvester part time.

So, for the first two years I operated the forage harvester. I hired one more truck driver and one other person to cut the crop. There was an apartment for housing at the Buckskin Ranch. Everett remodeled that for an additional house. Over the next two years I hired several different couples to help out, but none lasted longer that two or three months. Again, Bruce Bowe and Everett became my most reliable workers.

My grandson, Jack Roberts, and Kevin Kauffman were the ones that packed the sileage in the pits.

Pam Carter did a lot of the swathing for me, and in 2006 Rachel Ruddenklau came from New Zealand and operated my mower conditioner for an entire summer.

She was a great helper and also became a close family friend.

I took on the task of operating most of the pivot irrigation systems. We hired three irrigators to move the hand lines and the wheel lines. I would always check the pivots late at night before dark, and again at 5am every morning.

Often, I would have to go out in the middle of the night to check them. They were all designed to operate automatically, and even reverse directions, but I still needed to keep a close eye on them.

Because most of the systems were at Buckskin, Pat and I moved from the house at FRR to the large house at Buckskin. It had a very large yard; we purchased a ride-on mower; but it still took over four hours twice a week to mow the yard.

Pat, again, was a lot of help, and she would often accompany me on my pivot checks and help clean the screens and nozzles on the irrigation systems. We had to go up the hill five miles to adjust the water flow from the Buckskin lakes to the ranch.

It was very important that we did not waste any water, or we wouldn't have enough to last us all season.

There was a swimming pool at Buckskin, and Rachel and her boyfriend put that to good use.

Pat's granddaughter, Christine, visited us for six weeks in the summer, and Joreg often brought a friend from Austria to the ranch.

Several of those friends, he hoped could help out, or eventually take over part of the management. My commitment to Reinhart and Joreg, and to the ranch, was that I would always do my best to operate the ranches as effectively and efficiently as I could, always keeping both Reinhart's and Joreg's interests at the forefront.

Some of Joreg's friends had their own ideas on how to profit from helping out. Many wanted to operate the equipment, but not do any irrigation or manual labour.

One of these friends who visited always wanted a truck or a vehicle at his disposal.

We purchased a new rotary mower to cut hay at accost of $32,000.

Joreg asked me to allow his friend to operate it. I spent several hours showing him how everything worked, and then let him have a go of it on his own.

On his very first round, he hit one of the tires on the pivot tower doing about $5,000 damage, and another $10,000 to the mower machine conditioner, on this brand-new machine.

Andre, one of my employees, spend three days repairing it, but the machine was in bad shape. Andre made it clear that he would quit if any of Joreg's friends were ever allowed to operate machines again.

Andre was always up and working by 6am. He worked hard all day and was very good with the machines and the cattle.

I rented a skidsteer loader, to clean out two of my cattle sheds. I had never operated one before and ran it for three or four hours and then put Andre on it. He did more cleanout in half an hour than I had done in four hours.

He did not like working at the Springfield Ranch; and I soon had him a job at FRR working under Mike.

We tried to hire reliable help at Springfield, without much success. I would have a weekly meeting with the staff from all three ranches. Mike was doing a great job at FRR; however, his wife Monica interfered with employees at Springfield, putting me at odds with those employees.

Dwayne Halverson was a foreman at Springfield.

In 2008, Pat and I decided we could no longer handle the management and labour requirements at FRR. Several past injuries and health injuries simply did not allow us to be fully involved.

We approached Reinhart with our decision, and he said if he were going to step down, he would be selling the ranch. We worked out an agreement where we would be paid to continue on as president and director of all three ranches but not so much of the manual labour.

So, Reinhart asked me to list the ranch for sale. We worked out a fair agreement where we would receive a retirement benefit package when the ranch was sold. We got the ranch appraised, including all assets including land equipment and livestock.

I then listed the ranch with Barry Cline, a realtor, for $8.9 million. We also approached Joreg with our decision, and he, too asked us to continue on as president and director of Springfield and Buckskin.

He was, however, slow at coming up with a benefit package, or an amount he would pay us for doing this. He expected us to do this with payment only from Reinhart and FRR.

We spent a great amount of time working out a fair agreement, until he finally agreed on a four-year term at $25,000 every two years.

Barry Cline did receive a few inquiries, but nothing close to our asking price, so after one year, we listed it with Cascadia Realtors, with Irv Ridd as the agent.

Mike was also hired on as the day-to-day manager at FRR, and my assistant manager at Springfield and Buckskin.

The following winter, we took a trip to New Zealand. When we checked emails in Vancouver, there was an unexpected notice from Joreg that he would no longer work with Reinhart. He was going to take all his equipment, his share of the cattle, and operate Springfield and Buckskin as his own ranches.

He was going to hire legal council in Austria to work out the details. I felt this was unfair of him, after all the assistance Reinhart had given him.

I didn't know the agreement that Reinhart and Joreg had between them. Eventually Pat and I were asked to determine a fair settlement between the two brothers.

I spent over two years working out an agreement that was suitable and fair. Joreg was not easy to deal with. He insisted he be repaid the full cost of the cows he bought. No consideration was given for the older cows or bulls.

He wanted to be paid the full amount for any equipment he had purchased. In the end, Joreg took his own equipment, and Reinhart purchased what he needed to operate FRR. Reinhart got frustrated with Joreg's unfair approach, and just said to give him what he wanted.

I made it clear to Joreg that I would not work with him after the four-year agreement was completed.

I hired a young acquaintance of Joreg's, who was 23 years old and from Austria, to do the day-to-day management at Springfield. His name was Reinhart Kappis, and he had no experience with farming or ranching, or as a manager.

He tried to develop new irrigation and bought equipment that was not needed, including two new ¾ ton trucks, two new tractors and three ATVs. He lasted just over a year as manager.

Joreg then hired Gord Neal as his manager at Springfield.

We had seldom ever borrowed money to operate Joreg's interest on the ranch. Two years after I retired, BMO asked me to look over the books, as the Springfield and Buckskin were carrying a large debt load.

Pat got totally frustrated with Joreg's attitude, and in late 2010 she threw up her hands, and asked me to work everything out with Joreg. She no longer wanted to be involved, and in fact, went to New Zealand for three months. Eventually, Joreg paid us the $50,000 he owed us.

I also sold him Pat's Jeep, all our own furniture in the Buckskin house and any other personal stuff we could not keep.

That year Joreg also bought a small sawmill, and Everett was hired to build a new calving barn and garage and several corrals at Springfield.

Pat would not have a thing to do with Joreg from that time on.

In the fall of 2011, Kevin Reid was brought to the ranch as a potential buyer. He eventually formed a large company and bought the ranch under the name Blue Goose Cattle Company.

I was paid out what was owed me and continued on until the late spring of 2012 as president and director of Springfield and Buckskin. I was fully in charge of the sale of FRR, and was very grateful that we'd hired Mary MgGregor as our lawyer and final negotiator.

Final negotiations were very interesting. We were to receive the full price of what we asked for the ranch. In addition, they also bought the D8 Cat. They only thing they did not buy was the Avalanche truck. I bought that for $3,000, much to Joreg's annoyance, as he claimed he owned it, but had no proof that he paid any money toward the purchase of it.

Reinhart asked me to be in charge of the FRR sale for him, which meant I worked vey closely with Mary McGregor.

Kevin Reid visited the ranch several times from Ontario to express his interest in purchasing it. Over the next few months, he put together several investors, who gave us a letter of intent to purchase FRR.

Doug Sinclair from 70 Mile House was hired as the manager, or CEO of Blue Goose Cattle Company. He was also an architect out of Vancouver, B.C.

This group of investors borrowed $80,000,000 to purchase different ranches and became very involved with food production in both the U.S. and Canada.

When Doug Sinclair visited me and my crew to determine if we could make a final deal, he expressed interest in hiring all of my crew. The Blue Goose Cattle Company hired several different accountants, and lawyers in both the U.S. and Canada.

At this point, I made sure all negotiations and offers would be approved by Mary, to make sure everything was legal.

In early 2011, we were given a letter of intent by this group and given 30 days to reply to the letter. At this time, Irv Ridd subcontracted Richard Osborne to help them put the deal together.

I found Richard difficult to work with and had to make several changes to the letter of intent.

Mary was excellent in directing and keeping the possibility of the sale on the up and up.

Richard attempted to charge additional sales commissions, etc, and I kept Reinhart informed at every step, and advised him to be more firm and demanding.

He had full confidence in Pat and I working with Mary to move the sale forward, always at the $8.9 million amount.

Blue Goose gave us a down payment of $250,000, and we gave them 45 days to take full diligence and arrange for full payment. The final foreclosure date was to be May 8, 2011.

Reinhardt was spending a lot of time in Europe on his other businesses, so I was fully in charge.

Mary was able to contact him to sign some of the necessary paperwork.

At this time, Blue Goose had involved several large investors. They had eight accountants in Vancouver, two lawyers and various accountants in Toronto, and more in New York.

At times this was very interesting, but Mary was fully capable and an excellent lawyer.

The price of $8.9 million was never in question. We had an appraisal done, and an agreement on the cattle by Will Smith of B.C. Livestock.

Down payment and advances did change some from the original letter of intent. Reinhart's instructions were clear that we were not to change the terms of the final sale amount, or the date of the final payment. Everything moved ahead as planned until May 6, 2011.

Blue Goose attempted to change the closing offer, and demanded some tax concessions, that would have been advantageous to them. This would not alter the sale price, but some of the tax advantages would be advantageous to Blue Goose, but a detriment to Reinhart.

This would have resulted in a benefit of approximately $200,000 to Blue Goose Cattle investors.

Mary phoned me and asked me to contact Reinhart and suggest we accept the new demands from Blue Goose. I tried to get in touch with Reinhart, as did Mary. We left several messages for him to contact us, but he did not get back to us.

Mary suggested that we accept the changes the buyers were asking for, but I informed her that I couldn't do that without Reinhart's approval, as I had given him my word I would only accept the figures and the agreement we were originally given.

She was concerned that if we didn't accept the offer, they would not go ahead with the sale. However, I had given Reinhart my word. This went on all afternoon on May 7.

Mary phoned almost every 30 minutes, trying to convince me to proceed with the sale at Blue Goose wanted. She was quite adamant that they would back out of their offer. I told Mary I just could not back out of my agreement with Reinhart, and that I would only be able to proceed with the original offer.

As midnight approached, Mary was phoning every 15 minutes, suggesting I change my mind, but I just couldn't do it without Reinhart's approval.

At 11:55pm she phoned and said she had just got off the phone with the Blue Goose lawyers, and if I would not accept their offer with the changes they wanted, they would withdraw their offer.

Again, I refused to agree to their demands. Her advice was still that we give them what they wanted, because she was sure Reinhart would want the sale of the ranch to go ahead and suggested he might be pretty annoyed with me if I lost the sale.

The tax concession was very important to the buyers, but I also felt that it was important to Reinhart. Mary phoned me five minutes after midnight to inform me that Blue Goose had backed down and would be proceeding with the sale as originally agreed.

She had to confirm this with the Blue Goose lawyers, and phoned again three minutes later, and said, "Tim, I'm very surprised. The Blue Goose lawyers have been told to go ahead with the sale without the tax concessions they wanted."

She phoned me at 7am the next morning and simply said, "Tim, you somehow won. Do you realize this small-town lawyer has just out-maneuvered some of the best lawyers on Bay Street and Wall Street that had been representing the Blue Goose Cattle Company?"

Reinhart phoned me shortly afterward. He had talked to Mary, and she had filled him in on what had happened. He thanked me for the stance I had taken.

"I only have one question for you, Reinhart," I said. "And that is, 'What would you have done if I had lost the sale? How annoyed would you have been?'"

He said, "No, Tim; I would not have been annoyed with you. You did what was right, and exactly what I would have wanted you to."

Reinhart said he had left the negotiations in my hands for a reason and had every confidence I would do it right.

One month later, Blue Goose forwarded full payment for FRR to Mary McGregor. After consultation with Reinhart, she paid off all accounts, and any money owing, including the commission to the real estate agents, and any back loans.

Reinhart made it clear that the first cheque she signed was to go to me and Pat to honour the amount I was to receive.

Part of the agreement was that the Blue Goose accountants in Vancouver were to take over the books, including payroll, government deductions, and so on.

Pat and I make a special trip to Kamloops to take a gift and some flowers to Mary McGregor for all she had done. Mary was, and still is, one of the highest-regarded agriculture lawyers in B.C.

Once again, I was very fortunate that I had great people to work with me and assist me.

Reinhart never wanted to visit the ranch again. He had Pat and I remove all his personal belongings from his house, including some paintings.

I continued on as president and director for Joreg and his holdings until March 30, 2012.

Two of the best employees I had at Springfield were Ivan Sampson and Dwayne Sergeant.

Bruce Bowie continued to be one of the best employees I had at FRR. He worked there for over 18 years. Everett Byman was the most honest and reliable employee I had for over 10 years.

Pat and I purchased a house in Terra Ridge in Williams Lake in July 2011. We moved off the ranch and into that house in August 2011.

That winter, we took a trip to Saskatoon to visit Sandra and family, and also to Manitoba to visit Dan and his family. I was still busy handling the final settlement with Reinhart and Joreg.

I will always be very appreciative of how well my family, including my brothers and sisters, treated Pat. She always loved all of our grandkids and was always very proud of them.

Pat's son was living in New Zealand. He and his wife were having marital problems, and he had Pat over to stay with him. She only spent eight days there, however, and then went down to stay with Judith and Owen for three more weeks. She became interested in us perhaps moving to New Zealand, and in fact looked at several different houses there.

When she returned, she tried to work out her problems with WorkSafe B.C., as well as concerns she had with kidney stones, and with pains in her chest and sternum that were at times unbearable. Her diabetes was also causing her many problems, as did the Ecoli that just would not go away.

We took a bus trip to the Yukon, and Alaska in June and July of that year. We enjoyed that holiday very much, even though Pat was in almost constant discomfort. We went to Dawson City, Anchorage and Skagway.

We had left our car in Calgary, so on our return, we again drove to Saskatoon and Winnipeg. Pat's health continued to deteriorate. I lost her in August of 2012. This was a terrible loss for me. I could not handle being alone. Pat was cremated, and we had her funeral service at Pioneer Log

Complex in Williams Lake. My family all attended, and in fact, made most of the arrangements for me.

Sandra was the executor and did a fantastic job of settling all of Pat's affairs.

The next summer, we buried Pat's ashes in the Williams Lake cemetery. I purchased a large enough plot so that my ashes will be buried beside her.

I dedicate these memoirs to Pat, my partner for over 35 years. We were together in Lethbridge, at the Bobtail and Bar X and the FRR ranches. She was a very capable, talented and well-liked lady.

This poem was written by Frank Gleason for Pat on August 22, 2012. Frank was a well-known cowboy poet all over western Canada and the western U.S.

```
                  PAT, LOVED BY ALL WHO KNEW HER.

          SOMETIMES WHEN WE LOSE A LOVED ONE
          AND WE HAVE TO SAY GOOD-BYE
          YOU CAN'T BELIEVE THEIR TIME HAS COME
          AND YOU'LL SIT AND WONDER WHY.

          YES, SOMEONE YOU LOVED AND SHARED YOUR LIFE.
          YOU JUST CAN'T BELIEVE THEY'RE GONE,
          BUT, YOU TREATED HER WELL AS EVERYONE COULD TELL
          SO THAT'S BOUND TO MAKE YOU STRONG.

          BUT, LIFE YOU KNOW IS A GAMBLE
          AND WE LIVE EACH DAY BY CHANCE.
          SO, JUST THINK OF THE GOOD TIMES YOU HAD IN THE PAST
          WHEN YOU BOTH WORKED DOWN ON THE RANCH.

          SO, AT NIGHT JUST LOOK UP AT THE MOON
          WHEN THE STARS ARE TWINKLING BRIGHT
          THEN YOU'LL SEE PAT SMILING DOWN AT YOU
          SAYING DON'T WORRY TIM, THINGS ARE ALRIGHT.

          SO, IF WE BELIEVE WHAT WE'VE ALWAYS BEEN TOLD
          WELL, YOU'RE NOT REALLY LEFT ALL ALONE.
          SHE'LL BE WAITING UP THERE SO JUST SAY A PRAYER
          TIL THE DAY THE GOOD LORD CALLS YOU HOME.
```

Frank Gleason
Aug 22 2012

Poem for Pat by cowboy poet Frank Gleason

We had many challenges, made many improvements to the ranches and Pat was very active in the ranching communities. She treated people firmly but fairly.

Pat and I truly loved working together and visiting friends and family.

We did a lot of traveling in the U.S. and New Zealand and visited every province in Canada. We traveled through the Gulf of Mexico, as far south as Belize. The best tribute I can say of Pat is that she was a truly dedicated rancher's wife.

I thank Linda for all her help and encouragement in writing my memoirs. She has been my partner since 2013 and has helped me through my leg surgery and nursed me back to health though different injuries.

I often reminisced and told Linda of various events in my life. She felt it was important that I write it all down for my family, and particularly, my grandkids.

Linda is also a very capable, understanding person, and we enjoy each other's company. The last two chapters of my memoirs will include my life and travels with Linda.

Pesticides and noxious weeds at the ranches

One of the big problems we had at the FRR ranches was the influx of grasshoppers. This brought back a lot of memories from the 1950s, when we farmed in southern Alberta.

They did a tremendous amount of damage to our grain fields and hayfields.

I used various methods of control, and even hired a helicopter to spray insecticides such as Lindane and Sevin. We had at least three years of heavy infestations of grasshoppers.

On the ranch, we also experienced a lot of problems with noxious weeds, such as burdock, toadflax, wild mustard, nap weed and orange hock weed. We purchased an ATV and put a sprayer and large nozzle on it; Pat would drive this and I would sit on the back, spraying weeds.

I budgeted $10,000 every summer for that type of week control, and also another $50,000 each summer to control weeds by aerial spraying, even though I had moved 1,200 miles from where I was born, I still experienced many of the same challenges and problems in the ranches in B.C. as I did in Alberta.

The three ranches bordered each other. FRR was 105,000 acres, Springfield was 30,000 and Buckskin was 12,000, for a total of 147,000 acres. 20,000 of that was deeded, and 125,000 was Crown range.

I hired separate crews at each ranch, but because they were close, I was able to utilize a lot of the staff on all three ranches.

In the summer I employed 21 people, and the heaviest work load was in the spring and early summer when we were calving, doing turnout and gearing up for irrigation and haying.

In the winter, I cut the crew to around 10, and everyone helped with all the tasks. I organized roundup and weaning, with myself and four cowboys I'd have with me. That went over two months in the fall during roundup.

As president and manager of all three ranches, Pat and I did spend a lot of time in the office, and also on legal issues and planning – mainly in the winter.

As I wrap up writing about my memoirs, my lifestyle has changed. I now live in Williams Lake, and have had two operations since 2013. That puts limitations of some of my capabilities.

And as I lean off my saddle to close the corral gate for the last time, I feel I can relax and reminisce.

FRR has been sold, and Mike Altwasser now manages it. I feel comfortable in being able to occasionally pour a glass of scotch and look out the window at a snowstorm, instead of having to be out in the storm.

Life after Pat

After Pat's death in August, 2012, I continued to live at Terra Ridge by myself. Some of the residents were very friendly, but most I didn't associate with very much. Lucy and Harry Hauck, Lila, and the Geisbrechts were very good neighbours, as was Mike Stanza.

Some of the ranching community did visit and spent time with me. My kids and my brother and sister phoned often, and I truly appreciated all of this help, and their concerns.

Some of Pat's friends visited and phoned often, and Joyce Ward, her daughter Stacy and son-in-law Matt, and their grandson visited often, as did Dixie, Steve and their kids. I truly appreciated Steve's visits and his concerns.

Al Lay, Erik Reay and my friend Alden Fletcher from Taber phoned often, and Pat's friend Shannon Smith visited with her kids, Delaney and Austin. She was good company; she, too had some health problems.

Company and friends helped, but for the most part, I just passed the time alone, and had a difficult time coping with that.

In October, my niece Elsie passed away in Lacombe, and Dixie and I went to her funeral.

Later, I flew to Calgary and visited with Bev and Keith, and then went on to Lethbridge and Taber, visiting with Gerald and Marg, and Frank and Colleen.

This did help me start to heal. I made up my mind that I had to get more active, and I looked at several motor homes, thinking of doing some traveling.

My brother Gerald came to Williams Lake for two weeks, and as always, he was a big help to me, both as a brother and as a friend.

I gradually started to spend a lot of time on the computer. One day, I hooked up to Match.com, and found several other people looking for companionship. One of these was a lady living in Kelowna, named Linda.

She was taking care of her grandchildren while their mother worked in Ft. McMurray. Her granddaughter Austynn put her profile and photo on this site. After reading Linda's profile (and a few others) several times, I finally took the bold step of 'winking' at her on the internet.

She 'winked' back, and we eventually began talking on the telephone. It seemed that we had a lot in common, but most of all both of us were very, very lonely and were looking for companionship.

Linda had lost her husband to cancer a few years earlier.

I had a friend, Tom Caldoun, in West Bank who was moving to Arizona. He invited me to visit him, and I decided I would go to Kelowna and meet Linda at the same time.

A few weeks later, I traveled to West Bank, saw Tom, met Linda and stayed for two days. We talked a lot about our past partners, our past lives, and realized we were compatible in many ways.

Linda has a lot of the same interests at Pat: loves to cook, garden, and likes kids. We decided to visit again, and later, at Christmas, she came to Williams Lake on the bus to meet my family and spend Christmas with her brother at Forest Grove. She met all 19 of my grandkids.

We continued contact by telephone. I had an operation planned in Kamloops on my leg and ankle in late March and was concerned about that outcome. Rachel Ruddenklau in New Zealand wanted me to come to her wedding in Omaru, New Zealand in mid-February. I asked Dixie if she would travel with me to Rachel's wedding, as I was having a great deal of trouble walking.

Dixie and I flew to New Zealand for three weeks and met all the Ruddenklau family.

I really enjoyed our time at Rachel's wedding. At that time, I needed help to walk. This handicap helped a lot of airports, as I did get assistance boarding, and with traveling from place to place.

Denny Roberts, Steve's dad, drove us to Vancouver to meet our flight, and also picked us up on our return.

A Rancher's Story

I had convinced Linda to come to Williams Lake when I returned, so she came to my house a few days early and had it all cleaned up for my return. By this time my ankle was a real problem. I booked the operation to have my ankle completely rebuilt, and five pins put in my leg and foot.

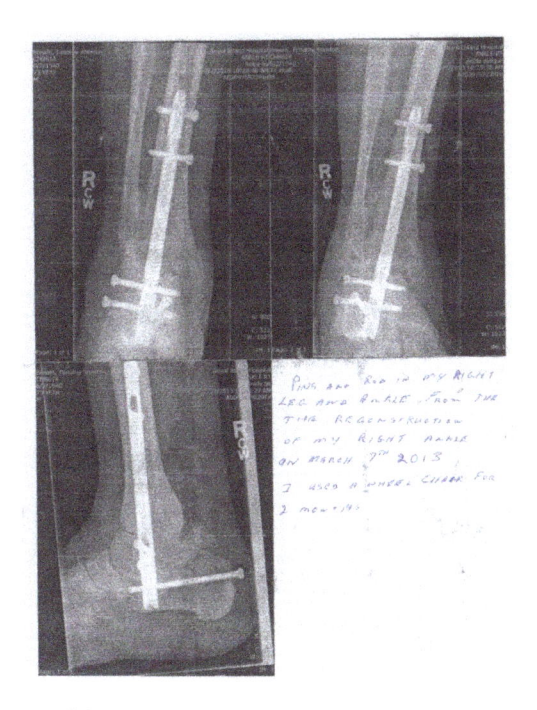

Pins and rods put in my ankle 2013

Brewin family 1998

Mom and grandkids

Tim and family 2007

Brewin family reunion 2017

Alfred's family 2017

Monica's family 2017

Rod's family 2017

Gerald's family 2017

Frank's family

Eleanor's family 2017

Tim's family 2017

Tim and Linda 2016

Brandy

Linda's family 2015

Frank, Gerald, Rod, Eleanor and Tim

Return of Owen and Judith 2017

In mid-March 2013 Linda stayed with me when I had the operations, and during that time my daughter Bev also came to Williams Lake and the two of them looked after me.

For the first few days, I was pushed around in a wooden office chair with rollers. After that, they arranged for a wheelchair. I could not do much on my own and was truly grateful for their help.

My ankle slowly improved so I could get around with crutches, a cane or an air boot for support.

After that I could get around a little on my own. In September of that year, Linda and I took a cruise and train trip to San Francisco and the Napa. I was slow at getting around, but really enjoyed that trip, as well as the train tours up to Seattle, and the bus ride home.

At Christmas time, we took a bus trip to Seattle through Oregon and Washington State. Linda had moved up to Williams Lake, and was living with me, looking after the house and the cooking.

In July 2014, we took a flight to Toronto, and a bus tour of Newfoundland and the Maritime provinces, including the New England states. We visited Ottawa, Montreal, Old Quebec, all of Nova Scotia, New Brunswick and P.E.I.

We were able to find a street Hurry Street, named after Linda's family in P.E.I. The ferry ride to Newfoundland was rough, but we really did enjoy ourselves.

The bus tour company decided to travel from Port Abasque to St. John's during the night, behind schedule.

We almost hit a cow moose and her calf on that trip and scared all of us on the bus.

We were not impressed with the bus driver, or our tour guide to take the chance of putting us all at risk.

Our trip also included Bona Vista, the old Cabot trail and the east coast of Newfoundland, as well as the Gros Morne National Park – all truly worth seeing.

Old Quebec City was truly great to see; however, Linda did fall and hit her head and spent several hours at the hospital. No one spoke English at the hospital, but Linda did make friends with a young girl using hand signals.

We got back to the hotel about 1am. One of the ladies on the tour was also a nurse. She was very good with Linda, and we became good friends with her and her husband, and often played crib with them.

We seen the old walled City of Quebec, the plain of Abraham. We shopped in the Old Quebec City, where I bought Linda a very nice purse that she was very proud of. We took a bus tour of Cape Breton and visited Rita MacNeil's restaurant.

We also toured the east coast of Nova Scotia. We had a special lobster dinner in P.E.I. and at night we traveled on the Bancroft, the home of Alexander Bell for a very enjoyable two days' stay, and a tour of central Nova Scotia.

We then traveled on to Halifax for three days, and spent a day at the Citadel, and Old Fort. We toured Luxenberg, seen the Bluenose sailing ship, went to Pier 21 and the shopping centre along the water front. The next day we went out to Peggy's Cove. Leaving Halifax, we traveled up to Moncton, onto the Bay of Fundy, and then to St. John for one night.

The following day we crossed into the U.S. We toured the states of Virginia, Maine and New York, seeing the beautiful and colourful fall tree colours.

Those states have a lot of Amish influence, such as large houses and dairy barns. They grow a tremendous amount of corn, potatoes and blueberries. Their dairy farms are huge.

The next day we traveled on up to Niagara Falls for a two-day stay. We went on the Maid of the Mist, under Niagara Falls, and spent a day viewing all of the sights and shopping in Niagara. The next day we crossed back into Canada and toured a lot of the fancy homes and farms on our way to the airport in Toronto.

We purchased a little ceramic bear at the Toronto airport that moves back and forth by solar power. When we were dropped off at the airport, Linda realized she had forgotten her camera on the bus. We had the bus company send it to their office in Edmonton, and they mailed it to us in Williams Lake.

That was a great 28-day tour. We made a lot of new friends and seen a lot of eastern Canada.

The next summer we took a trip in our camper trailer to Alberta, and stayed with my daughter Bev and son-in-law Keith's, where they were holding the 100th anniversary of the Jones farm. We ran in to Calgary to see Linda's son, Wes, then down to Waterton Park for four days where we met with Frank and Colleen. We then went to Purple Springs and stayed at their place for two more days.

We toured my old farm with Linda, then traveled on to Sandra and Dean's at Cupar, Saskatchewan for four days. We drove up through Saskatoon, staying overnight at a trailer park in North Battleford.

On the way to Sandra's, we stayed overnight at Maple Creek, Saskatchewan. I took Linda to a wine brewery near Maple Creek, and also to Old Fort Walsh. From North Battleford, we made our way on the Edmonton, staying overnight at Vermillion.

We then went on to a park west of Edmonton for three days. Linda's grandson and granddaughter came out for two days. Her son came out, too; he was in a court battle over custody of his son. Her brother, Bill, also came for a short visit. Linda's son, Colin, was living in Linda's house in Wabanman.

She eventually sold this house.

Leaving Wabanman, we went to Edson to visit Linda's sister, Marian and her sister, Kathy for three days. When we left Edson, I was driving, and the trailer hit a soft shoulder and rolled. It was completely demolished. We did have good insurance on it and loaded everything into a U-Haul for the trip back home to Williams Lake.

We have considered replacing that trailer, but I think we will purchase a motor home instead. Linda is a good driver, and often drives when we travel.

For Christmas 2013, we took a 'Christmas in Portland' bus trip. We did some sight seeing and shopping in Portland, and Christmas dinner was on a large tour boat. On New Years Eve there was a gathering put on by the bus company that was very poorly planned.

I went to the bar and bought two bottles of rum, so that at least we all had a New Years drink. We were disappointed that both Portland and Seattle did not seem to decorate and prepare their cities for Christmas as they do in Canada.

We also toured the space and aircraft centre outside of Seattle, seeing many of the spacecraft used in outer space.

We were booked for a spaghetti supper, but our bus driver got lost. Linda and I finally spotted the Old Spaghetti House, downhill from where we were. We got there an hour and a half late and were not treated that well because we were so late.

It was a great meal, though.

We spent a day shopping at the big shopping centre near Linwood. Three or four of our group got lost, and it took a couple of hours to find everyone.

That night, we had a great gathering at the hotel.

In Seattle, we also attended three different concerts. One night, coming back from shopping, the bus driver slammed on the brakes as he was pulling in to the hotel. Several of us were sent flying, and I dislocated my collar bone.

In 2015, we flew to Disneyland. We rented an electric scooter and seen all the sights. We took turns riding the scooter. Linda truly enjoyed seeing all the Disneyland characters. We also toured Universal Studios and went to Sea World in San Diego.

We bought a lot of souvenirs. Next, we took a bus trip to Yuma to visit my brother, Frank and sister-in-law Colleen. They go to Yuma every winter.

Our luggage got lost, with most of our souvenirs, and we never did get them back. The bus company was of very little help tracking our luggage. However, we really enjoyed Yuma with Frank and Colleen. They drove us to Palm Springs for our flight home.

The pilot, however, forgot to file his flight plan, so we sat in the airport in Palm Springs for five extra hours.

We were lucky to make our flight connections to San Francisco, to Vancouver, and back to Williams Lake.

Linda and I get along very well together. She is head of the social committee at Terra Ridge, putting on suppers and entertainment at our hall for residents and guests.

We have done a lot of traveling, but both have some health issues, so have become familiar with the drive to Kamloops and the Royal Inland Hospital.

I have lung problems, as does Linda, and I need oxygen at night. We are fortunate that our families have accepted us being together. All of the grandkids are great, and we love to visit. Linda's granddaughter has a one-year-old daughter, so we have a great-granddaughter. This is our first: her name is Jolene.

We have a chosen granddaughter in Norway, who also has a one-month old daughter, whose name is Aina.

We continue great friendships with the Ruddenklaus in New Zealand, and Judith and Owen visited us in June of 2017. We took a trip in my truck to the Yukon, Alaska and northern B.C. for 22 days. Unfortunately, I got pneumonia on that trip, and spent four days in the hospital on our return, where I finally got fitted with an oxygen concentrator.

Sasquatch at Pink Mountain 2017

Events that had an impact on my life:
1. Our house burning down when I was three years old
2. First year of WWII from 40-45
3. Hired man working for us wanted for murder
4. My dog Sport poisoned when I was five years old
5. Grasshopper plague when I was six years old
6. My brother Jack contracting polio when I was eight years old; his right arm paralyzed and in Edmonton hospital for over a year
7. Jack getting Brucellosis when he was about 25 years old
8. My niece Joan being shot and killed when I was 10 years old and she was 12
9. Eight calves stolen by neighbours and us having to go get them
10. Beet Webworm infesting crops when I was 16 years old
11. Three horses dying from overload of eating chipped grain when I was 14 years old
12. Dad rolling his car and sustaining head injuries when I was 17
13. My daughter Patty dying when she was 11 months old from heart failure
14. Losing my entire crop to hail in 1962
15. A woman being murdered when we were working at the Bobtail in 1993

16. Pat being threatened in the office of the Bobtail by the fellow who murdered that lady
17. Alfie and Helen's grandson being murdered
18. Jim Heaton being murdered at FRR
19. My dog Boyd dying in 2010
20. My horses Lester and Pete dying at FRR
21. Horses drowning at Aspen Valley Ranch
22. Horse being killed by a stick running in its stomach
23. Aspen house burning down in 2003
24. Lloyd house burning down in 2007
25. Pipeline and electric cable being stolen in 2004
26. Hay burning at FRR in 2001
27. Doug Chambers dying in 2004 after he murdered a boy in Merritt
28. My ankle being injured in 1976 and my shoulder injured in 1996 and the resulting operations; the ankle being reconstructed, with pins inserted in 2013
29. Cabin and meadows burning at Pre-emption in 2007 as a result of Jim Lowry starting the fire
30. FRR being sold, and the breakup of the ranches between Reinhart and Joreg
31. Pat dying in 2012
32. My brothers Norman, Alfred, Jack, Rod and Gerald dying, the death of sisters Marjorie and Monica and the deaths of my mother and dad

Grandkids and family

I am proud of all my grandkids. They have all done well, and for sure are a true source of pride, both and youngsters growing up and now as adults.

Bev and Keith's three sons, Greg, Michael and Carson, all did very well in school. They were very good at sports, such as football and basketball, and they won several championships. All three have attended and graduated from university, and all three are firefighters.

Greg is a crew chief on a First Responder crew, located out of Mackenzie, B.C. where he and his crew parachute out of a large aircraft into new fire breakouts. Michael and Carson are located on crews in Alberta as First Responders. They rappel out of helicopters and secure the location for the other firefighters. Greg often surveys the fires with Forestry and government officials to determine the best way to fight the fire.

Greg's girlfriend, Stephanie, is in her final year of schooling to become an R.N.; they make a fine young couple.

Dan and Georgie have three children. Conner is going to attend university this year in Calgary. He, too, excelled in school and at hockey and baseball growing up. He has been combining two jobs the last year in Okatokes, Alberta.

Their daughter Sarah did very well in school, as well as playing on the Ringette teams, both at provincial and national levels. She had a job in Calgary this past summer and will attend her second year of university in Calgary.

Their youngest daughter, Mackenzie, is in her final year of high school in Okotoks. She, too has always done well in school, and at sports, especially Ringette. She loves horses and is a very good polo player.

Sandra and Dean's two daughters Kaitlin and Megan go to school at Coupar, Saskatchewan. They also do very well in school and at sports. They're very involved in 4H and have started their own cow herd with 4H heifers. They show and sale 4H calves all over central Saskatchewan, and really do excel at 4H competitions.

Dixie and Steve have four children. The oldest is Camille, who just graduated from the University of Calgary. She, too has always done well in school and in 4H. she won Grand Champion with her steer project four years ago in Williams Lake. She has worked at various jobs the past three summers and does well at whatever she gets involved with.

Their son, Jack, always did well in 4H, and now works for Tolko in Williams Lake and is doing very well. Jack is a very dedicated and hard worker, and also helps out on his parents' ranch.

Ryan goes into Grade 11 this year at Williams Lake Secondary School. He loves to hunt and is very involved with rodeo and hockey. He also helps at the ranch and is a very good roper and great with the cattle. He often takes part with his dad in the ranch rodeo challenge and has done very well in 4H.

Will, their youngest son, does very well in school and 4H. He also competes in high school rodeos and is becoming a very good roper. He will attend WLSS this year.

Naomi and Pete have two children - Alexandria and Aurora, who attend school in Taber, and both do very well.

Linda's daughter, Denise, has two children: Austynn and Dylan. She also has a grandson from her son Colin. Colin's son, Raine, goes to school in Stoney Plain in Grade 5.

Austynn worked in Stoney Plain, Alberta as a nanny, and Dylan is going to school in Bar Head – they both do very well in school.

Dylan loves the outdoors and loves to read; Austynn has a two-year old daughter, so we have a great granddaughter named Jolene.

Good friends and employees

1. **Alden Fletcher**

    Aldon and I first met at age five. We went to school together from Grade 1, attended college together and have been good friends for over 70 years. Aldon was very active on municipal council and the hospital board. He and his wife, Milly, often visited. Our kids were in 4H and they were also good friends. Eldon helped me out a lot, and we were very supportive of each other. He was a good friend to all of the Brewin family, and highly respected by us all.

2. **Dave Mulner**

    I met David at about four years of age (he stole an ice cream cone from me). We attended school together, played sports together, enjoyed hunting and had respect for our friendships and our families.

3. **Frank Sitter**

    I met Frank in school at Grassy Lake. We played baseball, basketball and many sports together. He was well-liked and fun to be around, and he and his wife Rose farmed close beside my farm.

4. **Brian Anderson**

    Brian was a close neighbour, and active 4H leader, and we both served on the regional 4H council. Brian was great with kids.

5. **Matt Perin, Laddie Pavka, Louis Turcato and Terry Unruh** were friends and 4H leaders, as were **Brenda Engelsen, Pat Anderson, Pat and Joanne Lund, Terry Lund and John Stober.**
6. **Don and Marian Hamilton, and Patty and Darwin Lund** were also great friends to the Brewin family.
7. **Owen and Judith Ruddenklau** from New Zealand first worked for me in 1976. They were great friends, and we have often visited and traveled together. They were great friends of me, of Pat and also of Linda. Their daughter, Rachel and son, Paul, and his wife Tracy also worked for me and became very good friends.
8. **Don Howard** is a good friend from Olds College.
9. **Rick and Bonnie Petrie and Alec Trebasket and their sons Willie and Lance** are friends from the Bobtail Ranch.

Other friends and employees

Bruce Roberts

Bruce and his friend did the logging for me for two winters. They did an excellent job. Bruce also often stayed with Pat and I. We really enjoyed his company.

Katri Strooband

In 2009 we hired Katri and her boyfriend from Australia as trainees to work at FRR. They were very nice, hard-working young people. Much of their ummer was spent fencing and building corrals. They were both very capable and were trusted to work by themselves. They often visited with Pat and I and would enjoy helping out or just relaxing around the pool.

They had worked on a large, very unique station in Queensland, Australia, where crocodiles and poisonous snakes were concerns and challenges.

They did spend Christmas with us and Katri's mom and dad emailed often so we also got to know them well. When these two young people returned to Australia in late October, they purchased some cows and started their own farm, and built their own house.

Two years later, excessive rains caused flooding in their area. Most people had to abandon their houses because of the poisonous snakes and mold. Many houses were pumped out and simply burned down. This included Katri and Rob's.

Katri has put together an excellent video of FRR and their experiences while they worked there.

Her mother informed Pat of emails that Katri had received and concerns she had about malicious behaviour at FRR. I did have Katri send me two of these emails. There definitely was demeaning comments from a ranch employee that should have known better.

I took disciplinary action, eventually laying off the foreman at Springfield.

Reinhart was always very fair and concerned about the ranch employees. He made sure that no employee was every late in receiving their salary. He also worked with me to give very generous Christmas bonuses every year.

Both Reinhart and myself were hurt and dismayed about the purpose behind these demeaning comments.

I am truly grateful that Katri cared enough about the ranch and her fellow workers to draw this to my attention.

I do hope I can take advantage of Stroolands' offer to tour myself or any of my friends or family around the large stations in Australia.

Mabel Cromwell

We worked with Mable Cromwell many years. She was an accountant with P.M.T. in Williams Lake. She did the accounting for FRR for about 20 years. Mabel was really highly-regarded by myself, Pat and Reinhart. She was efficient and effective, and highly respected, not only by our ranch, but by several ranches in the Williams Lake area.

We relied on Mable to keep our ranch books in order. She did our income tax, and year-end statement. Pat and Mabel worked closely together, and Pat truly appreciated her direction and advice. They did, in fact, become good friends.

We also appreciated Gloria, the receptionist at P.M.T.

Mabel's husband and I both served on the Cariboo Cattlemen's Association board. She provided great service and advice when we sold FRR.

Tom and Jill Wasstrom

I hired many people while managing the FRR, or at Buckskin or Springfield. Usually we tried to find people with experience with both farming and cattle. If they had experience operating the D8 Cat, or the excavator, it was a bonus.

Tom Wasstrom worked for the ranch, helping with the cattle. He also did a lot work with the D8 Cat. He and Jill were a young couple who lived right on the ranch. Jill got along very well with Pat.

I employed thirty agricultural trainees from many different countries and many are good friends today. I also employed many neighbours on my farm at Purple Springs that are still good friends today.

LeRae Haynes

LeRae Haynes

I feel very fortunate that I was able to find LeRae to help me put my memories together. We'd meet about once a week. She's done the typing and given me suggestions on how to put my stories together. She's arranged the printing and helped with the layout of the book.

LeRae has worked as a reporter and writer for the Williams Lake Tribune and the Green Gazette magazine, has many interests and talents, and recently won the Hugo Stahl award for her volunteer efforts in the community – mainly involving music.

She's very good at music, sings and plays several instruments – and her favourite is the ukulele. She gives instruction to various musical groups, teaches music lessons and has written many songs, one of which she wrote for her grandfather. The lyrics are written below.

Linda and I have enjoyed listening to her music, her own stories and life experiences. We have gained a valuable and well-loved friend in LeRae Haynes.

Love You Through and Through

I remember the smell of chain oil and sawdust
His lunchbox made of tin
He'd fall asleep in church with his Bible in his lap
And to the very end
The very best thing about bein a kid
And the sweetest memory
Was ridin in the truck with Grandpa and his dog
To find the perfect Christmas tree

Dapper guy in suspenders and fedora
Singin skip skip skip to my lou
He'd hug you tight and swing you in a circle
Love you through and through
His family round the table was the greatest gift
Look in his face and you'd know
His loving heart as big as heaven
Would gently carry him home

He was Henry the 8th I am I am
With a laugh as big as the sky
Singing off-key and washing dishes
With a twinkle in his eye
He hung a tire swing in the willow tree
Did a crossword puzzle every day
Worked in his shop and played in his garden
And gathered his family to pray

When I hear the words Amazing Grace
I close my eyes and see your face
When I look for something good and true
In my heart there's you

Len Abblitt

Len was the brand inspector that we usually used when we sold our cattle. Len was reliable, thorough, and became a good friend. He also worked at the Williams Lake auction market, and often came out to the local ranches.

Throughout the years, I employed many people with special talents on their own. One of these was Steve Roberts. Steve is a great artist who made and sold his artwork at various fairs and events. He made and sold postcards, as well as framed artwork. Steve is a good cowboy, often competing or doing the pick-up work at various rodeos. He won the cowboy challenge several times at the O'Keefe Ranch.

His son, Ryan, also competes at these events.

Gordon Woods

Gordon woods played several musical instruments, and often played at local dances and entertained at western events.

Many of these men performed at rodeos, such as Bruce Bowie and Heaton – they were very good ball players. Mike McGuiness made and sold leather work and iron work he made on the forge. Sheldon Purdy was a trapper in his spare time.

Al Lay

A very good friend of mine is Al Lay, who was a Conservation officer in Williams Lake, in charge of predator control for many years. He worked closely with the cattlemen and the ranchers. Al was highly respected and appreciated.

I first met Al in 1996 at FRR, and we quickly developed a close friendship. I allowed him and his friend Rod Cook, and his son Jerid, to hunt on the ranch. I allowed them the use of a cabin on the ranch, which used to me a cabin used by the government surveyors.

Pat and I visited with Al and his friends often when they were up hunting. We played a lot of crib, and eventually I taught Al to count above two. We drank a lot of Crown Royal.

We played a lot of tricks on one another. We really enjoyed all of Al's stories, his memories and experiences with bears, wolves and other ranchers.

Our visits to the cabin with Al and his friends usually lasted until the early hours of the morning, often including the day's hunting experiences, and almost always a bottle of Crown Royal. Al loved to tease, and we loved to play tricks on them.

One time I was in gum boots instead of cowboy boots – Al got quite a kick out of this 'dirt farmer.' On our next trip to the cabin, he tied a pair of rubber boots to the back of my truck. Those boots took many trips back and forth to the cabin.

Pat loved to dress up dummies and sit them in Al's cabin. One time, we really scared the three of them when we set up three old man dummies at the table. I guess they got quite a scare when they came in after dark and seen three old men sitting at the table.

We would spot deer for them when they came up. There was one place we called 'the island', in a grove of trees. That was a special spot of Al's.

Once, we put an old easy chair and a dummy in this grove of trees. When Al scanned it with his binoculars, he got quite annoyed that someone else was in 'his' hunting spot.

It was the following day before they realized it was a dummy, and not a real person.

Al played a mean trick on Steve when he put some skunk scent on Steve's cowboy hat – you just don't get rid of that.

Al found an old kids' pink purse and laid it by the side of the road. I refused to pick it up, as I was sure it was a trick from Al. Pat, however, did pick it up and sure enough, it was a 'Ha ha, I got you!' from Al.

Over the years, countless tricks were played.

Duck Inn cabin FRR

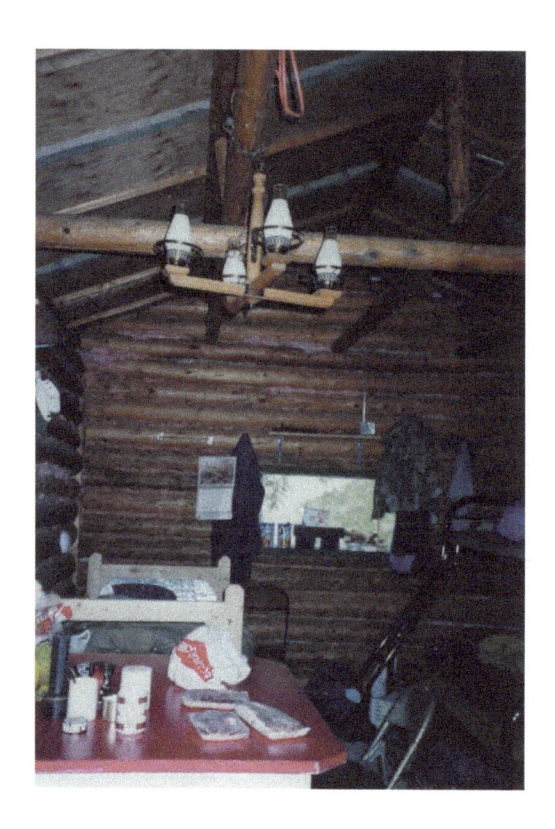

Al's hunting cabin

Tim's retirement cartoon from Al

Pat became very close with all the conservation officers: Al, Ken, Andy and Darrell. They all called her 'Mom.'

They are still close friends, and we have carried on that friendship now, including Linda.

Good friends and employees

Others who worked for me and who became friends include Sheldon Purdy, Bob Kelly, Tom Caldow and Andy McKay. I also want to make special mention of Carol Campbell, who did night calving for four years and operated the forage harvester.

Joyce Ward and her family were very special friends of Pat's for many years and remain good friends of mine and Linda's.

Shannon Smith worked for Pat and became a good friend.

Mike Altwasser, who took over the management at FRR when I retired, has become a very good friend.

Jim Heaton, who I trained to be ranch manager, was sadly killed when he was stabbed in the kidneys in a bar in Williams Lake. He was like a son, and his mom, Sherry, and dad Richard, are good friends.

Randy Johnson was a good friend who also worked for me part time, as well as Deiter Kellinghouse.

Cliff Dorion worked for me part time and became a friend, as did Will Smith, manager of B.C. Livestock in Williams Lake, and Wayne Jordan, an auctioneer and good friend.

Friends from FRR

1. **Bruce Bowe**
   Bruce was a good cowboy and also good with equipment and the cattle. He worked for FRR for 18 years, he was honest and loyal.
2. **Everett Byman**
   He was a great worker, was good with the equipment and the cattle, and also did most of the carpentry on the ranch.

I want to mention Dave and Joanne Weingart. Dave did a great deal of the mechanic work on the equipment at all three ranches, and Joanne ordered or arranged for most of the needed repairs. A huge recognition of thanks for keeping our equipment in good repair!

Eric Muirs had his own small excavator, and we often hired Eric to help with ditching and trenching. He's another great guy I owe thanks to.

Our closest neighbours, Garth and Margaret Lloyd, were always appreciated. Their grandson, Todd, worked for me for two summers.

Doug Haughtan was a John Deere salesman who helped me out many times.

Pam Carter worked for me for several years. She was a huge benefit in swathing, doing farm work and packing silage.

Wes and Marian Metzer helped out with the riding and sorting.

Larry and Wayne Jordan (auctioneers) were great to work with, as was Bruce Rolph, and Harold Reay.

Two friends that were important to Pat and I were Eric and Diane Reay. Eric often helped out at brandings and sorting.

Deiter Kellinghausen became a great friend and a reliable source of information. He had managed the C1 ranch at Alexis Creek for over 30 years.

Gene and Lorna Sapp were close neighbors who helped me a lot.

When we purchased the Springfield Ranch from Mike and Brenda O'Keef, they were great people to deal with – very honest and reliable.

George and Gordon Keener lived on Slater Mountain. The Springfield range enclosed much of Slater Mountain, and the Keeners were great neighbours and very active in the community.

Rudy and Randy Johnson were a big benefit to the ranch. The Johnson family originally developed the Buckskin Ranch to where it was one of the most progressive ranches in central B.C. when we purchased it. Rudy and Helen planted a beautiful maple tree that provided great shade and enjoyment to the Buckskin yard.

It presented shade to the kitchen and entire front of the house when we lived there.

Inspiration to write this book

I was inspired and encouraged to write my memoirs and life stories by several different people.

1. Greg Jones, my oldest grandchild often asked about my life growing up and had a keen interest in my early years.
2. Bev Jones, my oldest daughter and my greatest critic, encouraged me to put down on paper what I had done over the years.
3. Pat often told me to write a book.
4. Linda listened to my stories and also told me to write them down.
5. All of my kids and family members who just wanted to know what happened.
6. The Ruddenklaus wanted to know the truth; they know that I don't B.S. or exaggerate.

So, included here are mostly true stories. Some are embellished a wee bit, and there is perhaps a little B.S. but not much. They're mostly true happenings about what occurred.

Other information and inspiration in writing my story was that I hoped to show how one event led to another. I tried to show how the development of ranching in western Canada and Alberta influenced the direction my life took.

My mother, my dad and other family members started the farm and developed the original homestead.

I wanted to show that growing up a close family helped direct my early years, and my goals in life.

My early years as the youngest son, my school years, sports, the responsibilities of chores and helping on the farm influenced me growing up. Other influences were the close bond we had as a family, the Air Cadets, Boy Scouts and Mother Nature.

Working closely with Gerald, Frank, Eleanor and Rod and being given responsibility in developing the farm were also good lessons for me.

Raising pigs, starting my own farm, the SPF hogs, exotic cattle and running a business as a young farmer helped give me direction.

Irrigation, cattle, expansions, sugar beets, grain and new crops also played a huge role.

Developing my own farm with Marj and my children, working later on the farm with Dan, Bev, and later, Cher, all influenced my future.

The sale of my farm, moving to B.C. to manage the Bobtail Ranch, and later, the Bar X Ranch, developing the cow herds on these operations, the irrigation and range development all played a part.

Taking on the management, development and expansion of FRR, the herd development and irrigation expansion, range increases, the expansion of the Aspen Valley Ranch, Buckskin Ranch and later, the Springfield operation, were all important developments.

The many employees, neighbours and friends, plus government resource personnel, all played a part. Crimes, such as theft, and even murder, influenced my life. So, what I hope to show is how one event led to another, and how accidents and health also played a part.

Pat's help and direction played an important role, and the sale of FRR, Pat's death and the breakup of the ranches influenced my life.

As I wrap up writing about my memoirs, my lifestyle has changed. I now live in Williams Lake, and have had two operations since 2013. That puts limitations of some of my capabilities.

And as I lean off my saddle to close the corral gate for the last time, I feel I can relax and reminisce.

FRR has been sold, and Mike Altwasser now manages it. I feel comfortable in being able to occasionally pour a glass of scotch and look out the window at a snowstorm, instead of having to be out in that storm.

For me, there is no more pulling of backwards calves, riding in -30 weather, searching for cows or bulls, no more worrying about having to start the four-wheel drive tractor or loader to feed and put out sileage. No more needing to attend livestock or government meetings, no more sewing up animals after a wolf attack.

No more 25-mile-long cattle drives, no more doing night calving, no more going out in the middle of the night to check on the pivots. No more worrying about wolves killing calves, no more long, tiring days helping the vets with preg testing.

My thoughts now turn more to family and friends. Perhaps even Al will stop in and I can take another dollar from him playing crib.

I made many changes to all three ranches, with a lot of help from many people.

I do feel I have had a good, long ride.

Constant companions: Tim and Boyd
Boyd moved the cattle;
Tim sat in the saddle

CPSIA information can be obtained
at www.ICGtesting.com
Printed in the USA
LVHW070403070119
602944LV00001B/1/P

9 781525 539862